THE MORMON MENACE

BEING THE CONFESSION OF
JOHN DOYLE LEE - DANITE
AN OFFICIAL ASSASSIN OF THE
MORMON CHURCH UNDER THE LATE
BRIGHAM YOUNG

INTRODUCTION
By ALFRED HENRY LEWIS

D1738125

INTRODUCTION

THE MORMON PURPOSE

Almost a half century ago, being in 1857, John Doyle Lee, a chief among that red brotherhood, the Danites, was ordered by Brigham Young and the leading counselors of the Mormon Church to take his men and murder a party of emigrants then on their way through Utah to California. The Mormon orders were to "kill all who can talk," and, in their carrying out, Lee and his Danites, with certain Indians whom he had recruited in the name of scalps and pillage, slaughtered over one hundred and twenty men, women, and children, and left their stripped bodies to the elements and the wolves. This wholesale murder was given the title of "The Mountain Meadows Massacre." Twenty years later, in 1877, the belated justice of this Government seated Lee on his coffin, and shot him to death for his crimes.

In those long prison weeks which fell in between his arrest and execution, Lee wrote his life, giving among other matters the story of the Church of Mormon from its inception, when Joseph Smith pretended, with the aid of Urim and Thummim, to translate the golden plates, down to those murders for which he, Lee, was executed. Lee's confessions, so to call them, were published within a few months following his death. The disclosures were such that the Mormon Church became alarmed; the book might mean its downfall. In the name of Mormon safety Brigham Young, by money and other agencies, succeeded in the book's suppression. What copies had been sold were, as much as might be, bought up and destroyed, together with the plates and forms from which they had been printed.

In the destruction of this literature, so perilous to Mormons, at least two volumes escaped. These have been placed in my hands by certain patriotic influences, and are here reprinted as The Mormon Menace. Much that was shocking and atrocious has been eliminated in the editing, as unfit for modest ears .and eyes. What remains, however, will give a sufficient picture of the Mormon Church in its hateful attitude towards all that is moral or republican among our people. A black kitten makes a black cat; what the Mormon Church was under President Young it is under President Smith, and will be with their dark successors.

The purpose of the present publication of Lee's story is to warn American men, and more particularly American women, of the Mormon viper still coiled upon the national hearth. To-day, as in the days of Lee, the Mormon missionary is abroad in the world. He is in your midst; he makes his converts among your neighbors; within the month, on one detected occasion, he stood at the portals of your public schools and gave his insidious pamphlets, preaching Mormonism, into the hands of your children.

More, the Mormon Church has, in addition to its religious, its political side, and teaches not only immorality, but treason. On a far-away 5th of November a certain darksome Guy Fawkes and his confederates, all with a genius for explosives, planned to blow up the British Government by blowing up its parliament, and went some distance towards carrying out their plot. The Mormon Church of Latter-day Saints, with headquarters in Salt Lake City, is employed upon a present and somewhat similar conspiracy against this Government, with Senator Smoot as the advance guard or agent thereof in the halls of our national legislature.

As this is written, a Senate inquiry into this conspiracy wags slowly yet searchingly forward. Stripped of formality of phrase and reset in easier English, the question which the Senate Committee is trying to solve is this: Is the Mormon Church in conspiracy against the Government, with Senator Smoot's seat as a first fruit of that conspiracy? As corollary comes the second query: To which does Senator Smoot give primary allegiance, the Church or the nation?

By every sign and signal smoke of evidence the conspiracy charged exists, with President Smith of the Mormon Church its chief architect and expositor. Smoot takes his seat in the upper house of Congress with a first purpose of carrying forth, so far as lies within his hands, the plans of the conspirators. What is the purpose of the conspirators? To protect themselves and their fellow Mormons in the criminal practice of polygamy, and prevent their prosecution as bigamists by the Utah courts.

The inquiry has already uncovered Mormonism in many of its evil details, and retold most, if not all, of those stories of pious charlatanism and religious crime which, during seventy-five years of its existence, make up the annals of the Mormon Church. As a first proposal it was explained in evidence before the committee that in no sort had the Mormon Church abated or abandoned polygamy as either a tenet or a practice. Indeed, the present conspiracy aims to produce conditions in Utah under which polygamy may flourish safe from the ax of law. In the old days, when Brigham Young ruled, the Mormons were safe with sundry thousands of desert miles between the law and them. Then they feared nothing save strife within the Church, and that would be no mighty peril. Brigham Young would put it down with the Danites. He had his Destroying Angels, himself at their head, and when a man rebelled he was murdered.

Mormonism is not, when a first fanaticism has subsided, a religion that would address the popular taste. It is a religion of gloom, of bitterness, of fear, of iron hand to punish the recalcitrant. It demands slavish submission on the part of every man. It insists upon abjection, self-effacement, a surrender of individuality on the part of every woman. The man is to work and obey; the woman is to submit and bear children; all are to be for the Church, of the Church, by the Church, hoping nothing, fearing nothing, knowing nothing beyond the will of the Church. The money price of Mormonism is a tithe of the member's income - the Church takes a tenth. The member may pay in money or in kind; he may sell and pay his tenth in dollars, or he may bring to the tithing yard his butter, or eggs, or hay, or wheat, or whatever he shall raise as the harvest of his labors.

3

In the old time the President of the Church was the temporal as well as spiritual head. No one might doubt his "revelations" or dispute his commands without being visited with punishment which ran from a fine to the death penalty. When outsiders invaded their regions the Mormons, by command of Brigham Young, struck them down, as in the Mountain Meadows murders. This was in the day when the arm of national power was too short to reach them. Now, when it can reach them, the Church conspires where before it assassinated, and strives to do by chicane what it aforetime did by shedding blood. And all to defend itself in the practice of polygamy!

One would ask why the Mormons set such extravagant store by that doctrine of many wives. This is the great reason: It serves to mark the Church members and separate and set them apart from Gentile influences. Mormonism is the sort of religion that children would renounce, and converts, when their heat had cooled, abandon. The women would leave it on grounds of jealousy and sentiment; the men would quit in a spirit of independence and a want of superstitious belief in the Prophet's "revelations." Polygamy prevents this. It shuts the door of Gentile sympathy against the Mormon. The Mormon women are beings disgraced among the Gentiles; they must defend their good repute. The children of polygamous marriages must defend polygamy to defend their own legitimacy. The practice, which doubtless had its beginning solely to produce as rapidly as might be a Church strength, now acts as a bar to the member's escape; wherefore the President, his two counselors, the twelve apostles and others at the head of Mormon affairs, insist upon it as a best, if not an only, Church protection. Without polygamy the Mormon membership would dwindle until Mormonism had utterly died out. The Mormon heads think so, and preserve polygamy as a means of preserving the Church.

What the Mormon leaders think and feel and say on this keynote question of polygamy, however much they may seek to hide their sentiments behind a mask of lies, may be found in former utterances from the Church pulpit, made before the shadow of the law had fallen across it.

President Heber C. Kimball, in a discourse delivered in the Tabernacle, November 9, 1856 (Deseret News, volume 6, page 291), said: "I have no wife or child that has any right to rebel against me. If they violate my laws and rebel against me, they will get into trouble just as quickly as though they transgressed the counsels and teachings of Brother Brigham. Does it give a woman a right to sin against me because she is my wife? No; but it is her duty to do my will as I do the will of my Father and my God. It is the duty of a woman to be obedient to her husband, and unless she is I would not give a damn for all her queenly right and authority, nor for her either, if she will quarrel and lie about the work of God and the principles of plurality. A disregard of plain and correct teachings is the reason why so many are dead and damned, and twice plucked up by the roots, and I would as soon baptize the devil as some of you."

October 6, 1855 (volume 5, page 274), Kimball said: "If you oppose any of the works of God you will cultivate a spirit of apostasy. If you oppose what is called the spiritual wife doctrine, the patriarchal order, which is of God, that course will corrode you with apostasy, and you will go overboard. The principle

4

of plurality of wives never will be done away, although some sisters have had revelations that when this time passes away, and they go through the vale, every woman will have a husband to herself. I wish more of our young men would take to themselves wives of the daughters of Zion, and not wait for us old men to take them all. Go ahead upon the right principle, young gentlemen, and God bless you for ever and ever, and make you fruitful, that we may fill the mountains and then the earth with righteous inhabitants."

President Heber C. Kimball, in a lengthy discourse delivered in the Tabernacle on the 4th day of April, 1857, took occasion to say: "I would not be afraid to promise a man who is sixty years of age, if he will take the counsel of Brother Brigham and his brethren, that he will renew his youth. I have noticed that a man who has but one wife, and is inclined to that doctrine, soon begins to wither and dry up, while a man who goes into plurality looks fresh, young, and sprightly. Why is this? Because God loves that man, and because he honors his work and word. Some of you may not believe this - I not only believe it, but I also know it. For a man of God to be confined to one woman is a small business; it is as much as we can do to keep up under the burdens we have to carry, and I do not know what we should do if we only had one woman apiece."

President Heber C. Kimball used the following language in a discourse, instructing a band of missionaries about to start on their mission: "I say to those who are elected to go on missions, Go, if you never return, and commit what you have into the hands of God - your wives, your children, your brethren, and your property. Let truth and righteousness be your motto, and don't go into the world for anything else but to preach the gospel, build up the Kingdom of God, and gather the sheep into the fold. You are sent out as shepherds to gather the sheep together; and remember that they are not your sheep; they belong to Him that sends you. Then don't make a choice of any of those sheep; don't make selections before they are brought home and put into the fold. You understand that! Amen."

When the Edmunds law was passed, and punishment and confiscation and exile became the order, even dullwits among Mormons knew that the day of terror and bloodshed as a system of Church defense was over with and done. Then the Mormons made mendacity take the place of murder, and went about to do by indirection what before they had approached direct. Prophet Woodruff was conveniently given a "revelation" to the effect that polygamy might be abandoned. They none the less kept the Mormon mind in leash for its revival. The men were still taught subjection; the women were still told that wifehood and motherhood were their two great stepping-stones in crossing to the heavenly shore, missing which they would be swept away. Meanwhile, and in secret, those same heads of the Church - Smith, the President, Cluff, the head of the Mormon College, Tanner, chief of the Young Men's Mutual Improvement Association - took unto themselves plural wives by way of setting an example and to keep the practical fires of polygamy alive.

True, these criminals ran risks, and took what President Smith in his recent testimony, when telling of his own quintette of helpmeets, called "the chances of the law." To lower these risks, and diminish them to a point where in truth they would be no risks, the Mormon Church, under the lead of its bigamous President several years rearward, became a political machine. It looked over the future, considered its own black needs as an outlaw, and saw that its first step towards security should be the making of Utah into a State. As a territory the hand of the Federal power rested heavily upon it; the Edmunds law could be enforced whenever there dwelt a will in Washington so to do. Once a State, Utah would slip from beneath the pressure of that iron statute. The Mormons would at the worst face nothing more rigorous than the State's own laws against bigamy, enforced by judges and juries and sheriffs of their own selection, and jails whereof they themselves would weld the bars and hew the stones and forge the keys.

With that, every Mormon effort of lying promise and pretense of purity were put forward to bring statehood about. What Gentiles were then in Utah exerted themselves to a similar end, and made compacts, and went, as it were, bail for Mormon good behavior. In the end Utah was made a State; the Mormons breathed the freer as ones who had escaped that Edmunds statute which was like a sword of Damocles above their polygamous heads. To be sure, as a State Utah had her laws against plural marriages, and provided a punishment for the bigamist; the general government would consent to nothing less as the price of that statehood prayed for. But the Mormon criminals, the Smiths, the Lymans, the Tanners, and the Cluffs, were not afraid. They had gotten the reins of power into their own fingers, and made sure of their careful ability to drive ahead without an upset.

The Mormon Church, now when Utah was a State, went into politics more openly and deeply than before. Practically there are three parties in Utah - Republicans and Democrats and Mormons. The Gentiles are Democrats or Republicans; the Mormons are never anything but Mormons, voting on this side or on that, for one man or another, as the Mormon interest dictates and the Mormon President and the apostles direct. Every Mormon who has a vote occupies a double position; he is a Mormon in religion and a Mormon in political faith. In that way every office is filled with a Mormon, or with a Gentile who can be blind to Mormon iniquities. To-day a bigamist in Utah has no more to fear from the law than has a gambling-house keeper in the city of New York.

That Mormon conspiracy, whereof Smoot in the Senate is one expression, was not made yesterday. It had its birth in the year of the Edmunds law and its drastic enforcement. In that day, black for Mormons, it was resolved to secure such foothold, such representation in the Congress at Washington, that, holding a balance of power in the Senate or House, or both, the Congressional Democrats or Republicans would grant the Mormons safety for their pet tenet of polygamy as the price of Mormon support. The Mormons in carrying out these plans decided upon an invasion and, wherever possible, the political conquest of other States. They already owned Utah; they would bring - politically - beneath their thumb as many more as they might. With this thought they planted colonies in Nevada, in Colorado, in Idaho, in Wyoming, in Montana, in Oregon, in Arizona. As a refuge for polygamists, should the unexpected happen and a storm of law befall, they also planted colonies over the Mexico line in Chihuahua and Sonora.

Before going to the latter move they talked with Diaz; and that astute dictator said "Yes," with emphasis. Diaz welcomed the Mormons; they might be as polygamous as they pleased. He wanted citizens; and he was not blind to those beauties of enterprise and courage and hardihood that are the heritage of the Anglo- Dane. He bade the Mormons come to Mexico and make a bulwark of themselves between him and his American neighbors north of the Rio Grande. The Mormons hated the Americans; Diaz could trust them. The Mormons went to Mexico; there they are to-day in many a rich community, as freely polygamous as in the most wide-flung hour of Brigham Young. Diaz smiles as he reviews those prodigal crops of corn and cattle and children which they raise. They make his empire richer in men and money - commodities of which Mexico has sorely felt the want.

Once when a Methodist clergyman went to Diaz, remonstrated against that polygamy which he permitted, and spoke of immoralities, Diaz snapped his fingers.

"Do you see their children?" cried Diaz. "Well, I think more of their children than of your arguments."

From this Mexican nursery the Mormon President can, when he will, order an emigration into Nevada or any of those other States I've mentioned, to support the Church where it is weakest. Moreover, as related, the settlements in Mexico offer a haven of retreat should any tempest of prosecution beat upon the Utah polygamists through some slip of policy or accidental Gentile strength.

In Nevada, in Colorado, in Oregon, in Idaho, in every one of those States wherein the Church has planted the standards of Mormonism, the Mormon, as fast as he may, is making himself a power in politics. He is never a Democrat, never a Republican, always a Mormon. What sparks of independent political action broke into brief, albeit fiery, life a few years ago were fairly beaten out when Thatcher and Roberts were punished for daring to act outside the Mormon command.

Now, pretend what they will, assert what lie they choose, the Mormon President holds the Mormon vote, in whatever State it abides, in the hollow of his hand. He can, and does, place it to this or that party's support, according as he makes his bargain. He will use it to elect legislators and Congressmen in those States. He will employ it to select the Senators whom those States send to Washington. And when they are there, as Smoot is there, for the safeguarding of polygamy and what other crimes Mormonism may find it convenient to rest upon from time to time, those Senators and Representatives will act by the Mormon President's orders. "When the lion's hide is too short," said the Greek, "I piece it out with foxes." And the Mormons, in a day when the Danites have gone with those who called them into bloody being, and murder as a Churchly argument is no longer safe, profit by the Grecian's wisdom.

But the darkest side of Mormonism is seen when one considers the stamp of moral and mental degradation it sets upon those men and women who comprise what one might term the peasantry of the Church. Woman is, as the

7

effect of Mormonism, peculiarly made to retrograde. Instead of being uplifted she is beaten down. She must not think; she must not feel; she must not know; she must not love. Her only safety lies in being blind and deaf and dull and senseless to every better sentiment of womanhood. She is to divide a husband with one or two or ten or twenty; she is not to be a wife, but the fraction of a wife. The moment she looks upon herself as anything other than a bearer of children she is lost. Should she rebel - and in her helplessness she does not know how to enter upon practical revolt - she becomes an outcast; a creature of no shelter, no food, no friend, no home. Woman is the basis or, if you will, the source and fountain of a race; woman is a race's inspiration. And what shall a race be, what shall its children be, with so lowered and befouled an origin?

At the hearing before the Senate Committee President Smith, stroking his long white beard in the manner of the patriarchs, made no secret of his five wives, and seemed to court the Gentile condemnation. This hardihood was of deliberate plan on the part of President Smith. He was inviting what he would call "persecution." He did not fear actual prosecution in the Utah courts; as to the Federal forums, those tribunals were powerless against him now that Utah was a State. Being safe in the flesh, President Smith would bring upon himself and Mormonism the whole fury of the press. It would serve to quiet schism and bicker within the Mormon Church. An opposition or a "persecution" would act as a pressure to bring Mormons together. That pressure would squeeze out the last drop of political independence among Mormons, which to the extent that it existed might interfere with his disposal of the compact Mormon vote. In short, an attack upon himself and upon Mormonism by the Gentiles would tighten the hold of President Smith, close-herd the Mormons, and leave them ready politically to be driven hither and yon as seemed most profitable for Church purposes.

Gray, wise, crafty, sly, soft, one who carries mendacity to the heights of art, President Smith gives in all he says and does and looks the color of truth to this explanation of his frankness. He would not prodigiously care if Smoot were cast into outer Senate darkness. It would not be an evil past a remedy. He could send Smoot back; and send him back again. Meanwhile, he might lift up the cry of the Church persecuted; that of itself would stiffen the Mormon line of battle and multiply recruits.

President Smith looks forward to a time when one Senate vote will be decisive. He cannot prophesy the day; but by the light of what has been, he knows that it must dawn. About a decade ago the Democrats took the Senate from the Republicans by one vote - Senator Peffer's. In Garfield's day the Senate, before Conkling stepped down and out, was in even balance with a tie. What was, will be; and President Smith intends, when that moment arrives and the Senate is in poise between the parties, to have at least one Utah vote, and as many more as he may, to be a stock in trade wherewith to traffic security for his Church of Mormon and its crimes. Given a balance of power in the Senate - and it might easily come within his hands - President Smith could enforce such liberal terms for Mormonism as to privilege it in its sins and prevent chance of punishment.

8

There be those who, for a Mormon or a personal political reason, will find fault with this work and its now appearance in print; they will argue that some motive of politics underlies the publication. It is fair to state that in so arguing they will be right. The motive is three-ply - made up of a purpose to withstand the Mormon Church as a political force, limit its spread as a so-called religion, and buckler the mothers and daughters and sisters of the country against an enemy whose advances are aimed peculiarly at them. The morals of a people are in the custody of its women; and, against Mormonism - that sleepless menace to American morality - these confessions of Lee the Danite are set in types to become a weapon in their hands. It was the womanhood of the nation that compelled the present Senate investigation of Smoot and what Mormon influences and conspiracies produced him as their representative; and it is for a defense of womanhood and its purity that this book is made. The battle will not be wholly won with Smoot's eviction from his Senate seat; indeed, the going of Smoot will be only an incident. The war should continue until all of Mormonism and what it stands for is destroyed; for then, and not before, may wifehood or womanhood write itself safe between the oceans. Congress must not alone cleanse itself of Smoot; it must go forward to methods that shall save the politics of the country from a least of Mormon interference, and the aroused womanhood of the land should compel Congress to this work. He who would hold his house above his head must mind repairs, and the word is quite as true when spoken of a country.

Alfred Henry Lewis. New York City,
December 15, 1904.

CHAPTER I
THE STORMY YOUTH OF LEE

In justice to myself, my numerous family, and the public in general, I consider it my duty to write a history of my life. I shall content myself with giving facts, and let the readers draw their own conclusion therefrom. By the world at large I am called a criminal, and have been sentenced to be shot for deeds committed by myself and others nearly twenty years ago. I have acted my religion, nothing more. I have obeyed the orders of the Church. I have acted as I was commanded to do by my superiors. My sins, if any, are the result of doing what I was commanded to do by those who were my superiors in authority in the Church of Jesus Christ of Latter-day Saints.

My birthday was the 6th day of September, A.D. 1812. I was born in the town of Kaskaskia, Randolph County, Illinois. My father, Ralph Lee, was born in the State of Virginia. He was of the family of Lees of Revolutionary fame. He served his time as an apprentice and learned the carpenter's trade in the city of Baltimore. My mother was born in Nashville, Tennessee. She was the daughter of John Doyle, who for many years held the position of Indian Agent over the roving tribes of Indians in southeastern Illinois. He served in the War of the Revolution, and was wounded in one of the many battles in which he took part with the sons of liberty against the English oppressors.

At the time of my birth my father was considered one of the leading men of that section of country; he was a master workman, sober and attentive to business, prompt and punctual to his engagements. He contracted largely and carried on a heavy business; he erected a magnificent mansion, for that age and country, on his land adjoining the town of Kaskaskia.

This tract of land was the property of my mother when she married my father. My grandfather Doyle was a wealthy man. He died in 1809 at Kaskaskia, Illinois, and left his whole fortune to my mother and her sister Charlotte, by will. They being his only children, he divided the property equally between them.

My father and mother were both Catholics, were raised in that faith; I was christened in that Church. When about one year old, my mother being sick, I was sent to a French nurse, a negro woman. At this time my sister Eliza was eleven years old, but young as she was she had to care for my mother and do all the work of the household. To add to the misfortune, my father began to drink heavily and was soon very dissipated; drinking and gambling were his daily occupation. The interest and care of his family were no longer a duty with him; he was seldom present to cheer and comfort his lonely, afflicted wife.

The house was one mile from town, and we had no neighbors nearer than that. The neglect and indifference on the part of my father towards my afflicted mother served to increase her anguish and sorrow, until death came to her relief. My mother's death left us miserable indeed; we were (my sister and I) thrown upon the wide world, helpless, and, I might say, without father or mother. My father when free from the effects of intoxicating drink was a kind-hearted, generous, noble man, but from that time forward he was a slave to drink - seldom sober.

My aunt Charlotte was a spit-fire; she was married to a man by the name of James Conner, a Kentuckian by birth. They lived ten miles north of us. My sister went to live with her aunt, but the treatment she received was so brutal that the citizens complained to the county commissioners, and she was taken away from her aunt and bound out to Dr. Fisher, with whose family she lived until she became of age.

In the meantime the doctor moved to the city of Vandalia, Illinois. I remained with my nurse until I was eight years of age, when I was taken to my aunt Charlotte's to be educated. I had been in a family which talked French so long that I had nearly lost all knowledge of my mother tongue. The children at school called me Gumbo, and teased me so much that I became disgusted with the French language and tried to forget it - which has been a disadvantage to me since that time.

My aunt was rich in her own right. My uncle Conner was poor; he drank and gambled and wasted her fortune; she in return give him blixen all the time. The more she scolded, the worse he acted, until they would fight like cats and dogs. Between them I was treated worse than an African slave. I lived in the family eight years, and can safely say I got a whipping every day I was there.

My aunt was more like a savage than a civilized woman. In her anger she generally took her revenge upon those around her who were the least to blame. She would strike with anything she could obtain with which to work an injury. I have been knocked down and beaten by her until I was senseless, scores of times, and carry many scars on my person, the result of harsh usage by her.

When I was sixteen years old I concluded to leave my aunt's house - I cannot call it home; my friends advised me to do so. I walked one night to Kaskaskia; went to Robert Morrison and told him my story. He was a mail contractor. He clothed me comfortably, and sent me over the Mississippi River into Missouri, to carry the mail from St. Genevieve to Pinckney, on the north side of the Missouri River, via Potosie, a distance of one hundred and twenty-seven miles. It was a weekly mail. I was to receive seven dollars a month for my services. This was in December, 1828. It was a severe winter; snow unusually deep and roads bad. I was often until two o'clock at night in reaching my stations. In the following spring I came near losing my life on several occasions when swimming the streams, which were then generally over their banks. The Meramec was the worst stream I had to cross, but I escaped danger, and gave satisfaction to my employer.

All I know of my father, after I was eight years of age, is that he went to Texas in the year 1820, and I have never heard of him since. What his fate was I never knew. When my mother died my uncle and aunt Conner took all the property - a large tract of land, several slaves, household and kitchen furniture, and all; and, as I had no guardian, I never received any portion of the property. The slaves were set free by an act of the Legislature; the land was sold for taxes, and was hardly worth redeeming when I came of age; so I sold my interest in all the land that had belonged to my mother, and made a quit-claim deed of it to

Sidney Breeze, a lawyer of Kaskaskia, in consideration of two hundred dollars. I was born on the point of land lying between and above the mouth of the Okaw or Kaskaskia River and the Mississippi River, in what is known as the Great American Bottom - the particular point I refer to was then called Zeal-no-waw, the Island of Nuts. It was nineteen miles from the point of the bluffs to the mouth of the Okaw River; ten miles wide up at the bluffs and tapering to a point where the rivers united. Large bands of wild horses - French ponies, called "punt" horses - were to be found any day feeding on the ever green and nutritious grasses and vegetation. Cattle and hogs were also running wild in great numbers; every kind of game, large and small, could be had with little exertion. The streams were full of fish; the forests contained many varieties of timber; nuts, berries, and wild fruits of every description, found in the temperate zone could be had in their season.

Near by was the Reservation of the Kaskaskia Indians, Louis DuQuoin was chief of the tribe. He had a frame house painted in bright colors, but he never would farm any, game being so plentiful he had no need to labor. Nearly all the settlers were French, and not very anxious for education or improvement of any kind. I was quite a lad before I ever saw a wagon, carriage, set of harness, or a ring, a staple, or set of bows to an ox yoke. The first wagon I ever saw was brought into that country by a Yankee peddler; his outfit created as great an excitement in the settlement as the first locomotive did in Utah; the people flocked in from every quarter to see the Yankee wagon.

Everything in use in that country was of the most simple and primitive construction. There were no sawmills or gristmills in that region; sawed lumber was not in the country. The wagons were two-wheeled carts made entirely of wood - not a particle of iron about them; the hubs were of white elm, spokes of white oak or hickory, the felloes of black walnut, as it was soft and would bear rounding. The felloes were made six inches thick, and were strongly doweled together with seasoned hardwood pins; the linch pin was of hickory or ash; the thills were wood; in fact all of it was wood. The harness consisted of a corn husk collar, hames cut from an ash tree root, or from an oak; tugs were rawhide; the lines also were rawhide; a hackamore or halter was used in place of a bridle; one horse was lashed between the thills by rawhide straps and pins in the thills for a hold-back; when two horses were used, the second horse was fastened ahead of the first by straps fastened on to the thills of the cart. Oxen were yoked as follows: A square stick of timber of sufficient length was taken and hollowed out at the ends to fit on the neck of the ox, close up to the horns, and this was fastened by rawhide straps to the horns.

The people were of necessity self-sustaining, for they were forced to depend upon their own resources for everything they used. Clothing was made of home manufactured cloth or the skins of wild animals. Imported articles were procured at heavy cost, and but few found their way to our settlements. Steamboats and railroads were then unthought of, by us at least, and the navigation of the Mississippi was carried on in small boats that could be drawn up along the river bank by means of oars, spikes, poles, and hooks. The articles most in demand were axes, hoes, cotton cards, hatchels for cleaning flax, hemp and cotton, spinning wheels, knives, and ammunition, guns, and bar shears for plows. In exchange for such goods the people traded beef, hides, furs, tallow, beeswax, and honey. Money was not needed or used by anyone - everything was trade and barter.

The people were generous and brave. Their pleasures and pastimes were those usual in frontier settlements. They were hardy, and well versed in woodcraft. They aided each other, and were all in all a noble class of people, possessing many virtues and few faults. The girls were educated by their mothers to work, and had to work. It was then a disgrace for a young woman not to know how to take the raw material - the flax and cotton - and, unaided, manufacture her own clothing. It is a lamentable fact that such is no longer the case.

CHAPTER II
LEE BEGINS A CAREER

I formed a liking for Emily Conner. Emily was an orphan, and lived about four years at my aunt Charlotte's after her mother died, and until her father married again. She had a consoling word for me at all times when I was in trouble. From being friends, we became lovers and were engaged to be married, when my circumstances would permit. That winter I went to a school for three months.

Early in the spring the Indian war known as the Black Hawk war broke out, and volunteers were called for. I enrolled myself at the first call, in the company of Capt. Jacob Feaman, of Kaskaskia. The company was ordered to rendezvous at Fort Armstrong, Rock Island, where the troops were reorganized, and Capt. Feaman was promoted to colonel, and James Conner became captain of the company. I served until the end of the war, and was engaged in many skirmishes, and lastly was at the battle of Bad Axe, which I think took place on the 4th day of August, A. D. 1831, but am not certain as to the date.

The soldiers were allowed to go home about the 1st of September, 1831. Our company got to Kaskaskia, and were discharged, I think, on the 1st of September, 1831. I got back with a broken-down horse and worn-out clothing, and without money. I concluded to seek a more genial clime, one where I could more rapidly better my financial condition. I went to see and talk with Emily, the friend of my childhood, and the girl that taught me first to love. I informed her of my intentions. We pledged mutual and lasting fidelity to each other, and I bid her farewell and went to St. Louis to seek employment.

When I landed on the wharf at St. Louis I met a negro by the name of Barton, who had formerly been a slave to my mother. He informed me that he was a fireman on the steamboat Warrior, running the upper Mississippi, between St. Louis, Missouri, and Galena, Illinois. I told him I wanted work. He said he could get me a berth on the Warrior as fireman, at twenty-five dollars a month; but he considered the work more than I could endure, as it was a hard, hot boat to fire on. I insisted on making the effort, and was employed as fireman on the Warrior at twenty-five dollars per month. I found the work very hard. The first two or three times that I was on watch I feared I would be forced to give it up; but my spirit bore me up, and I managed to do my work until we reached the lower rapids near Keokuk. At this place the Warrior transferred its freight, in light boats, over the rapids to the Henry Clay, a steamer belonging to the same line.

The Henry Clay then lay at Commerce, now known as Nauvoo. I was detailed with two others to take a skiff with four passengers over the rapids. The passengers were Mrs. Bogges and her mother, and a lady whose name I have forgotten, and Mr. Bogges. The distance to the Henry Clay from where the Warrior lay was twelve miles. A large portion of the cargo of the Warrior belonged to the firm of Bogges & Co. When we had gone nearly halfway over the rapids my two assistants got drunk and could no longer assist me; they lay down in the skiff and went to sleep. Night was fast approaching, and there was no chance for sleep or refreshment, until we could reach Commerce or the Henry Clay. The whole labor fell on me, to take that skiff and its load of passengers to the steamer. Much of the distance I had to wade in the water and push the skiff, as was most convenient. I had on a pair of new calfskin boots when we started, but they were cut off my feet by the rocks in the river long before we reached the end of the journey.

After a deal of hardship I succeeded in getting my passengers to the steamer just as it became dark. I was wet, cold, hungry, and nearly exhausted. I sat down by the engine in my wet clothing and soon fell asleep, without bedding or food. I slept from exhaustion until near midnight, when I was seized with fearful crampings, accompanied by a cold and deathlike numbness. I tried to rise up, but could not. I thought my time had come, and that I would perish without aid or assistance.

When all hope had left me I heard a footstep approaching, and a man came and bent over me and asked if I was ill. I recognized the voice as that of Mr. Bogges. I said I was in the agonies of death, and a stranger without a friend on the boat. He felt my pulse, and hastened away, saying as he left me:

"Do not despair, young man, you are not without friends. I will return at once."

He soon returned, bringing a lantern and a bottle of cholera medicine, and gave me a large dose of the medicine; then he brought the captain and others to me. I was soon comfortably placed in bed, and from that time I had every attention paid me, and all the medical care that was necessary. Mr. Bogges told me that he had supposed I was one of the regular crew of the Henry Clay, and was among friends; that his wife had noticed that I appeared to be a stranger, and had seen me when I sat down by the engine alone; that after they retired his wife was restless and insisted on his getting up and finding me; this was the occasion of his assistance coming as it did.

Mr. Bogges had contracted for freighting his goods to Galena, where he resided; and had provided for the passage of himself, wife, and mother-in-law.

14

They would go by land from Commerce, as he dreaded the passage of the upper rapids in time of low water, as it then was.

After finishing the loading of the steamer I began to fire up to get ready for a start. While so engaged, Mr. Bogges came to me, and offered to employ me. He asked me then what wages I was getting. I told him twenty-five dollars.

"I will give you fifty dollars," said he.

We reached Galena in safety, and health. Now a new life commenced. Mr. Bogges introduced me to John D. Mulligan, his partner. I at once commenced my duties as bar-tender at the store. The business was such that I found it more than play. Many a time I did not get rest or sleep for forty-eight hours at a time. I have frequently taken in one hundred dollars in twenty- four hours for drinks, at five cents a drink. I paid attention to business, making the interest of my employers my interest. On account of my faithful services I was permitted to prepare hot lunches during the night, to sell to gamblers. What I made was my own. In this way I made from fifty to one hundred dollars a month extra.

One day while I was absent from the store a French half-breed, by the name of Shaunce got on a drunken spree and cleared out the store and saloon. Hearing the disturbance I ran to the store. I entered by the back door and went behind the counter. As I did so Shaunce ran to the counter and grabbed a large number of tumblers, and threw them about the house, breaking them all.

"Shaunce, you must either behave, or go out of the house," I said.

He jumped over the counter, caught me by the throat, and shoved me back against the counter, saying:

"You little dog, how dare you insult me!"

There was no time to swap knives. I must either receive a beating or do something to prevent it. I remembered the advice that my uncle Conner had given me about fighting.

"John, if you ever get in a fight with a man that overmatches you, take one of his hands in both of yours, and let him strike as he may, but get one of his fingers in your mouth and then bite it, and hold on until he gives up," he had said.

Acting on this advice, I succeeded in getting one of Shaunce's thumbs in my mouth. I held to it until I dislocated the thumb joint, when he yelled:

"Take him off!"

This little affair made a quiet man of Shaunce, and my employers were more pleased with me than ever before. They made me a present of fifty dollars for what I had done.

While with Bogges & Co. I made money, and was saving of what I earned. I did not gamble. I took good care of myself, and, having the respect of every person, I admit I was quite vain and proud. I was accused by the gamblers of being stingy with my money. So I thought I would do as others did, and commenced to give money to others as a stake to gamble with on shares. Soon I began to play. I won and lost, but did not play to any great extent. Mr. Bogges took me to task for gambling. He also showed me many of the tricks of the gamblers, and I promised him to quit the practice as soon as I got married.

In the early part of 1832 I received an affectionate letter from my Emily, desiring me to return to her, and settle down before I had acquired a desire for a rambling life. I then had five hundred dollars in money and two suits of broadcloth clothing. I was anxious to see Emily, so I settled up with Bogges & Co. and started for home. Emily was then living at her sister's house in Prairie de Roache; her brother-in-law, Thomas Blay, kept the tavern there. I boarded with them about two weeks, during which time I played cards with the Frenchman, and dealt "vantune," or twenty-one, for them to bet at. I was lucky, but I lived fast, and spent my money freely, and soon found that half of it was gone.

Emily was dissatisfied with my conduct. I proposed immediate marriage; Emily proposed to wait until the next fall, during which time we were to prepare for housekeeping. She wished to see if I would reform, for she had serious doubts about the propriety of marrying a gambler. She asked me to quit gambling, and if I had made that promise all would have been well, but I was stubborn and proud and refused to make any promise. I thought it was beneath my dignity. I really intended to never gamble after my wedding, but I would not tell her so; my vanity overruled my judgment. I said that if she had not confidence enough in me to take me as I was, without requiring me to give such a promise, I would never see her again until I came to ask her to my wedding.

This was cruel, and deeply wounded Emily; she burst into tears and turned from me. I never saw her again until I went to ask her to attend my wedding. I went up into the country and stopped with my cousins. While there I met the bride of my youth; she was the daughter of Joseph Woolsey and Abigail, his wife. I attended church, went to parties and picnics, and fell in love with Agathe Ann, the eldest girl. The old folks were op- posed to my marrying their daughter, but after suffering the tortures and overcoming the obstacles usual in such cases, I obtained the consent of the girl's parents, and was married to Agathe Ann Woolsey on the 24th day of July, A. D. 1833.

The expenses of the wedding ended all my money, and I was ready to start the world new and fresh. I had about fifty dollars to procure things to keep house on, but it was soon gone; yet it procured, about all we then thought we needed. I commenced housekeeping near my wife's father's, and had good success in all that I undertook. I made money, or rather I obtained considerable property, and was soon comfortably fixed.

CHAPTER III
LEE BECOMES A MORMON

After I moved to Luck Creek I was a fortunate man and accumulated property very fast. I look back to those days with pleasure. I had a large house and I gave permission to all sorts of people to come there and preach.

Methodists, Baptists, Campbellites, and Mormons all preached there when they desired to do so.

In 1837 a man by the name of King, from Indiana, passed by, or came to my place, on his way to Missouri to join the Mormons. He had been a New Light, or Campbellite preacher. I invited him to stay at my place until the next spring. I gave him provisions for his family, and he consented to and did stay with me some time.

Soon after that there was a Methodist meeting at my house. After the Methodist services were through I invited King to speak. He talked about half an hour on the first principles of the gospel as taught by Christ and his apostles, denouncing all other doctrines as spurious. This put an end to other denominations preaching in my house.

That was the first sermon I ever heard concerning Mormonism. The winter before, two elders, Durphy and Peter Dustan, stayed a few days with Hanford Stewart, a cousin of Levi Stewart, the bishop of Kanab. They preached in the neighborhood, but I did not attend or hear them preach. My wife and her mother went to hear them, and were much pleased with their doctrine. I was not a member of any Church, and considered the religion of the day as merely the opinions of men who preached for hire and worldly gain. I believed in God and in Christ, but I did not see any denomination that taught the apostolic doctrine as set forth in the New Testament. I read in the New Testament where the apostle Paul recommended his people to prove all things, then hold fast to that which is good; also that he taught that though an angel from heaven should preach any other gospel than this which ye have received, let him be accursed. This forbid me believing any doctrine that differed from that taught by Christ and his apostles. I wanted to belong to the true Church, or none.

When King began to preach at my house I noticed that every other denomination opposed him. I was surprised at this. I could not see how he could injure them if they were right. I had been brought up as a strict Catholic. I was taught to look upon all sects, except the Catholic, with disfavor, and my opinion was that the Mormons and all others were apostates from the true Church; that the Mormon Church was made up of the off-scourings of hell, or of apostates from the true Church. I then had not the most distant idea that the Mormons believed in the Old and New Testaments. I was astonished to hear King prove his religion from the Scriptures. I reflected. I determined, as every honest man should do, to fairly investigate his doctrines, and to do so with a prayerful heart.

The more I studied the question, the more interested I became. I talked of the doctrine to nearly every man I met. The excitement soon became general, and King was invited to preach in many places.

In the meantime Levi Stewart, one of my near neighbors, became interested in this religion, and went to Far West, Missouri, to investigate the question of Mormonism at headquarters. He joined the Church there, and when he returned he brought with him the Book of Mormon and a monthly periodical called the Elder's Journal.

17

By this time my anxiety was very great, and I determined to fathom the question to the bottom. My frequent conversations with Elder King served to carry me on to a conviction that the dispensation of the fullness of time would soon usher in upon the world. If such was the case I wished to know it; for the salvation of my never-dying soul was of far more importance to me than all other earthly considerations. I regarded the heavenly boon of eternal life as a treasure of great price. I left off my frivolity and commenced to lead a moral life. I began trying to lay up treasure in heaven, in my Father's rich storehouse, and wished to become an heir of righteousness, to inherit in common with the faithful children the rich legacy of our Father's Kingdom.

During that year our child, Elizabeth Adaline, died of scarlet fever. The night she lay a corpse I finished reading the Book of Mormon. I never closed my eyes in sleep from the time I commenced until I finished the book. I read it after asking God to give me knowledge to know if it was genuine and of Divine authority. By careful examination I found that it was in strict accord with the Bible and the gospel therein contained; that it purported to have been given to another people, who then lived on this continent, as the Old and New Testaments had been given to the Israelites in Asia. I also found many passages in the Bible in support of the forthcoming of such a work, preparatory to the gathering of the remnant of the House of Israel, and the opening glory of the Latter-day work, and the setting up of the Kingdom of God upon the earth for the reception of the Son of Man, and the millennial reign of Christ upon the earth a thousand years; all of which, to me, was of great moment. My whole soul was absorbed in these things.

My neighbor Stewart, who had just returned from Missouri, brought the most cheering and thrilling accounts of the power and manifestations of the Holy Spirit working with that people; that the spiritual gifts of the true believers in Christ were enjoyed by all who lived faithfully and sought them; that there was no deception about it; that everyone had a testimony for himself, and was not dependent upon another; that they had the gift of tongues, the interpretation of those tongues, the power of healing the sick by the laying on of hands, prophesying, casting out devils and evil spirits. All of which he declared, with words of soberness, to be true.

Stewart had been my playmate and my companion in former years. His word had great influence on me, and strengthened my conviction that the Book of Mormon was true - that it was a star opening the dispensation of the fullness of time. I believed the Book of Mormon was true, and, if so, everything but my soul's salvation was a matter of secondary consideration to me. I had a small fortune, a nice home, kind neighbors, and numerous friends, but nothing could shake the determination I then formed to break up, sell out, and leave Illinois and go to the Saints at Far West, Missouri.

My friends used every known argument to change my determination, but these words came into my mind, "First seek the righteousness of the Kingdom of God, then all things necessary will be added unto you "; and again, "What would it profit a man to gain the whole world and lose his own soul?" or, "What could a man gain in exchange for his soul?" I was here brought to the test, and my action was to decide on which I placed the most value - my earthly possessions and enjoyments or my reward in future, the salvation of my never-dying soul. I took up my cross and chose the latter. I sold out and moved to Far West. I took leave of my friends and made my way to where the Saints had gathered in Zion. Our journey was one full of events interesting to us, but not of sufficient importance to relate to the public. While on the journey I sold most of my cattle on time to an old man, a friend of Stewart's - took his notes, and let him keep them, which, as the sequel shows, was fortunate for me.

We arrived at Far West, the then headquarters of the Mormon Church, about the 4th day of June, 1838. The country around there for some fifteen or twenty miles, each way, was settled by Mormons. I do not think any others lived within that distance. The Mormons who had been driven from Jackson, Ray, and Clay counties, in 1833, settled in Caldwell and Daviess counties.

The night after our arrival at Far West there was a meeting to be held there. Stewart said to me:

"Let us go up and hear them speak with new tongues and interpret the same, and enjoy the gifts of the gospel generally, for this is to be a prayer and testimony meeting."

"I want no signs," I said. "I believe the gospel they preach on principle and reason, not upon signs - its consistency is all I ask. All I want are natural, logical, and reasonable arguments, to make up my mind from."

The Sunday after, I attended church in Far West Hall. The hall was crowded with people, so much so that I, with others, could not gain admittance to the building. I obtained standing room in one of the windows. I saw a man enter the house without uncovering his head. The Prophet ordered the Brother of Gideon to put that man out, for his presumption in daring to enter and stand in the house of God without uncovering his head. This looked to me like drawing the lines pretty snug and close; however, I knew but little of the etiquette of high life, and much less about that of the Kingdom of Heaven. I looked upon Joseph Smith as a prophet of God - as one who held the keys of this last dispensation, and I hardly knew what to think about the violent manner in which the man was treated who had entered the house of God without taking his hat off. But this did not lessen my faith; it served to confirm it. I was fearful that I might in some way unintentionally offend the great and good man who stood as God's prophet on the earth to point out the way of salvation.

We remained at the house of Elder Joseph Hunt, in Far West, several days. He was then a strong Mormon, and was afterwards first captain in the Mormon Battalion. He, as an elder in the Church, was a preacher of the gospel; all of his family were firm in the faith.

Elder Hunt preached to me the necessity of humility and a strict obedience to the gospel requirements through the servants of God. He informed me that the apostles and elders were our true teachers, and it was our duty to hear, learn, and obey; that the spirit of God was very fine and delicate, and was easily grieved and driven from us: that the more humble we were, the more of the Holy Spirit we would enjoy.

19

After staying in Far West about a week we moved about twenty miles, and settled on a stream called Marrowbone, at a place called afterwards Ambrosia. Sunday, June 17, 1838, I attended meeting. Samuel H. Smith, a brother of the Prophet, and Elder Daniel Cathcart preached. After meeting I and my wife were baptized by Elder Cathcart, in Ambrosia, on Shady Grove Creek, in Daviess County, Missouri. I was now a member of the Church, and expected to live in strict obedience to the requirements of the holy priesthood that ruled, governed, and controlled it. I must do this in order to advance in the scale of intelligence unto thrones, kingdoms, principalities, and powers, and through faithfulness and fidelity to the cause receive eternal increase in the mansions that would be prepared for me in my Father's kingdom.

Neighbor Stewart and myself each selected a place on the same stream, and near where his three brothers, Riley, Jackson, and Urban, lived. On my location there was a spring of pure, cold water; also a small lake fed by springs. This lake was full of fish, such as perch, bass, pickerel, mullet, and catfish. It was surrounded by a grove of heavy timber, mostly hickory and oak. We could have fish sufficient for use every day in the year if we desired.

My home on Ambrosia Creek reminded me of the one I had left on Luck Creek, Illinois; but it was on more rolling land, and much healthier than the Illinois home had proven to us. I knew I could soon replace, by labor, all the comfort I had abandoned when I started to seek my salvation. I felt that I had greatly benefitted my condition by seeking first the Kingdom of Heaven and its righteousness; all else, I felt, would be added unto me. But still I knew I must be frugal, industrious, and use much care. I improved my farm as rapidly as I could, and was soon so fixed that we were very comfortably established.

Meetings were held three times a week; also prayer and testimony meetings - at the latter sacrament was administered. In these meetings, as well as in everything I was called upon to do, I tried hard to give satisfaction. I was a devout follower from the first. Whatever duty was assigned me I tried to discharge with a willing heart and ready hand. This disposition, on my part, coupled with my views of duty, my promptness and punctuality, soon brought me to the notice of the leading men of the Church.

The motives of the people who composed my neighborhood were pure; they were all sincere in their devotions, and tried to square their actions through life by the golden rule - "Do unto others as you would they should do unto you." The word of a Mormon was then good for all it was pledged to or for. I was proud to associate with such an honorable people.

Twenty miles northeast of my home was the settlement of Adam-on-Diamond. It was on the east bank of Grand River, near the Three Forks. Lyman White, one of the twelve apostles, was president of that Stake of Zion. In July, 1838, Levi Stewart and myself concluded to visit the settlement of Adam-on-Diamond. We remained over night at the house of Judge Mourning. He was a Democrat. He told us that at the approaching election the Whigs were going to cast their votes, at the outside precincts, early in the day, and then rush in force to the town of Gallatin, the county seat of Daviess County, and prevent the Mormons from voting. The Judge requested us to inform our people of the facts in the case, and for us to see that the Mormons went to the polls in force, prepared to resist and overcome all violence that might be offered. He said the Whigs had no right to deprive the Mormons of their right of suffrage, who had a right to cast their votes as free and independent Americans.

The two political parties were about equally divided in Daviess County. The Mormons held the balance of power, and could turn the scale whichever way they desired. I had heard of Judge Mourning as a sharp political worker, and I then thought he was trying to carry out an electioneering job for his party.

We visited our friends at Adam-on-Diamond, and returned home. While on this trip I formed the acquaintance of Solomon McBrier, and purchased some cattle from him. He wished to sell me quite a number, but as I did not want to be involved in debt I refused to take them. I had a perfect horror of debt, for I knew that when a man was in debt he was in nearly every respect a slave, and that if I got in debt it would worry me and keep my mind from that quiet repose so necessary for contemplating the beauties of nature and communing with the Spirit regarding holy subjects.

Just before the election of August, 1838, a general notice was given for all the brethren of Daviess County to meet at Adam-on- Diamond. Every man obeyed the call. At that meeting the males over eighteen years of age were organized into a military body, according to the law of the Priesthood, and called The Host of Israel. The first rank was a captain with ten men under him; next was a captain of fifty - that is, he had five companies of ten; next, the captain of a hundred, or of ten captains and companies of ten. The entire male membership of the Mormon Church was then organized in the same way.

This, as I was informed, was the first organization of the military force of the Church. It was so organized by command of God, as revealed through the Lord's prophet, Joseph Smith. God commanded Joseph Smith to place the Host of Israel in a situation for defense against the enemies of God and the Church of Jesus Christ of Latter-day Saints.

At the same Conference another organization was formed - it was called the Danites. The members of this order were placed under the most sacred obligations that language could invent. They were sworn to stand by and sustain each other; to sustain, protect, defend, and obey the leaders of the Church, under any and all circumstances unto death; and to disobey the orders of the leaders of the Church, or divulge the name of a Danite to an outsider, or to make public any of the secrets of the order of Danites, was to be punished with death. And I can say of a truth, many have paid the penalty for failing to keep their covenants.

They had signs and tokens for use and protection. The token of recognition was such that it could be readily understood, and it served as a token of distress by which they could know each other from their enemies, although they were entire strangers to each other. When the sign was given it must be responded to and obeyed, even at the risk or certainty of death. The Danite that would refuse to respect the token, and comply with all its requirements, was stamped with dishonor, infamy, shame, disgrace, and his fate for cowardice and treachery was death.

21

This sign or token of distress is made by placing the right hand on the right side of the face, with the points of the fingers upward, shoving the hand upward until the ear is snug between the thumb and forefinger. I here pause, and ask myself the question:

"Am I justified in making the above statement?"

Those who think I am not should wait until they read the whole story. It is my purpose and intention to free my mind and bring to light some of the secret workings of the Priesthood.

To return to the election at Gallatin: The brethren all attended the election. All things seemed to pass off quietly, until some of the Mormons went up to the polls to vote. I was then lying on the grass with McBrier and a number of others.

As the Mormons were going to the polls a drunken brute by the name of Richard Weldorp stepped up to a little Mormon preacher by the name of Brown and said:

"Are you a Mormon preacher?"

"Yes, sir, I am."

"Do you Mormons believe in healing the sick by laying on of hands, speaking in tongues, and casting out devils?"

"We do," said Brown.

Weldon then said, "You are a liar. Joseph Smith is an impostor."

With this, he attacked Brown, and beat him severely. Brown did not resent it, but tried to reason with him; but without effect.

At this time a Mormon by the name of Hyrum Nelson attempted to pull Weldon off Brown, when he was struck by half a dozen men on the head, shoulders, and face. He was soon forced to the ground. Just then Riley Stewart struck Weldon across the back of the head with a billet of oak lumber and broke his skull. Weldon fell on me, and appeared lifeless. The blood flowed freely from the wound. Immediately the fight became general.

Gallatin was a new town, with about ten houses, three of which were saloons. The town was on the bank of Grand River, and heavy timber came near the town, which stood in a little arm of the prairie. Close to the polls there was a lot of oak timber which had been brought there to be riven into shakes or shingles, leaving the heart, taken from each shingle-block, lying there on the ground. These hearts were three square, four feet long, weighed about seven pounds, and made a very dangerous, yet handy weapon; and when used by an enraged man they were truly a class of instrument to be dreaded.

When Stewart fell the Mormons sprang to the pile of oak hearts, and each man, taking one for use, rushed into the crowd. The Mormons were yelling:

"Save him!" and the settlers yelled:

"Kill him!"

The sign of distress was given by the Danites, and all rushed forward, determined to save Stewart, or die with him. One of the mob stabbed Stewart in the shoulder. He rose and ran, trying to escape, but was again surrounded and attacked by a large number of foes.

The Danite sign of distress was again given by John L. Butler, one of the captains of the Host of Israel. Butler was a brave, true man, and a leader that it was a pleasure to follow where duty called. Seeing the sign, I sprang to my feet and armed myself with one of the oak sticks. I did this because I was a Danite, and my oaths that I had taken required immediate action on my part in support of the one giving the sign. I ran into the crowd.

As I reached it I saw Nelson fighting for life. He was surrounded by a large number who were seeking to murder him; but he had a loaded whip, the lash wrapped around his hand, using the handle, which was loaded with several pounds of lead, as a weapon of defense. He was using it with effect, for he had men piled around him in all shapes.

As I approached a man sprang to his feet. He had just been knocked down by Nelson. As the man was rising Nelson gave him a blow across the loins with the handle of his whip, which had the effect of straightening out the villain on the grass and rendered him an inoffensive spectator during the remainder of the play.

Capt. Butler was then a stranger to me, and until I saw him give the Danite sign of distress I believed him to be one of the Missouri ruffians who were our enemies. In this contest I came near committing a serious mistake. I had raised my club to strike a man, when a Missourian rushed at him and struck him with a loaded whip, and called him a cursed Mormon. The man then gave the sign, and I knew how to act.

Capt. Butler was attacked from all sides, but being a powerful man he used his oak club with effect and knocked a man down at each blow that he struck, and each man that felt the weight of his weapon was out of the fight for that day at least. Many of those that he came in contact with had to be carried from the field for surgical aid. In the battle, which was spirited, but short in duration, nine men had their skulls broken, and many others were seriously injured in other ways. The severe treatment of the mob by the Danites soon ended the battle.

Three hundred men were present at this difficulty, only thirty of whom were Mormons, and only eight Mormons took part in the fight. I was an entire stranger to all who were engaged in the affray, except Stewart, but I had seen the sign, and, like Samson when loaning against the pillar, I felt the power of God nerve my arm for the fray. It helps a man a great deal in a fight to know that God is on his side.

After the violence had ceased Capt. Butler called the Mormons to him, and as he stood on a pile of building timber he made a speech to the brethren. He said that his ancestors had served in the War of the Revolution to establish a free and independent government - one in which all men had equal rights and privileges; that he professed to be half white and free born, and claimed a right to enjoy his constitutional privileges, and would have his rights as a citizen, if he had to fight for them; that as to his religion, it was a matter between his God and himself, and no man's business; that he would vote, and would die before he would be driven from the polls.

Several of the Gentile leaders then requested us to lay down our clubs and go and vote. This Capt. Butler refused, saying:

"We will not molest anyone who lets us alone, but we will not risk ourselves again in that crowd without our clubs."

The result was the Mormons all voted. It is surprising what a few resolute men can do when united.

It may be well for purposes of explanation to refer back to the celebration of the Declaration of Independence on the 4th of July, 1838, at Far West. That day Joseph Smith made known to the people the substance of a Revelation he had received from God. It was to the effect that all the Saints throughout the land were required to sell their possessions, gather all their money together, and send an agent to buy up all the land in the region round about Far West, and get a patent for the land from the Government, then deed it over to the Church; then every man should come up there to the land of their promised inheritance and consecrate what he had to the Lord.

In return the Prophet would set apart a tract of land for each Saint - the amount to correspond with the number of the Saint's family - and this land should be for each Saint an everlasting inheritance. In this way the people could, in time, redeem Zion (Jackson County) without the shedding of blood. It was also revealed that unless this was done, in accordance with God's demand, as required by Him in the Revelation then given to the people through his Prophet, Joseph Smith, the Saints would be driven from State to State, from city to city, from one abiding place to another, until the members would die and waste away, leaving but a remnant of the Saints to return and receive their inheritance in Zion (Jackson County) in the last days.

Sidney Rigdon was then the mouthpiece of Joseph Smith, as Aaron was of Moses in olden times. Rigdon told the Saints that day that if they did not come up as true Saints and consecrate their property to the Lord, by laying it down at the feet of the apostles, they would in a short time be compelled to consecrate and yield it up to the Gentiles; that if the Saints would be united as one man, in this consecration of their entire wealth to the God of Heaven, by giving it up to the control of the Apostolic Priesthood, then there would be no further danger to the Saints; they would no more be driven from their homes on account of their faith and holy works, for the Lord had revealed to Joseph Smith that He would then fight the battles of His children, and save them from all their enemies; that the Mormon people would never be accepted as the children of God unless they were united as one man, in temporal as well as spiritual affairs, for Jesus had said unless ye are one, ye are not Mine; that oneness must exist to make the Saints the accepted children of God; that if the Saints would yield obedience to the commands of the Lord all would be well, for the Lord had confirmed these promises by a Revelation which He had given to Joseph Smith, in which it was said:

"I, the Lord, will fight the battles of my people, and if your enemies shall come up against you, spare them, and if they shall come up against you again, then shall ye spare them also; oven unto the third time shall ye spare them; but if they come up against you the fourth time, I, the Lord, will deliver them into your hands, to do with them as seemeth good unto you; but if you then spare them it shall be accounted unto you for righteousness."

The words of the apostle, and the promises of God, as then revealed to me, made a deep impression on my mind, as it did upon all who heard the same.

24

We that had given up all else for the sake of the gospel felt willing to do anything on earth that it was possible to do to obtain the protection of God, and have and receive His smile of approbation. Those who, like me, had full faith in the teachings of God, as revealed by Joseph Smith, His Prophet, were willing to comply with every order, and to obey every wish of the Priesthood.

The majority of the people, however, felt like Ananias and Sapphira - they dare not trust all to God and His Prophet. They felt that their money was as safe in their own possession as it was when held by the Church authorities. A vote of the people was had to determine - the question whether they would consecrate their wealth to the Church, or not. The vote was taken and was unanimous for the consecration. I soon found out that the people had voted as I have often known them to do in Mormon meetings since then; they vote to please the Priesthood, then act to suit themselves. I never thought that was right or honest; men should vote their sentiments, but they do not at all times do so. I have been the victim of such hypocrites.

The vote, as I said, was taken. It was done by a show of hands, but not a show of hearts. By the readiness with which all hands went up in favor of consecration it was declared that the people were of a truth God's children, and, as such, would be protected by Him. The Prophet and all his Priesthood were jubilant, and could hardly contain themselves; they were so happy to see the people such dutiful Saints.

Sidney Rigdon on that day delivered an oration, in which he said the Mormons were, as a people, loyal to the Government, obedient to the laws, and as such they were entitled to the protection of the Government in common with all other denominations, and were justified in claiming as full protection, in their religious matters, as the people of any other sect; that the Mormons had suffered from mob rule and violence, but would no longer submit to the mob or unjust treatment that had so long followed them. Now and forevermore would they meet force with force.

"We have been driven from Kirkland," said he; "from Jackson County, the true Zion; and now we will maintain our rights, defend our homes, our wives and children, and our property from mob rule and violence. If the Saints are again attacked, we will carry on a war of extermination against our enemies, even to their homes and firesides, until we despoil those who have despoiled us, and give no quarter until our enemies are wasted away. We will unfurl to the breeze the flag of our nation, and under that banner of freedom we will maintain our rights, or die in the attempt."

At the end of each sentence Rigdon was loudly cheered; and when he closed his oration I believed the Mormons could successfully resist the world. But this feeling of confidence faded away as soon as a second thought entered my mind. I then feared that the days of liberty for our people had been numbered. First, I feared the people would not give up all their worldly possessions, to be disposed of by and at the will and pleasure of three men. In the second place, I doubted the people being so fully regenerated as to entitle them to the full and unconditional support and favor of God that had been promised through the Revelation to Joseph Smith, in favor of the Latter-day Saints. I knew that God

25

was able and willing to do all He had promised, but I feared that the people still loved worldly pleasures so well that God's mercy would be rejected by them, and all would be lost.

About three days after the proclamation of Rigdon had been made there was a storm of rain, during which the thunder and lightnings were constant and terrible. The liberty pole in the town was struck by lightning and shivered to atoms. This evidence from the God of nature also convinced me that the Mormon people's liberties, in that section of the country, were not to be of long duration.

CHAPTER IV - THE SAINTS BESET WITH TROUBLES

The Saints did not consecrate their possessions as they had so recently voted they would do; they began to reflect, and the final determination was that they could manage their worldly effects better than any one of the apostles; in fact, better than the Prophet and the Priesthood combined. Individual Saints entered large tracts of land in their own names, and thereby secured all of the most desirable land round about Far West. These landed proprietors became the worst kind of extortionists, and forced the poor Saints to pay them large advances for every acre of land that was settled, and nothing could be called free from the control of the money power of the rich and headstrong Mormons who had defied the revelations and wishes of God.

So things went from bad to worse, until the August election at Gallatin referred to. The troubles of that day brought the Church and Saints to a standstill; business was paralyzed; alarm seized the stoutest hearts, and dismay was visible in every countenance. The Prophet issued an order to gather all the people at Far West and Adam-on-Diamond, under the leadership of Col. Lyman White, for the purpose of protecting the people from mob violence, and to save their property from lawless thieves who were roaming the country in armed bands.

The Gentiles and Mormons hastened to the executive of the State. The Gentiles asked for a military force to protect the settlers from Mormon violence. The Mormons requested, an investigating committee to inquire into the whole subject and suggest means necessary for future safety to each party. Also they demanded military protection from the mobs and outlaws that infested the country.

The Governor sent troops to keep order. They were stationed about midway between Far West and Adam-on-Diamond. A committee was also appointed and sent to Gallatin to inquire into the recent disturbances. This committee had

26

full power to send for witnesses, make arrests of persons accused of crime, and generally to do all things necessary for a full and complete investigation of the entire affair.

Many arrests were made at the request of the committee. The persons so arrested were taken before Justice Black, of Daviess County, and examined; witnesses were examined for both parties, and much hard and false swearing was done on both sides. After a long and fruitless examination the committee adjourned, leaving the military to look after matters until something would turn up to change the feeling of danger then existing. It was thought by the committee that all would soon become quiet and peace would be restored.

The Gentiles of the country were dissatisfied with the action of the committee and in no way disposed to accept peace on any terms; they determined that, come what would, the Mormons should be driven from the State of Missouri. Letters were written by the Gentiles around Far West to all parts of the State, and elsewhere, giving the most fearful accounts of Mormon atrocities. Some of the writers said it was useless to send less than three or four men for each Mormon, because the Mormons felt sure of heaven if they fell fighting, hence they did not fear death; that they fought with the desperation of devils.

Such reports spread like wildfire throughout northern Missouri, and thence all over the States of the Mississippi Valley, and resulted in creating a feeling of the most intense hatred in the breasts of all the Gentiles against the Mormons. Companies of volunteers were raised and armed in every town throughout northern Missouri, and commenced concentrating in the vicinity of the Mormon settlements. The troops sent by the Governor to guard the settlers and preserve order soon took part with the mob, and all show for legal protection was gone, so far as Mormons were concerned. I had built a cabin in the valley of Adam-on-Diamond, at the point where the Prophet said Adam blessed his posterity after being driven from the Garden of Eden.

The condition of the country being such that we could not labor on our farms, I concluded to go and hunt for wild honey. Several of my neighbors were to join me in my bee hunt, and we started with our teams, and traveled northeasterly until we reached the heavy timber at the three forks of Grand River. We camped on the middle fork of Grand River, and had fine success in securing honey.

We had been out at camp only two or three days when we discovered signs of armed men rushing through the country. On the 3d of October, 1838, we saw a large number of men that we knew were enemies to the Mormons on their way, as we supposed, to attack our people at the settlements. I concluded to go and meet them, and find out for certain what they were really intending to do. I was forced to act with caution, for, if they discovered that we were Mormons, our lives would be taken by the desperate men composing the mob who called themselves State volunteers. I took my gun and carrying a bucket on my arm started out to meet the people and learn their intentions. I met them just after they had broken camp on Sunday morning.

27

As soon as I saw them I was certain they were out hunting for Mormons. I concluded to pass myself off as an outsider, the better to learn their history. My plan worked admirably. I stood my ground until a company of eighteen men rode up to me, and said:

"You move early."

"Not so early, gentlemen; I am not moving any sooner than you are. What are you all doing in this part of the country, armed to the teeth as you are? Are you hunting for Indians?"

"No," said they, "but we wish to know where you are from, and what you are doing."

"I am from Illinois; there are four of us who have come out here to look up a good location to settle. We stopped on Marrowbone, and did think of staying there, until the settlers and Mormons got into a row at Gallatin, on election day. After that we concluded to strike out and see what this country looked like. I am now going to cut a bee tree that I found yesterday evening, and I brought my gun along so that if I met an old buck I could secure some venison to eat with my honeycomb."

As I got through they all huddled around me and commenced to relate the horrors of Mormonism. They advised me to have nothing to do with the Mormons, for said they:

"As old Joe Smith votes, so will every Mormon in the country vote, and when they get into a fight they are just the same way; they stick together. When you attack one of the crew you bring every one of them after you like a nest of hornets."

To this I replied that I had heard a little of the fuss at Gallatin, but did not suppose I had got the right of the story, and would be glad if they would tell me just how it was. I should like to learn the facts from an eyewitness. Several of the men spoke up and said they were there and saw it all. They then told the story, and did the Mormons more justice than I expected from them.

They said, among other things, that there was a large rawboned man there who spoke in tongues, and that when the fight commenced he cried:

"Charge, Danites!"

They then said the Mormons must leave the country.

"If we do not make them do so now, they will be so strong in a few years they will rule the country as they please. Another band of men will come along soon; and they will then go through the Mormon settlements and burn up every house, and lynch every Mormon they find. The militia has been sent to keep order in Daviess County, but will soon be gone, and the work of destroying the Mormons begin."

"If they have done as you say they have, pay them in their own coin," I said.

The company then passed on, and I returned with a heavy heart to my friends. I advised making an immediate start for home, and in a few minutes we were on our way.

While coming up from home we had found four bee trees, that we left standing, intending to cut them down and get the honey as we went back. When we got on the prairie, which was about eight miles across, the men with me

28

wanted to go and get the honey. I was fearful that the people I had met in the morning would attack the settlements, and I wanted to go directly home and let trees and honey alone.

While we were talking the matter over a single blackbird came to us, apparently in great distress. It flew around each one of us, and would alight on the head of each one of our horses, and especially on my horses' heads, and it even came and alighted on my hat, and would squeak as though it was in pain, and turn its feathers up, and acted as if it wished to warn us of danger. Then it flew off towards the settlements where I wished to go.

All admitted that these were strange actions for a bird, but they still insisted on going to cut the bee trees. I was persuaded to go with them. We had gone a quarter of a mile further when the blackbird returned to us and went through the same performance as before, and again flew off toward the settlement.

This was to me a warning to go home at once; that there was danger there to my family. I then proposed that we all join in prayer. We did so, and I prayed to the Author of our existence, and asked that if it was His will for us to go home at once, and if the blackbird had been sent as a warning messenger, to let it return again, and I would follow it. We then traveled on some two miles, when the messenger returned the third time and appeared, if possible, more determined than before to turn us towards home. I turned my team and started, as straight as I could go, for Adam-on-Diamond.

As we passed over the prairie we saw the smoke rising from many farms and houses in the vicinity of where we had left our bee trees. This smoke showed us that our enemies were at work, and that had we kept on in the course we were first intending to travel we would have fallen into the hands of the lawless and lost our lives.

Before we got home the news of the attack upon the settlements had reached there. It was also reported, and we afterwards learned that the report was true, that many of the Mormon settlers had been tied to trees and whipped with hickory withes, some of them being horribly mangled by the mob. This conduct on the part of the Gentiles roused every Mormon to action, and the excitement was very great.

Joseph the Prophet was then sent for. Col. White called together every man and boy that could carry arms. When the forces were assembled Col. White made a war speech. As he spoke he stood by his fine brown horse. There was a bearskin on his saddle. He had a red handkerchief around his head, regular Indian fashion, with the knot in front; he stood bareheaded, in his shirt sleeves, with collar open, showing his naked breast. He held a large cutlass in his right hand. His manner of address struck terror to his enemies, while it charged his brethren with enthusiastic zeal and forced them to believe they were invincible and bullet-proof. We were about three hundred and seventy-five strong. I stood near Col. White while he was speaking, and I judge of its effect upon others by the way it affected me.

While our Colonel was in the midst of his speech the aid-de-camp of the militia colonel came up with a dispatch to Col. White, to the effect that the militia had become mutinous and could no longer be controlled, but were going to join the mob; that the colonel would disband his forces, and would then go and report to the Governor the true condition of the country; that Col. White must take and make use of all the means in his power to protect the people from the mob, for the Government officers were powerless to aid him.

The aid did not deliver his message, for as he rode up close to where Col. White was standing speaking to his men, he stopped and listened a short time; then he wheeled his horse and rode back to the militia camp and reported that Col. White had fifteen thousand men under arms, in battle array, and would be upon their camp in less than two hours; that he was then making a speech to the army, and that it was the most exciting speech he had ever listened to in his life; that he meant war, and of the most fearful kind, and the only safety for their forces was in instant retreat. The soldiers broke camp and left in haste. I cannot say that the colonel commanding the militia was alarmed, or that he fled through fear of being overcome; but it suited him to leave, for he was anxious to prevent a collision between his troops and the men under Col. White.

Joseph, when informed of the danger of the settlers from mob violence, sent Maj. Seymour Brunson, of Far West, with fifty men to protect the settlers who lived on the two forks of the Grand River. Col. White kept his men in readiness for action. A strong guard was posted round the settlement; a point was agreed upon to which place all were to hasten in case of alarm. This point of meeting was east of the town, under the bluffs, on the main road leading from Mill Port to Adam-on-Diamond.

This road ran between the fields and bluff. We expected to be attacked every hour. A few nights afterwards the alarm was given, and every man rushed to the field. When I reached the command I found everything in confusion. The officer in command tried to throw two companies across the road, but the firing was heavy and constant from the opposing forces, who had selected a strong point for the purpose of attack and defense. The flash of the rifles and the ringing reports that echoed through the hills at each discharge of the guns added to the confusion, and soon forced the Mormons to take up their position in the fence corners and elsewhere, so they could be in a measure protected from the bullets of the enemy. Soon there was order in our ranks, and we were prepared to dislodge our opponents or die in the attempt, when two men came at the full speed of their horses, shouting:

"Peace! peace! Cease firing, it is our friends."

Chapman Duncan, the adjutant of Col. White, was the one who shouted peace. We were then informed that the men we had taken for a part of the Gentile mob were no other than the command of Maj. Brunson, who had been out on Three Forks to defend the settlers, and that he had been ordered back to the main body of the Hosts of Israel. They had intended to stop at Mill Port, but finding it deserted they concluded to alarm the troops at Adam-on-Diamond, so as to learn whether they would fight or not. I admit that I was much pleased to learn that danger was over and we were facing friends and not enemies; yet I was mad to think men would impose upon us in that way. The experiment was a dangerous one, and likely to be very serious in its consequences. The other men with me were equally wroth at the insult offered by those who had been so foolish as to question our bravery.

The withdrawal of the State militia was the signal for the Gentiles to give vent to the worst of their inclinations. The Mormons, at command of the Prophet, at once abandoned their homes, taking what could be carried with them, and hastened to either Far West or Adam-on-Diamond for protection and safety. Some few refused to obey orders, and they afterwards paid the penalty for disobedience by giving up their lives to the savage Gentiles who attacked and well-nigh exterminated them.

Armed men roamed in bands all over Caldwell, Carroll, and Daviess counties; both Mormons and Gentiles were under arms, doing injury to each other when occasion offered. The burning of houses, farms, and stacks of grain was generally indulged in by each party. Lawlessness prevailed, and pillage was the rule.

The Prophet Joseph said it was a civil war, and that by the rules of war each party was justified in spoiling his enemy. This opened the door, and men of former quiet became perfect demons in their efforts to spoil and waste away the enemies of the Church. I then found that men are creatures of circumstances, and that the occasion calls forth the men needed for each enterprise.

I also soon saw that it was the natural inclination of men to convert to their own use that which others possessed. What perplexed me most was to see how religion had not the power to subdue that passion in man, but at the first moment when the restrictions of the Church were withdrawn the most devout in our community acted like natural-born thieves.

Being young, stout, and having plenty of property, I fitted myself out in first-class style. I had good horses and plenty of the best of arms. I joined in the general patrol duty, and took part in daily raids made under either Maj. Brunson or Capt. Alexander McRay. I saw much of what was being done by both parties. I also made several raids under Capt. Jonathan Dunham, alias Black Hawk. I remember one incident that was amusing at the time, as it enabled us to determine what part of our forces would fight on the field and face the enemy, and also those who preferred to fight with their mouths.

Early in the morning, while Maj. Brunson's men were marching along, shivering in the cold - for it was a dark, cloudy morning late in October, 1838 - we saw a company of horsemen some three miles away. We concluded they were Missourians, and made for them at full speed. They halted and appeared willing to fight. When our command got within three hundred yards of them many of our pulpit braves found out all at once that they must stop and dismount to fix their saddles or for some other reason. The remainder of us rode on until within one hundred and fifty yards of the other force, and were drawn up in line of battle. Maj. Brunson rode forward and hailed them, saying,

"Who are you?"

"Capt. McRay," was the reply. "Who are you?"

"Maj. Brunson."

They met and shook hands. Seeing this the pulpit braves rushed up in great haste and took their places in the ranks, and lamented because we did not have an enemy to overcome.

So it is through life - a coward is generally a liar; those men were cowards, and lied when they pretended they would like to fight. All cowards are liars, but many liars are brave men.

While I was engaged with the Mormon troops in ranging over the country, the men that I was with took a large amount of loose property, but did not while I was with them burn any houses or murder any men. Yet we took what property we could find, especially provisions, fat cattle, arms, and ammunition. But still many houses were burned and much damage was done by the Mormons, and they captured a howitzer and many guns from the Gentiles. Frequent attacks were also made upon the Mormon settlements.

The Mormons made an attack on Gallatin one night, and carried off much plunder. I was not there with them, but I talked often with others and learned all the facts about it. The town was burned down, and everything of value, including the goods in two stores, carried off by the Mormons. I often escaped being present with the troops by loaning my horses and arms to others who liked that kind of work better than I did. Unless I had adopted that course I could never have escaped from being with the Hosts of Israel, for I was one of the regular Host, and could not avoid going when ordered, unless I furnished a substitute, which sometimes was accepted, but not always.

Once a company went from Adam-on-Diamond and burned the house and buildings belonging to my friend McBrier. Every article of movable property was taken by the troops; he was utterly ruined. This man was an honorable man, but mere good character, and properly, had no effect on those who were working to build up the Kingdom of God.

The Mormons brought in every article that could be used, and much that was of no use or value was hauled to Adam-on-Diamond. Such acts had the effect of arousing every Gentile in the three counties of Caldwell, Carroll, and Daviess, as well as to bring swarms of armed Gentiles from other localities.

Brother Lyman White, with three hundred men, was called to defend Far West. I went with his command. The night White reached Far West the battle of Crooked River was fought. Capt. David Patton, alias Fear Not, one of the twelve apostles, had been sent out by the Prophet with fifty men to attack a body of Missourians who were camping on the Crooked River. Capt. Patton's men were nearly all, if not every one of them, Danites. The attack was made just before daylight in the morning. Fear Not wore a white blanket overcoat, and led the attacking party. He was a brave, impulsive man. He rushed into the thickest of the fight, regardless of danger - really seeking it to show his men that God would shield him from all harm. But he counted without just reason upon being invincible, for a ball soon entered his body, passing through his hips. The wound was fatal; but he kept on his feet and led his men some time before yielding to the effects of the wound.

The Gentiles said afterwards that Capt. Patton told his men to charge in the name of Lazarus:

"Charge, Danites, charge!"

As soon as he uttered the command which distinguished him they gave the Danite captain a commission with powder and ball, and sent him on to preach to the spirits.

In this battle several men were killed and wounded on both sides. I do not remember all of the names of the Danites that were killed, but I do remember that a man by the name of Banion was killed, and one by the name of Holbrook wounded. I knew a man by the name of Tarwater, on the Gentile side, that was cut up fearfully. He was taken prisoner. The Danites routed the Gentiles, who fled in every direction. The night being dark, Holbrook and another Danite met and had a hand-to-hand fight, in which they cut each other fearfully with their swords before they discovered that they were friends.

After the Gentiles retreated the Mormons started for Far West, taking Tarwater along as a prisoner. After traveling several miles they halted in a grove of timber and released Tarwater, telling him he was free to go home. He started off, and when he was some forty yards from the Mormons Parley P. Pratt, then one of the twelve apostles, stepped to a tree, laid his gun up by the side of the tree, took deliberate aim, and shot Tarwater. He fell and lay still. The Mormons went on and left him lying where he fell.

CHAPTER V
THE MORMON WAR

After 1844 it was my habit to keep a journal, in which I wrote at length all that I considered worthy of remembering. Most of my journals, written up to 1860, were called for by Brigham, under the plea that he wished the Church historian to write up the Mormon history, and wanted my journals to aid him in making the history perfect. As these journals contained many things not intended for the public eye concerning the Mormon leaders and all I knew of the Mountain Meadows Massacre, and what led to it, they were never returned to me.

To proceed: I was at Far West when the Danites returned. They brought Capt. Patton with them. He died that night, and his death spread a mantle of gloom over the entire community. It robbed many of their fond hope that they were invincible. If Fear Not could be killed, who then might claim immunity from the missiles of death hurled by Gentile weapons?

Up to this time I firmly believed what the Prophet and his apostles had said on that subject. I had considered that I was bullet-proof, that no Gentile ball could ever harm me or any Saint, and I believed that a Danite could not be killed by Gentile hands. I thought that one Danite would chase a thousand Gentiles, and two could put ten thousand to flight.

Alas! my dream of security was over. One of our mighty men had fallen, and by Gentile hands. My amazement at the fact was equal to my sorrow for the death of the great warrior apostle. I had considered that all the battles between Danites and Gentiles would end like the election fight at Gallatin, and the only ones to be injured would be the Gentiles.

We had been promised and taught by the Prophet and his Priesthood that henceforth God would fight our battles, and I looked as a consequence for a bloodless victory on the side of the Lord, and that nothing but disobedience to the teachings of the Priesthood could render a Mormon subject to injury from Gentile forces. I believed as our leaders taught us, that all our sufferings and persecutions were brought upon us by the all-wise God of Heaven as chastisement to bring us together in unity of faith and strict obedience to the requirements of the Gospel; and the feeling was general that all our sufferings were the result of individual sin, and not the fault of our leaders and spiritual guides.

We, as members of the Church, had no right to question any act of our superiors; to do so wounded the Spirit of God, and would lead to our own loss and confusion. Still, I was thunderstruck to hear Joseph the Apostle say at the funeral of Capt. Patton that the Mormons fell by the missiles of death the same as other men. He also said that the Lord was angry with the people, for they had been unbelieving and faithless; they had denied the Lord the use of their earthly treasures, and placed their affections upon worldly things more than upon heavenly things; that to expect God's favor we must blindly trust him; that if the Mormons would wholly trust in God the windows of heaven would be opened and a shower of blessings sent upon the people; that all the people could contain of blessings would be given as a reward for obedience to the will of God as made known to mankind through the Prophet of the ever-living God; that the Mormons, if faithful, obedient, and true followers of the advice of their leaders, would soon enjoy all the wealth of the earth; that God would consecrate the riches of the Gentiles to the Saints.

This and much more he said to induce the people to obey the will of the Priesthood. I believed all he said, for he supported it by quotations from Scripture, and if I believed the Bible, as I did most implicitly, I could not help believing in Joseph, the prophet of God in these last days, Joseph declared that he was called of God and given power and authority from heaven to do God's will; that he had received the keys of the holy Priesthood from the apostles Peter, James, and John, and had been dedicated, set apart, and anointed as the prophet, seer, and revelator, and sent to open the dispensation of the fullness of time, according to the words of the apostles; that he was charged with the restoration of the House of Israel, and to gather the Saints from the four corners of the earth to the land of promise, Zion, the Holy Land (Jackson County), and to the setting up of the Kingdom of God preparatory to the second coming of Christ in the last days. Every Mormon, true to his faith, believed as fully in Joseph and his holy character as he did that God existed.

The Prophet Joseph was a most extraordinary man; he was rather large in stature, some six feet two inches in height, well built, though a little stoop-shouldered, with prominent and well- developed features, a Roman nose, light chestnut hair, upper lip full and rather protruding, chin broad and square, and an eagle eye, and on the whole had something in his manner and appearance that was bewitching and winning; his countenance was that of a plain, honest man, full of benevolence and philanthropy and void of deceit or hypocrisy. He was resolute and firm of purpose, strong as most men in physical power, and all who saw were forced to admire him, as he then looked and existed. In the sports of the day, such as wrestling, he was over the average. Very few of the Saints had the strength needed to throw the Prophet in a fair tussle. In every gathering he was a welcome guest, and always added to the amusement of the people, instead of dampening their ardor.

During the time that we were camping at Adam-on-Diamond, waiting to see what would be the result of the quarrel between our Church and the Gentiles, one Sunday morning (it had rained heavily the night before and the air was cold) the men were shivering over a few firebrands, feeling out of sorts and quite cast down. The Prophet came up while the brethren were moping around and caught first one and then another and shook them up, and said:

"Get out of here, and wrestle; jump, run, do anything but mope around; warm yourselves up; this inactivity will not do for soldiers."

The words of the Prophet put life and energy into the men. A ring was soon formed, according to the custom of the people. The Prophet stepped into the ring, ready for a tussle with any comer. Several went into the ring to try their strength, but each one was thrown by the Prophet, until he had thrown several of the stoutest of the men present. Then he stepped out of the ring and took a man by the arm and led him in to take his place, and so it continued - the men who were thrown retiring in favor of the successful one. A man would keep the ring so long as he threw his adversary.

The style of wrestling varied with the desires of the parties. The Eastern men, or Yankees, used square hold, or collar and elbow; those from the Middle States side hold, and the Southern and Western men used breeches hold and old Indian hug or back hold. If a man was hurt he stood it without a murmur; it was considered cowardly and childish to whine when thrown or hurt in the fall.

While the sport was at its height Sidney Rigdon, the mouthpiece of the Prophet, rushed into the ring, sword in hand, and said that he would not suffer a lot of men to break the Sabbath day in that manner. For a moment all were silent. Then one of the brethren, with more presence of mind than the others, said to the Prophet:

"Brother Joseph, we want you to clear us from blame, for we formed the ring by your request. You told us to wrestle, and now Brother Rigdon is bringing us to account for it."

The Prophet walked into the ring and said, as he made a motion with his hand:

"Brother Sidney, you had better get out of here and let the boys alone; they are amusing themselves according to my orders. You are an old man. You go and get ready for meeting and let the boys alone." Just then catching Rigdon off his guard, as quick as a flash he knocked the sword from Rigdon's hand, then caught him by the shoulder, and said: "Now, old man, you must go out, or I will throw you down."

Rigdon was as large a man as the Prophet, but not so tall. The prospect of a tussle between the Prophet and the mouthpiece of the Prophet was fun for all but Rigdon, who pulled back like a crawfish; but the resistance was useless, the Prophet dragged him from the ring, bareheaded, and tore Rigdon's fine pulpit coat from the collar to the waist; then he turned to the men and said:

"Go in, boys, and have your fun. You shall never have it to say that I got you into any trouble that I did not get you out of."

Rigdon complained about the loss of his hat and the tearing of his coat. The Prophet said to him:

"You were out of your place. Always keep your place and you will not suffer: but you got a little out of your place and you have suffered for it. You have no one to blame but yourself."

After that Rigdon never countermanded the orders of the Prophet, to my knowledge; he knew who was boss.

An order had been issued by the Church authorities commanding all the members of the Mormon Church to leave their farms and take such property as they could remove and go to one of the two fortified camps - that is Far West or Adam-on-Diamond. A large majority of the settlers obeyed, and the two camps were soon full of people who had deserted home again for the sake of the gospel.

There was a settlement on Log Creek, between three and five miles east from Far West. It was quite a rich settlement. A man named Haughn had just completed a good flouring mill on the creek. The morning after the battle of Crooked River Haughn came to Far West to consult with the Prophet concerning the policy of the removal of the settlers on Log Creek to the fortified camps.

Col. White and myself were standing by when the Prophet said to him:

"Move in, by all means, if you wish to save your lives."

Haughn replied that if the settlers left their homes all of their property would be lost, and the Gentiles would burn their houses and other buildings. The Prophet said:

"You had much better lose your property than your lives; one can be replaced, the other cannot be restored; but there is no need of your losing either if you will only do as you are commanded."

Haughn said that he considered the best plan was for all of the settlers to move into and around the mill, and use the blacksmith's shop and other buildings as a fort in case of attack; in this way he thought they would be perfectly safe.

"You are at liberty to do so if you think best," said the Prophet.

Haughn then departed, well satisfied that he had carried his point. The Prophet turned to Col. White and said:

"That man did not come for counsel, but to induce me to tell him to do as he pleased; which I did. Had I commanded them to move in and leave their property they would have called me a tyrant. I wish they were here for their own

36

safety. I am confident that we will soon learn that they have been butchered in a fearful manner."

At this time the Missourians had determined to exterminate the whole of the Mormon people. Governor Lilburn W. Boggs issued orders to that effect. I think Gen. Clark was the officer in command of all the Gentile forces. Gen. Atchison and Col. Doniphan each commanded a division of from three to four thousand men, and they soon besieged Far West. The Mormons fortified the town as well as they could, and took special care to fortify and build shields and breastworks, to prevent the cavalry from charging into the town. The Gentile forces were mostly camped on Log Creek, between Far West and Haughn's Mill, about a mile from Far West, and about half a mile south of our outer breastworks.

Our scouts and pickets guards were driven in and forced to join the main ranks for safety. The Mormon troops were placed in position by the officers, so as to guard every point. We all had a large supply of bullets, with the patching sewed on the balls to facilitate the loading of our guns, which were muzzle loaders. The Mormon force was about eight hundred strong, poorly armed; many of the men had no guns; some had single-barrel pistols and a few homemade swords. These were our implements of war.

So situated, we were still anxious to meet the enemy, and demanded to be led out against our foes. Our men were confident that God was going to deliver the enemy into our hands, and so we had no fears. I was one of the advance force, and as I lay behind some timber, with my cap-box open, and bullets lying on the ground by my side, I never had a doubt of being able to defeat the Gentile army.

The troops lay and watched each other several days, then the Gentiles made two efforts to force their way into the town by stratagem; but seeing our forces in order they did not come within range of our guns. The Mormons stood in the ranks, and prayed for the chance of getting a shot; but all to no effect. The same evening we learned of the massacre at Haughn's Mill. The description of this massacre was such as to freeze the blood of each Saint, and force us to swear that revenge should come some day.

The massacre was reported about as follows to us at Far West. When the Gentile mob attacked the Mormons at the mill the Mormons took shelter in the blacksmith shop and other buildings. The mob took advantage of the banks of the creek and the timber, and very nearly surrounded the shop, which was built of logs, and served as a slaughterhouse instead of a shelter or protection.

The mob, while protected as they were, shot down the Mormons at their leisure. They killed eighteen and wounded as many more; in fact, they killed and wounded everyone who did not run away during the fight and take refuge in the woods. After shooting down all that could be seen, the mob entered the blacksmith shop and there found a young lad who had secreted himself under the bellows. One of the men said:

"Don't shoot; it is but a small boy."

"It is best to hive them when we can," was the reply.

Thus saying, they shot the little fellow.

There was an old man in the settlement by the name of McBride, who had been a soldier in the Revolutionary War; he was killed by being hacked to pieces with a corncutter while begging for his life. The dead and wounded were thrown into a well together. Several of the wounded were afterwards taken out of the well by the force that went from Far West, and recovered from their wounds. So great was the hatred of the mob that they saved none, but killed all who fell into their hands at that time. I received my information of the massacre from David Lewis, Tarleton Lewis, William Laney, and Isaac Laney; they were Kentuckians, and were also in the fight, but escaped death.

Isaac Laney was shot seven times, the seven shots leaving thirteen ball holes in his person; five of the shots were nearly in the center of the chest; one entered under the right arm, passed through the body and came out under the left arm; yet, strange as it appears, he kept his feet, and ran some three hundred yards to a cabin, where a woman raised a loose plank of the cabin floor and he lay down while she replaced the boards.

The mob left, and in about two hours Laney was taken from under the cabin floor nearly lifeless. He was then washed, anointed with oil, the elders praying for his recovery, according to the order of the Holy Priesthood, and he was promised, through prayer and faith in God, speedy restoration. The pain at once left him, and for two weeks he felt no pain at all. He then took cold, and the wound in his hips pained him for some two hours, when the elders repeated their prayers and again anointed him, which had the effect desired. The pain left him, and never returned. I heard Laney declare this to be a fact, and he bore his testimony in the presence of many of the Saints. I saw him four weeks after the massacre and examined his person. I saw the wounds, then healed. I felt of them with my own hands, and I saw the shirt and examined it, that he had on when he was shot, and it was cut in shreds. Many balls had cut his clothing that had not touched his person.

The massacre at Haughn's Mill was the result of the brethren's refusal to obey the wishes of the Prophet. All the brethren so considered it. It made a deep and lasting impression on my mind, for I had heard the Prophet give the counsel to the brethren to come into the town. They had refused, and the result was a lesson to all that there was no safety except in obeying the Prophet.

Col. George M. Hinkle had command of the troops at Far West, under the Prophet Joseph. He was from Kentucky, and considered a fair-weather Saint. When danger came he was certain to be on the strong side. He was a fine speaker, and had great influence with the Saints. Previous to the attack on Far West Col. Hinkle had come to an understanding with the Gentile commanders that in case the danger grew great they could depend on him as a friend and one through whom they could negotiate and learn the situation of affairs in the camp of the Saints. When our scouts were first driven in Col. Hinkle was out with them, and when they were closely pursued he turned his coat wrong side out and wore it so.

This was a peculiar move, but at the time it did not cause much comment among his men; but they reported it to the Prophet, and he at once became suspicious of the Colonel. The Prophet, being a man of thought and cool reflection, kept this information within a small circle, as it was a bad time to ventilate an act of that kind.

The Prophet concluded to make use of the knowledge he had gained of Hinkle's character, and employ him to negotiate between the two parties. I do not believe that Joseph had the least idea that he, with his little handful of men, could stand off the army that had come up against him. I know that now, but at the time I was full of religious zeal and felt that the Mormon Hosts of Israel were invincible. Joseph wished to use Hinkle to learn the designs of the Gentiles, so that he could prepare for the worst. Col. Hinkle was therefore sent by Joseph to have an interview with the Gentiles.

The Colonel returned and reported to Joseph the terms proposed by the Gentile officers. The terms offered were as follows: Joseph and the leading men of the Church, Rigdon, Lyman White, P. P. Pratt, Phelps, and others, were to give themselves up without delay; the remainder of the men were to surrender themselves and their arms by ten o'clock the following day, the understanding being that all would be tried for treason against the Government, and for other offenses.

The Prophet took advantage of this information, and had every man that was in imminent danger leave the camp for a place of safety. The most of those in peril went to Illinois. They left at once, and were safe from all pursuit before the surrender took place, as they traveled north and avoided the settlements.

When the brethren had left for Illinois, as just stated, Joseph called his remaining troops together and told them they were a good lot of fellows, but they were not perfect enough to withstand so large an army as the one now before them; that they had stood by him, and were willing to die for and with him, for the sake of the Kingdom of Heaven; that he wished them to be comforted, for God had accepted their offering; that he intended to, and was going to offer himself up as a sacrifice, to save their lives and to save the Church. He wished them to be of good cheer, and pray for him, and to pray that he and the brethren that went with him might be delivered from their enemies. He then blessed his people in the name of the Lord. After that he and the leading men, six in number, went direct to the camp of the enemy.

They were led by a Judas, Col. G. M. Hinkle. I stood upon the breastworks and watched them go into the camp of the enemy. I heard the yells of triumph of the troops as Joseph and his companions approached. It was with great difficulty that the officers could restrain the mob from shooting them down as they entered. A strong guard was then placed over them to protect them from mob violence.

The next morning a court-martial was held, at which Joseph and his six companions who had surrendered with him were sentenced to be shot. The execution was to take place at eight o'clock the next morning. When the sentence of the court-martial was announced to them, Col. Lyman White said:

"Shoot and be damned!"

Gen. Atchison and Col. Doniphan arrived with their divisions the same day, soon after the court-martial had been held. Col. Doniphan, in particular, remonstrated against the decision. He said it was nothing more nor less than cold-blooded murder, and that every name signed to the decision was signed in blood, and he would withdraw his troops and have nothing to do in the matter if the men were to be shot. Gen. Atchison sustained Col. Doniphan, and said the wiser policy would be, inasmuch as they had surrendered themselves as prisoners, to place them in the Richmond jail and let them take the due course of the law; let them be tried by the civil authorities of the land. In this way justice could be reached and parties punished according to law, and thus save the honor of the troops and the nation. This timely interposition on the part of Col. Doniphan and Gen. Atchison changed the course and prevented the hasty action of an infuriated mob calling itself a court, and composed of men who were the bitter enemies of Joseph and his followers.

The next day a writing desk was prepared, with two secretaries or clerks; it was placed in the middle of the hollow square formed by the troops. The Mormons were marched in double file across the center of the square, where the officers and men who had remained in Far West surrendered themselves and their arms to Gen. Clark, Commander-in-Chief of the Missouri militia, then in arms against the Saints at Far West. I was among the number that then surrendered. I laid down a good Kentucky rifle, two good horse pistols, and a sword.

After stacking our arms we were marched in single file between a double file of the militia, who stood in a line from the secretary's desk extending nearly across the square, ready to receive us, with fixed bayonets. As each man came up he stepped to the desk and signed his name to an instrument recapitulating the conditions of the treaty, which were substantially as follows: We were to give a deed to all our real estate, and to give a bill of sale of our personal property, to pay the expenses of the war that had been inaugurated against us; also a committee of twelve should be appointed, one for Far West and one for Adam-on-Diamond, who were to be the sole judges of what would be necessary to remove each family out of the State. All of the Mormons were to leave Missouri by the 1st of April, A. D. 1839. The rest of the property of the Mormons was to be taken by the Missouri troops to pay the expenses of the war. When the committee had examined into affairs and made the assignment of property that the Mormons were to retain, a pass would be given by the committee to each person as an evidence that he had gone through an investigation both as to his conduct and property. The prisoners at Far West were to be retained and not allowed to return home until the committee had reported and given the certificate that all charges had been met and satisfied. I remained a prisoner for nine days, awaiting the action of the committee.

While such prisoner I witnessed many scenes of inhumanity even more degrading than mere brutality itself. The mob of the militia was mostly composed of men who had been neighbors of the Mormons. This mob rifled the city, took what they wished, and committed many cruel and shameful deeds. These barbarous acts were done because they said the Mormons had stolen their goods and chattels, and while they pretended to search for stolen property they ravished women and committed other crimes at will.

40

One day, while we were standing by a log fire trying to keep warm, a man came up and, recognizing Brother Riley Stewart, said:

"I saw you knock Dick Weldon down at Gallatin."

With this he sprang and caught at an ax that had been stuck in a log. While trying to get the ax out, as it stuck fast in the log, Stewart ran. The man succeeded in getting the ax loose; he then threw it with all his force at Stewart. Fortunately the ax struck him only a glancing blow on the head, not killing him, but giving him a severe wound.

The night after he was wounded Stewart broke through the guard and escaped to his wife's people in Carroll County, fifty miles south of Far West. As soon as the citizens heard that Stewart had arrived they notified his wife's brothers and father that an armed mob intended to take him out and whip him severely, and then tar and feather him. His friends warned him of the fact, and he attempted to make his escape, but the mob was on the watch. They caught him, and, holding two pistols at his head, forced him to take off his coat, kneel down, and receive fifty lashes. These were given him with such force that they cut through his linen shirt. After this whipping he returned to Far West and took his chances with the rest of us.

One day a soldier of the mob walked up to a house near where I was standing. The house was occupied by an old widow woman. The soldier noticed a cow in the little shed near the house. He said that he thought it was a Danite cow; that he wanted to have the honor of killing a Danite, or something that belonged to a Danite. The old widow came to the door of her cabin and begged him to spare her cow, saying it was her only dependence for milk, that she had no meat, and if her cow was killed she must suffer.

"Well, then," said he, "you can eat the cow for a change."

He then shot the cow dead, and stood there and tantalized the old woman while she cried over her loss.

While we were standing in line, waiting our turn to sign the treaty, a large company of men, painted like Indians, rode up and surrounded us. They were a part of the men who were in the fight at the town of Gallatin on the day of election. They abused us in every way they could with words. This treatment was hard to bear, but we were powerless to protect ourselves in any way.

CHAPTER VI
LEE LOCATES THE GARDEN OF EDEN

Among other matters I had a fine gray mare that attracted the attention of many of the mob. I was allowed to take her to water while closely guarded by armed men. One day as I took her to water I was spoken to by several, who said they were sorry for a man like me, who appeared to be honest and peaceably disposed; that they knew that I and many honest men were deluded by Joseph Smith, the impostor. But they thanked God he would delude no more people; that he would certainly be shot; that I had better quit my delusion and settle down by the officer in command, who was then talking to me, in Carroll County, and make a home for my family; that I would never have peace or quiet while I remained with the Mormons. I heard him through. Then I said:

"No man has deceived me. I am not deceived by Joseph Smith, or any other man. If I am deceived it is the Bible that has deceived me. I believe that Joseph Smith is a prophet of God, and I have the Bible as my authority in part for this belief. And I do not believe that Joseph Smith will be shot, as you seem to think. He has not finished his work yet."

As I finished my remarks the officer became enraged, and said:

"That is the way with all you Mormons. You might as well try to move a mountain as to turn a Mormon from his delusion. Blow the brains out of this fool!"

In an instant several guns were leveled on me. I imagined I felt the bullets piercing my body.

The soldiers would certainly have shot me down if the officer had not immediately countermanded his order, by saying:

"Hold on, boys, he is not worth five charges of ammunition."

"Gentlemen," I said, "I am your prisoner, unarmed and helpless, and I demand your protection. But if you consider there is any honor in treating a man and an American prisoner in this way, you may do it."

As we returned to camp the man said:

"We will make it hot for the Mormons yet before we are done with them, and if you have not got enough of them now, you will have, and you will remember my words when it is too late to serve you."

"I may," said I; "when I do I will own up like a little man. But until I am so convinced I will never turn my coat."

"Well," said he, "you are not so bad, after all. I like a firm man."

The Mormons were locked in the public schoolhouses and kept without rations being issued to them. The grain fields and gardens that belonged to the Mormons were thrown open to the stock and wasted. Our cattle and other stock were shot down for sport and left for the wolves and birds of prey to devour. We were closely guarded, and not allowed to go from our quarters without an escort. We were nearly starved for several days, until I obtained permission to go out and bring in some of the cattle that the soldiers had killed for sport. The weather was cold and the snow deep, so the meat was good. I also got permission to gather in some vegetables, and from that time, while we remained prisoners, the men had plenty to eat, yet often it was of a poor quality. While a prisoner I learned that the loud and self- conceited men were of little account when danger stared them in the face.

Arrangements had been made to carry the treaty into effect. It was found necessary to send Gen. Wilson with five hundred men to Adam-on-Diamond to compel the surrender and the signing of the treaty, as had been done at Far West, and the people of that place were to be treated just as we had been. I was

42

recommended to Gen. Wilson by the officer who had ordered his men to blow my brains out, as a suitable man for a guide to Adam-on-Diamond. He said that I was as stubborn as a mule, but still there was something about me he respected; that he believed I was honest, and certainly no coward. Gen. Wilson said:

"Young man, do you live at Adam-on-Diamond?"

"I cannot say that I do; but I did once, and I have a wife and child there that I would like to see; but as to a home, I have none left."

"Where did you live before you came here?"

"In Illinois," I answered.

"You will soon see your wife and child. I shall start in the morning with my division for Adam-on-Diamond. You are at liberty to select two of your comrades and go with me as guide to pilot us there. Be ready for an early start and report to my adjutant."

"Thank you, sir, I will do as you request," said I.

The next morning I selected two good men. Brother Levi Stewart was one, but I have forgotten who the other man was. The day was cold and stormy, a hard north wind blowing, and the snow falling rapidly. It was an open country for thirteen miles, with eighteen inches of snow on the ground. We kept our horses to the lope until we reached Shady Grove timber, thirteen miles from Far West. There we camped for the night by the side of Brother Waldo Littlefield's farm. The fence was burned for camp-fires, and his fields of grain were fed to the horses, or rather the animals were turned loose in the fields. After camp was struck I went to Gen. Wilson and said:

"General, I have come to beg a favor of you. I ask you in the name of humanity to let me go on to Adam-on-Diamond to-day. I have a wife and helpless babe there. I am informed that our house was burned, and she is out in this storm without shelter. You are halfway there; the snow is deep, and you can follow our trail" - it had then slackened up, or was snowing but little - "in the morning; there is but one road to the settlement."

He looked at me for a moment, and then said:

"Young man, your request shall be granted; I admire your resolution." He then turned to his aid, who stood trembling in the snow, and said, "Write Mr. Lee and his two comrades a pass, saying that they have gone through an examination at Far West, and were found innocent."

After receiving my pass I thanked the General for his humane act, and with my friends made the journey, through the snow, to Adam- on-Diamond. As we neared home the sun shone out brightly. When I got in sight of where my house had been I saw my wife sitting by a log fire in the open air, with her babe in her arms. Some soldiers had cut a large hickory tree for firewood for her, and built her a shelter with some boards I had had dressed to weather-board a house, so she was in a measure comfortable. She had been weeping, as she had been informed that I was a prisoner at Far West, and would be shot, and that she need not look for me, for she would never see me again.

When I rode up she was nearly frantic with delight, and as soon as I reached her side she threw herself into my arms and then her self-possession gave way

43

and she wept bitterly; but she soon recovered herself and gave me an account of her troubles during my absence.

The next evening Gen. Wilson and his command arrived and camped near my little shanty. I started at once to report to Gen. Wilson. On my way to him I passed my friend McBrier, who had trusted me for some cattle. I still owed him for them. I told him why I had been unable to pay him, and wished him to take the cattle back, as I still had all of them except one cow that had died of the murrain; that it was an honest debt, and I wished to pay it. I asked him to go to my shanty with me, and said he could take what cattle were left and a black mare that was worth seventy-five dollars, and an eight-day clock that was worth twenty-five dollars, for my note.

"I have not got your note," said he.

"Who has it?" I asked.

"I do not know; I supposed you had it."

"I never saw it since I gave it to you."

"Well," said he, "my house was burned, and all my property either burned or taken from me, and your note was in the house when it was burned."

"Well," said I, "it matters not with me. If you will take the property and give me a' receipt against the note, so that it cannot be collected the second time, I will settle the debt." He then said:

"I thought you were in the party that burned the house, and had taken your note, but I am now satisfied to the contrary, and that you are an innocent man. All I ask is for you to renew the note. The property of the Mormons will be held to pay their debts and the expenses of the war, and I will get my pay in that way. You just renew the note, and that will settle all between us."

McBrier introduced me to a number of the soldiers as an honest Mormon. This worked well in my favor, and pleased me much, for it satisfied me more than ever that honesty was the best policy. I had done nothing that I considered wrong. I did not have to run and hide, or screen any act of mine from the public gaze.

My wife had been treated well personally during my absence; no insults had been offered to her, and I was well pleased with that. I was treated with respect by Gen. Wilson and his men. True, I was associated with the people that had incurred the displeasure of the authorities, and my neighbors were then receiving fearful punishment for all they had done. The punishment, however, was in a great part owing to the fault of the people. When the Gentiles found any of their property they became very abusive.

Every house in Adam-on-Diamond was searched by the troops for Gentile property. They succeeded in finding very much of the Gentile property that had been captured by the Saints in the various raids they made through the country. Bedding of every kind and in large quantities was found and reclaimed by the owners. Even spinning wheels, soap barrels and other articles were recovered. Each house where property was found was certain to receive a Missouri blessing, that is to say, the torch, from the troops.

The men who had been most active in gathering plunder had fled to Illinois, to escape the vengeance of the mob, leaving their families to suffer for their deeds. By the terms of the treaty all the Mormons were to leave Daviess County within fifteen days, but they were allowed to stay through the winter in Caldwell County; but all had to depart from Missouri before the first day of the next April. There were but a few families that met with the kind treatment that mine did. The majority of the people were censured and persecuted as much as they were able to stand and live.

In justice to the Prophet Joseph I cannot say that I ever heard him teach or even encourage men to steal little things. He told the people to wait until the proper time came to take their rights.

"Then," said he, "take the whole State of Missouri like men."

When the people at Adam-on-Diamond had signed the treaty and complied with the stipulations, the committee of twelve commenced their duties. When it came my turn to receive the property necessary to take me out of the State I was told to fit myself out comfortably. I told them that I had a wife and one child; that I had two good wagons, one a heavy one-horse wagon, with thills, and that I had a large mare which was equal to a common span; that the mare and wagon would do me. I wanted some bedding and our clothing, and some other traps of little value. I had a good milk cow that I wished to give to a friend who had lost all his cattle. His wife had died a short time before, leaving a little babe that must have milk. I told them they could take the rest of my property and do with it as they did with that of the brethren. I was worth then in property, at a fair valuation, four thousand dollars.

The officers were astonished at me, and said they did not, wish to oppress a man who acted fairly. They told me to take my large wagon and two of my best horses, and all the outfit that I wanted. I thanked them for their kindness. I was permitted to give the cow to my friend, and I had the privilege of taking such articles as I wished. I fitted up with just what would take me to Illinois, and left the remainder as a spoil for the enemies of the Church. I did not regret the loss of my property; I gave it up as the price of my religious freedom.

Before I speak of other things I will say a few words of the country we were then in. Adam-on-Diamond was at the point where Adam came and settled and blest his posterity after being driven from the Garden of Eden. This was revealed to the people through Joseph the Prophet. The Temple Block in Jackson County, Missouri, stands on the identical spot where once stood the Garden of Eden. When Adam and Eve were driven from the Garden they traveled in a northwesterly course until they came to a valley on the east side of Grand River. There they tarried for several years, and engaged in tilling the soil. On the east of the valley there is a low range of hills. Standing on the summit of the bluffs a person has a full view of the beautiful valley that lies below, dotted here and there with groves of timber. On the top of this range of hills Adam erected an altar of stone, on which he offered sacrifice unto the Lord. There was in our time (1838) a pile of stone there, which the Prophet said was a portion of the altar on which Adam offered sacrifice. Although these stones had been exposed to the elements for many generations, still the traces remained to show the dimensions and design of the altar. After Adam had offered his sacrifice he went up the valley some two miles, where he blessed his posterity

45

and called the place the Valley of Adam-on-Diamond, which, in the reformed Egyptian language, signifies Adam's Consecrated Land. It is said to be seventy-five miles, in a direct course, from the Garden of Eden to Adam-on-Diamond. Those ancient relics and sacred spots of earth are held holy by the greater portion of the Latter-day Saints. These things, and much more concerning the early days, were revealed to the Prophet Joseph.

On the 20th day of November, 1838, I took leave of my home and the sacred ground of Adam-on-Diamond and started as a banished man to seek a home in Illinois. We went to my farm on Shady Grove Creek, and stayed over night. We found everything as we had left it, nothing having been interfered with. I killed a large hog and dressed it to carry with us to eat on the journey. The snow was fully twenty inches deep, weather very cold, and, taken all in all, it was a disagreeable and unpleasant trip.

We went to the settlement on Log Creek and stopped with the family of Robert Bidwell. He had plenty of property. This man had good teams, and had reaped where he had not sown, gathered where he had not strewn. He was engaged in removing families of his helpless brethren to Quincy, Illinois, who had not teams to move themselves, but who had a little money that he was after, and he got all they had. For some reason unexplained to me he had been permitted to keep all of his property; none of it was taken by the troops.

While at Bidwell's I bought a crib of corn, about two hundred bushels, for a pocketknife. I built a stable for my mare, a crib for the corn, and hauled wood enough to do the family the rest of the winter. I also attended to Bidwell's stock and worked all the time for him. They had five children, which made considerable work for the women folks; my wife worked for them all the time.

During this time we had nothing but corn to eat. The hog I killed at my farm was diseased, and I had to throw the meat away. Notwithstanding our constant work for Bidwell's family, they never gave us a drop of milk or a meal of victuals while we remained there. Mrs. Bidwell fed six gallons of milk to their hogs each day. I offered to feed the hogs corn for milk, so we could have milk to eat with our boiled corn, but she refused the offer, saying they had all the corn they needed. They did have provisions of every kind in abundance, but not a particle of food could we obtain from them.

Prayer meetings were frequently held at their house. They had plenty of tallow, but Mrs. Bidwell would not allow a candle to be burned in the house unless some other person furnished it. One night at prayer meeting I chanced to speak upon the subject of covetousness, and quoted the twelfth chapter of Paul to the Corinthians, where he speaks of members of the Church of Christ being united. I was feeling bad to see so much of the covetousness of the world in some of the members of the Church, and I talked plainly upon the subject.

The next morning Mrs. Bidwell came into our room and said that my remarks at the meeting the evening before were directed at her, and she wanted me to understand that if I did not like my treatment there she desired us to go where we would fare better. This inhuman and unwelcome language did not sit well on an empty stomach, and was more than I could bear. I burst into tears. Yet I pitied the ungrateful woman. As soon as I could control my feelings I said:

46

"Sister Bidwell, I will take you at your word. I will leave your house as soon as I can get my things into my wagon, but before I leave you I wish to say a few words for you to ponder on when we are gone. In the first place, you and I profess to be members of the same Church; for the sake of our faith my family has been broken up and driven from a comfortable home in this inclement season of the year. We came here seeking shelter from the stormy blasts of winter, until the severity of the weather was past, when we intended to leave this State. You have been more fortunate than your brethren and sisters who lived in Daviess County. You are allowed to live in your own house, but we are homeless wanderers. Now you drive us from the shelter of your roof for a trivial offense, if offense it was. But I assure you that you are only angry because my words were the truth. Woe unto you who are angry and offended at the truth. As you do unto others, so will your Heavenly Father do unto you. Inasmuch as you have done this unchristian act, you will yet be houseless and homeless - you will be one day dependent upon those that you now drive from your door."

At first she mocked me, but soon her tune changed and she commenced to cry. She then begged me not to get angry with what a woman said. I told her I could not undo what I had said - that I should start at once for Quincy, Illinois.

We left the house of that stingy and selfish family, intending to go direct to Illinois. We traveled until we arrived at the house of a man by the name of Morris; they had a much smaller house than Bidwell's, but they would not listen to our continuing our journey during the severe cold weather. We accepted their invitation, and stayed there about two weeks. This family possessed the true Christian spirit, and treated us while there as kindly as if we had been their own children.

While staying with Brother Morris I attended several meetings at Far West. Old Father Smith, the father of the Prophet, led the meetings. He also directed the exodus of the Saints from Missouri to Illinois.

Thomas B. Marsh was at that time President of the twelve apostles, and I think Brigham Young was second and Orson Hyde the third on the roll. The great opposition to our people and Church caused the two pillars, Marsh and Hyde, to become weak-kneed and turn over to the enemy. Col. G. M. Hinkle, Dr. Averard, Judge W. W. Phelps, and others of the "tall" men of the Church followed suit. I remember going with Brother Levi Stewart to some of those fallen angels (in the days of our prosperity they had looked like angels to me) to inquire what to do and what was to be the future conduct of our people. G. M. Hinkle said that it was his opinion our leaders, the Prophet Joseph and those with him in prison, would be either hanged or imprisoned for life - that the members of the Church would scatter to the four winds, and never gather again in this dispensation.

We then went to Joseph's father and asked him for counsel. He told us that the Saints would gather again in Illinois. We asked him at what point, and he said:

"I do not know yet, but the further north we go the fewer poisonous serpents we will find."

He then advised us to attend private meetings and be set apart to the ministry. Public meetings could not be held by the terms of the treaty. We did attend private meetings, and I was ordained in the Quorum of Seventies, under the hands of Joseph Young and Levi Hancock. Stewart was ordained to the lesser Priesthood, which gave him authority to preach and baptize, but not to confirm.

The office that I held gave me authority to preach, baptize, and confirm by the laying on of hands, for the reception of the Holy Ghost, and to ordain and set apart Elders, Priests, Teachers, and Deacons, and to ordain a Seventy or High Priest, as the office of a Seventy belongs to the Melchisedek Priesthood; yet a Seventy or High Priest is generally ordained and set apart by the presidents of the several quorums.

After we were ordained we attended a private feast and blessing meeting, at which my wife and I got our Patriarchal Blessing, under the hands of Isaac Morley, Patriarch. This office properly belongs to those that are ordained and set apart to that calling, to bless the fatherless and the widow especially; but he can bless others who ask it and pay one dollar for the blessing. Often the widow and the poor are blessed free, but this is at the option of the Patriarch. My Patriarchal Blessing was in the following form:

"Brother John Doyle Lee: In the name of Jesus of Nazareth, and by virtue and authority of the Holy Priesthood, in me vested, I lay my hands upon thy head, and confer upon thee a Patriarchal or Father's Blessing. Thou art of Ephriam, through the loins of Joseph, that was sold into Egypt. And inasmuch as thou hast obeyed the requirements of the gospel of salvation, thy sins are forgiven thee. Thy name is written in the Lamb's Book of Life, never more to be blotted out. Thou art lawful heir to all the blessings of Abraham, Isaac, and Jacob in the new and everlasting covenant. Thou shalt travel until thou art satisfied with seeing. Thousands shall hear the everlasting gospel proclaimed from thy lips. Kings and princes shall acknowledge thee to be their father in the new and everlasting covenant. Thou shalt have a numerous posterity, who shall rise up and bless thee. Thou shalt have houses and habitations, flocks, fields, and herds. Thy table shall be strewed with the rich luxuries of the earth, to feed thy numerous family and friends who shall come unto thee. Thou shalt be a counselor in Israel, and many shall come unto thee for instruction. Thou shalt have power over thine enemies. They that oppose thee shall yet come bending unto thee. Thou shalt sit under thine own vine and fig tree, where none shall molest or make thee afraid. Thou shalt be a blessing to thy family and to the Church of Jesus Christ of Latter-day Saints. Thou shalt understand the hidden things of the Kingdom of Heaven. The spirit of inspiration shall be a light in thy path and a guide to thy mind. Thou shalt come forth in the morning of the first resurrection, and no power shall hinder, except the shedding of innocent blood, or consenting thereto. I seal thee up to eternal life. In the name of the Father, and of the Son, and of the Holy Ghost, Amen, and Amen."

To a true believer in the faith of the Latter-day Saints a blessing of this kind, from under the hand of a Patriarch, was then, and is now, next to a boon of eternal life. A Patriarch is a man highly favored of God, possesses the gift of discerning spirits, and can read the present and future destiny of men. Patriarchal blessings strengthen, stimulate and encourage true Saints to press on to perfection while passing through this world of sorrows, cares and disappointments.

Having been ordained and blessed, my next step was to arm myself with the Armor of Righteousness, and in my weakness pray for strength to face a frowning world. I had put my hands to the plow and I was determined that, with God's help, I would never turn back to the sinful elements of the world, the flesh, and the devil.

CHAPTER VII
THE SAINTS GATHER AT NAUVOO

About the middle of February, 1839, I started back for Fayette County, Illinois, with my family, in company with Brother Levi Stewart and Riley Helm, two of my old Illinois neighbors. While traveling through Missouri we were kindly treated by most of the people; many of them requested us to stop and settle down by them. I refused to do so, for I knew there was no safety for a true Saint in that State at that time.

When we crossed the Mississippi River at Quincy, and touched Illinois soil, I felt like a new man, and a free American citizen again. At this place I found many of the Saints who had preceded us camped along the river. Some had obtained employment; all appeared happy in the faith and strong in the determination to build up the Kingdom. Here I parted with Riley Helm, as his team had given out and he could go no farther. I gave him twenty-five cents in money - all that I had in the world - and twelve pounds of nails, to buy food with until he could get aid from some other quarter. I had laid in enough provisions at Brother Morris' to last me until I could reach my old home again. I started from Quincy by way of Mr. Vanleven's, the man I sold my cattle to, taking his note, when going to join the Saints.

Without meeting with any remarkable adventures, I arrived at Mr. Vanleven's house and was kindly received by him. He had the money ready for me, and paid me in full all he owed on the cattle. I now saw that some honesty yet remained in the world. I took two hundred dollars and left the rest of it with my friend and banker, so that it would be safe in case I met another storm of oppression. I then went to Vandalia, Illinois, and put up with my wife's sister's husband, Hickerson. He was in good circumstances. I left my wife with her sister, after laying in a supply of provisions for her and our child. I then commenced preparing for a mission. I did not know where I was to go, but I felt it my duty to go forth and give my testimony to the truth of the gospel as revealed by Joseph, the prophet of the everlasting God. Brother Stewart was to go with me, he having made arrangements for the comfort of his family during his absence.

The time I started on my first mission was about the 1st of April, 1839. I bade adieu to my little family and started forth, an illiterate, inexperienced man, without purse or scrip. I could hardly quote a passage of Scripture, yet I went forth to say to the world that I was a minister of the gospel, bearing a message from on High, with the authority to call upon all men to repent, be baptized for the remission of their sins, and receive the Holy Spirit by the laying on of hands. I had never attempted to preach a discourse in my life. I expected trials, and I had them to undergo many times.

Brother Stewart and myself started forth on foot, with our valises on our backs. We walked about thirty miles the first day, and as night was approaching we called at a house for lodging. They had been having a log rolling there that day, and quite a number of people were around the house. We asked for lodging and refreshments.

Our request was carried back to the supper-room to the man of the house, and we stood at the gate awaiting the reply. Presently the man came out and said that no Mormon preacher could stay in his house; and if we wished to save our scalps we had better be making tracks lively.

Brother Stewart took him at his word, and started off at a double quick. I followed, but more slowly. We made no reply to that man's remarks. A mile further on we again called for lodging.

The man could not keep us, as he was poor, and his family sick; but he directed us to a house half a mile from the traveled road, where he said a man lived that was an infidel, but would not turn a hungry man from his door.

We went to the house and asked for entertainment. The man said he never turned a man from his door hungry, but would as soon entertain horse thieves as Mormon preachers; that he looked upon all Mormons as thieves, robbers, and scoundrels. There was determination in his voice as he addressed us in this manner. He held his rifle in his hand while speaking. Then he said:

"Walk in, gentlemen. I never turn the hungry away." He addressed his wife, a very pretty, unassuming lady, and said, "Get these men some supper, for I suppose they feel pretty lank."

There was a good supper soon on the table; but I could not eat. Brother Stewart ate his supper, and soon was enjoying himself talking to the family. He was a great talker; liked to hear himself talk. They requested me to eat, but I thanked them, and said rest would do me more good than eating. I soon retired, but did not sleep. I was humiliated; my proud spirit was broken and humbled; the rough words used toward me had stricken me to the heart. At daylight we were on our way again.

About ten o'clock we arrived at a little town, and went to the public pump to get a drink. While there a woman came to the pump and asked us if we were Mormon preachers. We told her we were, but had never preached yet. She invited us to her house, saying she owned the hotel; that she was a widow; that she would inform the people of the town we were there, and as it was the Sabbath we could preach in her house, for she wished to hear the strange doctrine. We consented to remain, and went home with her and had something to eat.

At 11 o'clock, a. m., I made my debut to quite an attentive audience. I both quoted and made Scripture. I had been fasting and praying until I had become as humble as a child. My whole mind and soul were swallowed up in the gospel. My most earnest desire was to impart to others the knowledge that I had of the truths of the gospel.

When I began to speak I felt an electric thrill through my whole system. I hardly knew what I said, but the people said I spoke from inspiration; none of the audience noticed my mistakes in quoting Scripture.

After dinner my companion, Stewart, proposed to travel on, and, I agreeing with him, we left the town, although the people wished us to stay and preach again. I had but little confidence in myself, and concluded to preach but seldom, until I got over my timidity or man-fearing feeling that most beginners are subject to. But I have now been a public speaker for thirty-five years, and I have not yet entirely gotten over that feeling.

We started for Cincinnati, and traveled two days and a half without food. My boots hurt my feet and our progress was quite slow. The third night we applied to a tavern keeper for lodging and food. He said we were welcome to stay in his house free, but he must have pay for what we eat.

We sat in the hall all night, for we were much reduced by hunger and fatigue. That was a miserable night indeed. I reflected the matter over and over again, scrutinized it up one side and down the other. I could not see why a servant of God should receive such treatment - that if I was in the right faith, doing the will of God, He would open up the way before me, and not allow me to perish under the sore trials then surrounding me. I had seriously considered the propriety of walking back to where the kind landlady gave us our last meal, but was soon comforted, for these words came into my mind:

"He that putteth his hands to the plow, and then looketh back, is not fit for the Kingdom of Heaven;" "If ye were of the world, then the world would love its own, but because I have chosen you out of the world, the world persecuteth you;" "Ye, and all who live godly in Christ Jesus, shall suffer persecution, while evil men and seducers wax worse and worse, deceiving and being deceived."

The Son of God Himself, when He entered upon the duties of His mission, was led into the wilderness, where He was tempted forty days and nights, and when He was hungry and asked for bread He was told, substantially, that if His mission was of God that God would feed Him, that if hungry He could turn the stones to bread and eat. I remembered that similar sayings had been thrown into our teeth. These thoughts passed through my frame like electricity - or to use the language of one of the old prophets, it was like fire shut up in my bones; I felt renewed and refreshed from head to foot, and determined to trust in the Arm that could not be broken; to conquer and subdue the passions of my nature, and by the help of God to try and bring them in subjection to the will of the Spirit, and not of the flesh, which is carnal, sensual, and devilish. I determined that there should be no lack on my part.

Daylight came at last, and we renewed our journey. I put a double guard over those evil passions that were sown thickly in my sinful nature. The passion most dreaded by me was the lust of the flesh; that I knew to be the worst enemy to my salvation, and I determined to master it, I have walked along in silence for hours, with my heart lifted up to God in prayer, pleading with Him to give me power over my passions and sinful desires, that I might conquer and drive from my mind those besetting sins that were continually warring with the Spirit, which, if cherished or suffered to remain, would wound and grieve the Spirit and drive it away. It is written, "My Spirit will not dwell in an unholy temple." Jesus said to His followers that their bodies were the temples of the Living God; that if they who had charge of those temples, or bodies, allowed them to become unholy, He would destroy that body; while to those who guarded their temples, and kept them pure and holy, He and His Father would come and take up their abode and dwell with them as a constant companion forever, even unto the end, guiding them in all truth and showing them things past, present, and to come. From day to day I kept my mind in a constant strain upon this subject. Notwithstanding, the tempter was ever on the alert, and contested every inch of ground with me.

Often, while I was in the most solemn reflections, the tempter would place before me some lovely female, possessing all the allurements of her sex, to draw my mind from the contemplation of holy things. For a moment humanity would claim the victory; but quick as thought I would banish the vision from my mind and plead with God for strength and power to resist the temptations that were besetting me and enable me to cast aside the love of sinful pleasures. The words of the Apostle Paul were appropriate for me at that and in future time, when he declared that he died daily to crucify the deeds of the flesh. So it was with me. I was convinced that I could not serve two masters, God and Mammon. When I tried to please the one I was certain to displease the other. I found that I must give myself up wholly to God and His ministry and conduct myself as a man of God, if I would be worthy of the name of a messenger of salvation. I must have the Spirit of God accompany my words and carry conviction to the honest in heart. In this way I grew in grace from day to day, and I have never seen the hour that I regretted taking up my cross and giving up all other things to follow and obey Christ, my Redeemer and Friend. I do most sincerely regret that I ever suffered myself to be captivated by the wiles of the devil, contrary to my better judgment.

Brigham teaches that the will and acts of the people must all be dictated by him, and delights in hearing the apostles and elders declare to the people that he, Brigham, is God. He claims that the people are answerable to him as to their God, that they must obey his every beck and call. It matters not what he commands or requests the people to do, it is their duty to hear and obey. To disobey the will of Brigham is a sin against the Holy Ghost, and an unpardonable sin to be wiped out only by blood atonement. I must now resume my narrative, but I will hereafter speak of Brigham more at length.

We left the Fasting Hotel, as I called it, and traveled to Hamilton, Ohio, then a neat little town. As we arrived in the center of the town I felt impressed to call at a restaurant, kept by a foreigner. It was then noon. This was the first house we had called at since morning.

As we entered the proprietor requested us to unstrap our valises and sit down and rest, saying we looked very tired. He asked where we were from, and where we were going. We answered all his questions. He then offered us refreshments; we informed him that we had no money, and had eaten nothing for three days. He said it made no difference to him; that if we had no money we were more welcome than if we had plenty of it. We ate a hearty meal, and he gave us a drink of cider. He then filled our knapsacks with buns, cheese, sausages, and other things, after which he bid us godspeed.

We traveled on with hearts full of gratitude to God, the bountiful Giver Who had opened the heart of the stranger that had just supplied our wants, and we felt grateful to and blessed the man for his generous actions. While passing through Cincinnati we were offered refreshments by a lady that kept an inn. We crossed the Ohio River at Cincinnati, and stopped over night at a hotel on the Kentucky side of the river. We then traveled through Kentucky and into Overton and Jackson counties, Tennessee. I now bear testimony, though many years have passed since then, that from the moment I renewed my covenant to deny myself to all unrighteousness and live the life of a man devoted to God's work on earth, I have never felt that I was alone, or without a Friend powerful to aid, direct, and shield me at all times and during all troubles.

While in Tennessee I stopped with my friend Levi Stewart at the houses of his relatives in Overton and Jackson counties, and preached several times. My friend Stewart was blessed with a large bump of self-esteem. He imagined that he could convert all of his relatives at once; that all he had to do was to present the gospel, and they would gladly embrace it. He appeared to forget that a prophet was not without honor, save in his own country and among his own kinfolk.

Brother Stewart, though I was his superior in the Priesthood, if not in experience and ability, looked upon me as a cipher, fit for nothing. The rough treatment and slights that I received from him were more than humiliating to a man of fine feelings and a spirit such as I possessed. I said nothing to him, but I poured out my soul in secret prayer to my Heavenly Father, asking Him to open the door for my deliverance, so that my proud spirit, which was bound down, might soar in a free element.

One Sunday we attended a Baptist meeting. We sat facing the preacher, but at the far side of the house. My mind was absorbed in meditating upon my future labors. Gradually I lost consciousness of my surroundings, and my whole being seemed in another locality. I was in a trance, and saw future events. What I then saw was to me a reality, and I will describe it as such. I traveled in a strange land and among a people that I had never seen. I was kindly received by the people, and all my wants were supplied without my having to ask for charity. I traveled on, going over a mountainous country. I crossed a clear, handsome river, and was kindly received by the family of the owner of the ferry at that river. I stayed with this family for some days. I then recrossed the river and called at a house, where I asked for a drink of water, which was given me. I held quite a conversation with two young women. They informed me that there was no minister in the neighborhood; also that their father had gone in pursuit of a

Mormon preacher who had passed that way a few days before. A few days passed, and I saw myself in the midst of a congregation, to whom I was preaching. I also baptized a large number and organized a flourishing branch of the Church, and was in charge of that people. I was very popular with, and almost worshiped by, my congregation. I saw all this, and much more, when my vision closed. My mind gradually changed back, and I found myself sitting in the meetinghouse, where I had been just forty minutes before.

This was an open-day vision, in which the curtains of heaven were raised and held aside from futurity to allow me to look into the things which were to come. A feeling of heavenly rapture filled my being, so much so that, like the apostle who was caught up into the third heaven, I did not know whether I was in the body or out of it during my vision. I saw things that it would be unlawful for men to utter. While the vision lasted my soul was lighted up as if illuminated with the candle of God. When the vision closed the hallowed influence gradually withdrew, yet leaving sufficient of its glorious effect upon my soul to justify me in feeling and knowing that I was then chosen of God as a servant in His earthly kingdom; and I was also made to know, by my sensations, that my vision was real, and would soon be verified in every particular.

At the close of the church services we returned to our lodgings. Brother Stewart asked me if I was sick. I said:

"No, I am not sick, but I feel serious; yet I am comfortable."

That evening, after I had given some time to secret prayer, I retired to rest. Very soon afterwards the vision returned, though somewhat varied. I was in the midst of a strange people, to whom I was propounding the gospel. They received it with honest hearts, and looked upon me as a messenger of salvation. I visited from house to house, surrounded by friends and kindred spirits with whom I had once been familiar in another state of existence. I was in the spirit, and communing with the host of spirits that surrounded me; they encouraged me to return to the body and continue to act the part that my Master had assigned me. No person, except those who have entered by pureness of heart into constant communion with God, can ever enter into the joyous host with whom I then, and in after life, held intercourse.

When I came to myself in the morning I determined to travel until the end of time to find the people and country that God had shown me in my vision; and I made my arrangements to start forth again, knowing that God now went with me. I started off after having a talk with Brother Stewart. He tried to dissuade me from going, saying I had little experience, not sufficient to warrant my traveling alone; that we had better remain together where we were for a season, for we had a home there, and could study and inform ourselves more thoroughly before starting out among strangers. I told him that in and of my own strength I was but a weak vessel; but my trust was in God, and unless He would bless my labors I could not accomplish much. That I was God's servant, engaged in His work, therefore I looked to Him for strength and grace sufficient to sustain me in my day of trial. That I trusted in the arm of God alone, and not in one of flesh. I started off in a southwesterly course, over the Cumberland

Mountains, and went about seventy miles through a heavily timbered country. I found many species of wild fruit in abundance along the way.

Springs of pure, cold water were quite common. I passed many little farms and orchards of cultivated fruit, such as cherries, peaches, pears, and apples. As I proceeded the country became familiar to me, so much so that I soon knew I was on the very ground I had seen in my vision in the Baptist church. I saw the place where I had held my first meeting, and my joy was great to behold with my eyes what I had seen through a glass darkly. I turned aside from the road, and beneath the spreading branches of the forest trees I lifted my heart with gratitude to God for what He had done for me. I then went to the house where I had seen the multitude assembled when I was preaching.

There I saw the two young women that I had beheld in my vision. They appeared to me as though I had known them from infancy, they so perfectly accorded with those whom I had seen while God permitted me to peer into futurity. Yes, I saw the women, but their father was gone from home. I asked for a drink of water, and it was handed to me, as I had seen it done in my vision. I asked them if there had ever been any Mormon preachers in that country. They said there had not been any there. The young women were modest and genteel in behavior. I passed on to the Cumberland River, was set over the river by the ferryman, and lodged in his house.

So far all was as God had shown me; but I was still at the outer edge of my familiar scenery. I stayed about a week with the ferryman. His name was Vanleven, a relative of my friend and banker in Illinois. I made myself useful while there. I attended the ferry and did such work as I could see needed attending to. I also read and preached Mormon doctrines to the family.

On the fifth day after reaching the ferry I saw five men approaching. I instantly recognized one of them as the man I had seen in my vision - the man that took me to his house to preach. My heart leaped for joy, for God had sent him in answer to the prayers I had offered up, asking that the man should be sent for me. I crossed the men over and back again, and although I talked considerably to the man about what was uppermost in my mind, he said nothing about my going home with him. I was much disappointed. I retired for secret prayer, and asked God, in the name of His Son, Jesus Christ, to aid me, and to send the man whom I had seen in my vision back for me. Before I left my knees I had evidence that my prayer was answered.

The next morning at daylight I informed my friends that I must depart in search of my field of labor. They asked me to stay until breakfast, but I refused. One of the negroes put me over the river, and directed me how to cross the mountains on the trail that was much shorter than the wagon road. I stopped in a little cove and ate a number of fine, ripe cherries. I then went on until I reached what to me was enchanted ground. I met the two sisters at the gate, and asked them if their father was at home.

"No, he is not at home," said the ladies, "he has gone to the ferry to find a Mormon preacher, and see if he can get him to come here and preach in this neighborhood."

They then said I must have met him on the road. I told them that I had come over the mountain trail, and said I was probably the man he had gone for. They replied:

"Our father said that if you came this way, to have you stop and stay here until his return, and to tell you that you are welcome to preach at our house at any time."

This was on Friday. I took out my pencil and wrote a notice that I would preach at that place on the following Sunday, at 10 o'clock, a. m. I handed it to the girls. They agreed to have the appointment circulated. I passed on and preached at a place twelve miles from there, and returned in time for my appointment.

When I arrived within sight of the place of meeting I was filled with doubt and anxiety. I trembled all over, for I saw that a vast concourse of people had come to hear an inexperienced man preach the gospel. I went into the grove and again prayed for strength and assistance from my Father in Heaven, to enable me to speak His truth aright. I felt strengthened and comforted. As I arose from prayer these words came into my mind:

"Truth is mighty and will prevail."

Thereafter I waited until the hour arrived for preaching; then I approached the place where I had once been in a vision.

This meeting place was in a valley, near a cold, pure spring; on either side was a high, elevated country; in the center of this valley there stood a large blacksmith and wagon shop, surrounded with a bower of brushwood to protect the audience from the sun. This bower, in which I was to preach, would seat one thousand people.

In the center of the bower they had erected a framework or raised platform for a pulpit. I took my place and preached for one hour and a half. My tongue was like the pen of a ready writer. I scarcely knew what I was saying. I then opened the doors of the Church for the admission of members. Five persons joined the Church, and I appointed another meeting for that night. I again preached, when two more joined the Church.

The next day I baptized the seven new members. I then arranged to hold meetings at that place three times a week. I visited around the country, seeking to convert sinners. The first converts were leading people in that county.

Elisha Sanders and his wife and daughter were the first to receive the gospel. Sanders was a farmer; he had a large flour mill, owned a woodyard, and was engaged in boat building on the Cumberland River. Caroline C. Sanders had volunteered to publish the appointment of my first meeting, which I left with the daughters of Mr. Smith. I labored at this place two months, and baptized twenty-eight persons, mostly the heads of families. I then organized them into a branch of the Church.

Brother Sanders fitted up a room very handsomely for me, in which I could retire for study, rest, and secret prayer. I was made to feel at home there, and knew that God had answered my prayers. I had the knowledge that God's Spirit accompanied my words, carrying conviction to the hearts of sinful hearers, and giving me souls as seals to my ministry.

Brother Stewart soon preached himself out in his relatives' neighborhood. He heard of my success, and came to me. He said that the people where he had been preaching were an unbelieving set. I introduced him to the members of my congregation, and had him preach with me a few times, which gratified him very much.

One Sunday we were to administer the ordinance of baptism. Several candidates were in attendance. Brother Stewart was quite anxious to baptize the people. I was willing to humor him. So I said:

"My friends, Brother Stewart, a priest of the New Dispensation, will administer the ordinance of baptism."

The people stood still; none would come forward for him to baptize them. They said they would not be baptized until I would baptize them myself. I told them I would act if they desired it. So I baptized the people, and Brother Stewart was much offended with them. He had not yet learned that he that exalteth himself shall be cast down, and he that humbleth himself shall be exalted. I then called on the people for a contribution, to get some clothing for Brother Stewart. I had concluded to have him return home, and wished to reclothe him before he started, for he was then in need of it. The contribution was more liberal than I expected.

After Brother Stewart departed I stayed there some three weeks. Then I made up my mind to go home and visit my family. Brother Sanders invited me to go to Gainsborough with him, whore he presented me with a nice supply of clothing. Sister Sanders presented me with a fine horse, saddle, and bridle, and twelve dollars in money. The congregation gave me fifty dollars, and I had from them an outfit worth over three hundred dollars. I at first refused to accept the horse, but Sister Sanders appeared so grieved at this that I finally took it. I left my congregation in charge of Elder Julien Moses, and started for my family about the 1st of October, 1839. I promised to call on my flock the next spring, or send a suitable minister to wait upon them.

When I reached Vandalia I found my family well. God had raised up friends for them in my absence. The Saints were then gathering at Commerce, that is to say Nauvoo, Hancock County, Illinois. I visited my sister's family that fall; they then lived about one hundred miles north of Vandalia. I preached often through Central Illinois, and that fall I baptized all of my wife's family, except her father. He held out and refused the gospel until he was on his deathbed; then he demanded baptism, but being in a country place he died ere an elder could be procured to baptize him. By the rules of our Church a person can be baptized for the dead, and later he was saved to eternal life by the baptism of one of his children for the salvation of his soul.

CHAPTER VIII
LEE AS A MISSIONARY

Shortly after my return to Illinois I built a house for my family. During the winter I entered into a trading and trafficking business with G. W. Hickerson. We would go over the country and buy up chickens, butter, feathers, beeswax, and coon skins, and haul them to St. Louis, and carry back calicoes and other goods in payment for the articles first purchased. We made some money that way.

While carrying on this trade I drew the remainder of my money from my friend, Vanleven, and began my preparations for joining the Saints. About the middle of April, 1840, I succeeded in securing a good outfit, and with my old friend Stewart again joined the Saints at Nauvoo. I felt it to be God's will that I must obey the orders of the Prophet, hence my return to the society of the brethren.

Joseph and his two counselors, his brother Hyrum and Sidney Rigdon had been released from jail in Richmond, Missouri, and were again at the head of the Church and directing the energies of the brethren. It was the policy of Joseph to hold the city lots in Nauvoo at a high price, so as to draw money from the rich, but not so high as to prevent the poor from obtaining homes. The poor who lost all their property in following the Church were presented with a lot free in the center of the city. The Prophet told them not to sell their lots for less than eight hundred to one thousand dollars, but to sell for that when offered; then they could take a cheaper lot in the outskirts of the city and have money left to fix up comfortably.

All classes, Jews and Gentiles, were allowed to settle there, one man's money being as good as another's. No restrictions were placed on the people; they had the right to trade with anyone that suited them. All classes attended meetings, dances, theaters, and other gatherings, and were permitted to eat and drink together. The outsiders were invited to join in all of our amusements. Ball was a favorite sport with the men, and the Prophet frequently took a hand in the game. He appeared to treat all men alike, and never condemned a man until he had given him a fair trial to show what was in him.

Among the first things was the laying of the foundation of the Temple. When this was done each man was required to do one day's work in every ten days, in quarrying rock or doing other work for the structure. A company was sent up the Mississippi River to the Pineries to get out lumber for the Temple and other public buildings. The money for city lots went into the Church treasury to purchase materials for the Temple which could not be supplied by the Saints' own labor.

At the conference in April, 1840, the Prophet delivered a lengthy address upon the history and condition of the Saints. He reminded the brethren that all had suffered alike for the sake of the gospel. The rich and the poor had been brought to a common level by persecution; many of the brethren owed debts that they had been forced to contract in order to get out of Missouri alive. He considered it unchristianlike for the brethren to demand the payment of such debts; he did not wish to screen anyone from the just payment of his debts, but he did think that it would be for the glory of the Kingdom if the people, of their own will, freely forgave each other all their existing indebtedness, one to the other, renew their covenants with Almighty God and with each other, refrain from evil, and live their religion. By this means God's Holy Spirit would support and bless the people.

The people were then asked if they were in favor of thus bringing about the year of jubilee. All that felt so inclined were asked to make it known by raising their hands; every hand in the audience was raised. The Prophet declared all debts of the Saints, to and from each other, forgiven and wiped out. He then gave the following words of advice to the people:

"I wish you all to know that because you were justified in taking property from your enemies, while engaged in war in Missouri, which was needed to support you, there is now a different condition of things. We are no longer at war, and you must stop stealing. When the right time comes we will go in force and take the whole State of Missouri. It belongs to us as our inheritance; but I want no more petty stealing. A man that will steal petty articles from his enemies will, when occasion offers, steal from his brethren too. Now I command you, that you who have stolen must steal no more. I ask all the brethren to renew their covenants, and start anew to live their religion. If you will do this, I will forgive you your past sins."

The vote was taken on this proposition, and resulted in the unanimous decision of the people to act as requested by the Prophet. He then continued, saying that he never professed to be a perfect man.

"I have my failings and passions to contend with the same as has the greatest stranger to God. I am tempted the same as you are, my brethren. I am not infallible. All men are subject to temptation, but they are not justified in yielding to their passions and sinful natures. There is a constant warfare between the two natures of man. This is the warfare of the Saints. It is written that the Lord would have a tried people - a people that would be tried as gold is tried by the fire, even seven times tried and purified from the dross of unrighteousness. The chances of all men for salvation are equal. True, some have greater capacity than others, yet the chances for improving our minds and subduing our passions by denying ourselves to all unrighteousness and cultivating the principles of purity are the same; they are within the reach of every man; all have their free agency; all can lay hold of the promises of eternal life, if they will only be faithful and comply with God's will and obey the Priesthood in these last days. Never betray anyone, for God hates a traitor, and so do I. Stand by each other; never desert a friend, especially in the hour of trouble. Remember that our reward consists in doing good acts, and not in long prayers like the Scribes and Pharisees of old, who prayed to be seen of men. Never mind what men think of you, if your hearts are right before God. It is written, 'Do unto others as you would that others should do unto you.' The first commandment is, 'Thou shalt love the Lord thy God with all thy heart, mind, and strength.' The second commandment is, 'Thou shalt love thy neighbor as thyself.' Upon these two hang all the law and the prophets."

To more deeply impress these truths upon the minds of his people the Prophet gave them an account of the man who fell among thieves and was relieved by the stranger; and he also taught us from the Scriptures, as well as by the revelations that he had received from God, that it is humane acts and deeds of kindness, justice and words of truth, that are accounted to man for righteousness; that prayers, made to be heard by men, and hypocritical groans are displeasing to God.

The Prophet talked to us plainly, and fully instructed us in our duty and gave the long-faced hypocrites such a lecture that much good was done. I had at that time learned to dread a religious fanatic, and I was pleased to hear the Prophet lay down the law to them. A fanatic is always dangerous, but a religious fanatic is to be dreaded by all men - there is no reason in one of them. I cannot understand how men will blindly follow fanatical teachers. I always demanded a reason for my belief, and hoped I never would become a victim of fanaticism.

During the summer of 1840 I built a house and such other buildings as I required on my lot on Warsaw street, and was again able to say I had a home. The brethren were formed into military companies that year in Nauvoo. Col. A. P. Rockwood was drillmaster. Brother Rockwood was then a captain, but was afterwards promoted to be colonel of the Host of Israel. I was then fourth corporal of the company. The people were regularly drilled and taught military tactics, so that they would be ready to act when the time came for returning to Jackson County, the land of our inheritance. Most of my wife's relatives came to Nauvoo that year, and settled near my house.

In 1841 I was sent on a mission through Illinois, Kentucky, and Tennessee. I also visited portions of Arkansas. I traveled in company, on that mission, with Elder Franklin Edwards. I was then timid about speaking in towns or cities. I felt that I had not a sufficient experience to justify me in doing so.

My comrade had less experience than I had, and the worst of it was he would not study to improve his mind, or permit me to study in quiet. He was negligent, and did not pay sufficient attention to secret prayer, to obtain that nearness to God that is so necessary for a minister to have if he expects his works to be blessed with Divine favor. I told him he must do better, or go home. He promised to do better; also agreed that he would do the begging for food and lodging, and I might do the preaching. I accepted the offer, and in this way we got along well and pleasantly for some time.

At the crossing of the Forkadeer River we stayed over night with the ferryman, and were well entertained. When we left the ferry the old gentleman told us we would be in a settlement of Methodist people that evening, and they were set in their notions and hated Mormons as badly as the Church of England hated Methodists, and if we got food or shelter among them he would be mistaken. He told us to begin to ask for lodging at least an hour before sundown, or we would not get it.

In the after-part of the day we remembered the advice of the morning and stopped at every house. The houses were about half a mile apart. We were refused at every house. The night came on dark and stormy, the rain fell in torrents, while heavy peals of thunder and bright flashes of lightning were constant, or seemed so to me. The timber was very heavy, making the night darker than it would otherwise have been. The road was badly cut up from heavy freight teams passing over it, and the holes were full of water. We fell into many holes of mud and water, and were well soaked.

About ten o'clock we called at the house of a Methodist class leader, and asked for lodging and food. He asked who we were. We told him that we were Mormon preachers. As soon as he heard the name Mormon he became enraged, and said no Mormon could stay in his house. We started on. Soon afterwards we heard him making efforts to set his dogs on us. The dogs came running and barking, as a pack of hounds always do.

Brother Edwards was much frightened; but I told him not to be scared, I would protect him. So when the dogs came near us I commenced to clap my hands and shouted as though the fox was just ahead of us; this caused the dogs to rush on and leave us in safety. In this way we escaped injury from the pack of ten or more dogs that the Methodist had put on our trail.

At the next house we were again refused shelter and food. I asked for permission to sit under the porch until the rain stopped.

"No," said the man, "if you were not Mormons I would gladly entertain you, but as you are Mormons I dare not permit you to stop around me."

This made twenty-one houses that we had called at and asked for lodging, and at each place we had been refused, simply because we were Mormons.

About midnight my partner grew very sick of his contract to do the begging and resolved to die before he would ask for aid from such people again. I told him I would have both food and lodging at the next place we stopped. He said it was useless to make the attempt, and I confess that the numerous refusals we had met with were calculated to dishearten many a person; but I had faith in God. I had never yet gone to Him in a humble and penitent manner without receiving strength to support me, nor had He ever sent me empty-handed from Him. My trust was in God, and I advanced to the next house, confident that I would not ask in vain.

As we approached the house we discovered that the negroes were having a dance. I asked where their master was; they pointed out the house to me. We walked to the house and up on the porch. The door was standing open; a candle was burning, and near the fire a woman was sitting holding a sick child on her lap. The man was also sitting near the fire. Our footsteps attracted their attention; our appearance was not inviting as we stood there wet, muddy, and tired. I spoke in a loud voice, saying:

"Sir, I beseech you, in the name of Jesus Christ, to entertain us as servants of the living God. We are ministers of the gospel, we travel without purse or scrip; we preach without hire, and are now without money; we are wet, weary, and hungry; we want refreshment, rest, and shelter."

The man sprang to his feet, but did not say a word. His wife said:

"Tell them to come in."

"We will do you no harm; we are friends, not enemies," I said.

We were invited in. Servants were called, a good fire was made and a warm supper placed before us. After eating we were shown to a good bed. We slept until near ten o'clock in the morning. When we did awaken our clothes were clean and dry, and breakfast was ready and waiting for us. In fact, we were as well treated as it was possible to ask.

This family had lately come from the State of Virginia, intending to try that climate for a year, and then, if they liked it, purchase land and stay there permanently. After breakfast the gentleman said:

"You had a severe time of it among the Christians yesterday and last night. As you are ministers, sent out to convert sinners, you cannot do better than to preach to these Christians, and seek to convert them."

He offered to send word all over the settlement and notify the people, if we would stay and preach that night. We accepted his offer, and remained, thus securing the rest that we so much needed, thanking God for still remembering and caring for us, His servants.

Agreeably to arrangements, we preached in the Methodist meeting-house to a very attentive audience upon the first principles of the gospel. We alluded to the treatment of Christ and His followers by the Pharisees and Sadducees, the religious sects of those days, and said that we preached the same gospel, and fared but little better. This meeting-house had been built conjointly by Methodists and Universalists. Members from both persuasions were present. Our neighbor who had fed and cared for us leaned to the latter faith.

At the close of our remarks the class leader who had set the hounds on our track was the first to the stand to invite us home with him. I told him that the claims of those who did not set their dogs on us, after they had turned us from their doors hungry, were first with me - that his claims were an after consideration. He said it was his negro boys that sent the hounds after us; he would not be bluffed. He said that one of us must go with him - that if I would not go Brother Frank must go. I told him that Elder Edwards could use his own pleasure, but I would hold a meeting that night with our Universalist brethren; and thus we parted.

Elder Edwards went to spend the night with the class leader, while I attended a meeting with the friends who had invited me home with them. I had a good time. Of their own accord they made up a collection of a few dollars as a token of their regard for me. I was to meet Elder Edwards at the house of my friend who took us in at midnight from the storm, an hour before sun; but he did not put in an appearance for an hour after. When he got within talking distance I saw by his features that he had been roughly dealt with. His first words were:

"He is the wickedest old man that I ever met with, and, if he don't repent, God will curse him."

That was enough, and I began to laugh. I conceived what he had to encounter the long night before. He said:

"If the Lord will forgive me for going this time, I will never go again unless you are along." I said to him:

"Brother Frank, experience teaches a dear school, yet fools will not learn at any other. I knew what treatment you would receive, and refused to go. If you had been a wise man you would have taken the hint and kept away from him."

We made our way through to Overton County, Tennessee. Here I advised my friend Edwards to return to Nauvoo, and gave him money to pay his fare on a steamer, for he was not cut out for a preacher.

At Carlisle, the county seat of Overton County, I met with a young man, an elder, by the name of Dwight Webster. Though but little experienced, yet he was a man of steady habits and an agreeable companion. We held a number of meetings in this part of the country. Brother Webster and I baptized several persons, and made a true friend of a wealthy merchant, named Armstrong, who welcomed us to his house and placed us under his protection. He also owned a large establishment in Louisville, Kentucky. He was an infidel, though an honorable gentleman. His wife Nancy, and her sister Sarah, were both baptized.

While here I received a letter from Brother James Pace, one of my near neighbors in Nauvoo, requesting me to visit his brother, William Pace, and his relatives in Rutherford County, Tennessee. Elder A. O. Smoot and Dr. David Lewis succeeded us in this county, and in Jackson County, Tennessee, and added many to those whom we had already baptized.

Brother Webster and I made our way through to Stone River, preaching by the way, as opportunity occurred. Here I handed my letter of introduction to William Pace, brother of my neighbor, James Pace, who received us kindly and procured us the liberty of holding forth in the Campbellite chapel.

Here we were informed that the Campbellite preachers were heavy on debate; that none of the other sects could stand before them, and that no one dare meet them in public or private discussion. I replied that my trust was in God, that the message I had to bear was from Heaven; that if it would not bear the scrutiny of man I did not want to stand by it; but if it was of God He would not suffer His servants to be confounded.

"Truth is mighty and will prevail; Error cannot stand before Truth. If these men can overthrow the gospel which I preach, the sooner they do it the better for me. I do not wish to deceive anyone, or to deceive myself. If anyone can point out an error in the gospel which I preach, I am willing to drop that error, and exchange it for truth."

The hour came, and Brother Webster and I both spoke. We spoke on the first principles of the Gospel of Christ, as taught by the Saviour and His apostles.

Before sitting down I extended the courtesy of the pulpit to any gentleman that wished to reply or offer any remarks either for or against what we had set forth. Parson Hall, the presiding Campbellite minister, was on his feet in a moment and denounced us as impostors. He said we were holding forth a theory that was fulfilled in Christ; that the canon of Scripture being full, these spiritual gifts that were spoken of in the New Testament were done away with, being no longer necessary. As for the story of the "Golden Bible" (Book of Mormon), that was absurd in the extreme, as there were to be no other books or revelations granted. He quoted the Revelations of St. John in his support, where they read:

"He that addeth to, or diminisheth from the words of the prophecies and this Book, shall have the plagues herein written added to his torment," or words to that effect. I followed him in the discussion, and quoted John where it reads:

"He that speaketh not according to the law and the testimony hath no light in him." I said that my authority and testimony were from the Bible, the book of the law of the Lord, which all Christian believers hold as a sacred rule of their faith and practice.

To that authority I hoped my worthy friend would not object. I illustrated my position by further quotations from the criptures, and when our meeting was over the people flocked around Brother Webster and myself in a mass, to shake hands with us and invite us to their houses - the Methodists, Baptists, and Presbyterians especially.

The planters in this county were mostly wealthy, and prided themselves on being hospitable and kind to strangers, especially to ministers of the gospel. We went from house to house and preached two and three times a week. We saw that the seed had already been sown in honest hearts, and we were near to them.

Knowing the danger of being lifted up by self-approbation, I determined to be on my guard, attend to secret prayer, and to reading and keeping diaries. When at our friend Pace's house Brother Webster and I would frequently resort to a lonely grove to attend to prayer and read to ourselves.

CHAPTER IX
MORMONISM AND ITS ORIGIN

Only a short time after the events narrated it was arranged that Parson Hall and myself should hold another discussion in the Campbellite chapel. Parson Hall did not want to meet me in discussion, but he must do so or lose his flock, as all the people had become interested in the subject of Mormonism. We met at the appointed time, and chose two umpires to act as moderators of the meeting. The subject to be discussed was:

"Are apostles, prophets, and teachers, together with the spiritual gifts spoken of and recorded by the Apostle Mark in his 16th chapter, necessary to the Church now as they were then?"

In his closing speech Parson Hall became very abusive and denounced the Mormons to the lowest regions of darkness, and called the Prophet Joseph a vile impostor. I replied to him and closed the discussion. It had been agreed that the Old and New Testaments should be the only authorities to be quoted by us. The umpires refused to decide as to which one of us had the best of the discussion. They said it rested with the people to decide for themselves. It was evident, however, that the people were with me. The principal topic of conversation was about this strange Mormon doctrine.

Parson Hall's flock was by no means satisfied with his course. He said the Mormon doctrine was the strongest Bible doctrine he had ever heard of, and he feared the consequences of a further discussion. But this would not satisfy the people, who wanted to hear and learn more of it; so another discussion was agreed upon, in which Parsons Curlee and Nichols were to assist Parson Hall, and prompt him. The subject was:

"Is the Book of Mormon of Divine origin, and has it come forth in direct fulfillment of prophecy? And was Joseph Smith inspired of God?"

We selected three judges; the hall was thronged. I felt the responsibility of my situation, but I put my trust in God to give me light and utterance to the convincing of the honest and pure in heart. The discussion lasted many hours. I showed conclusively, both from the Old and New Testaments, that, in accordance with Scripture and prophecy, the ten tribes of Israel had been broken up and scattered upon the face of the earth. That sure and indisputable evidence had been found and produced by which it was certain that the North American Indians were descendants from the ten tribes of Israel. I showed this from many customs and rites prevalent among the Indians, and there could be no doubt, in any rational mind, that these tribes had sprung from the remnants of the scattered ten tribes of Israel. The prophecies of the Old and New Testaments, the traditions and history of the Indians so far as known, their solemn religious rites and observances, were conclusive evidence of this fact.

And God has repeatedly promised that, in His own good time, these tribes of Israel, this chosen people, should be again gathered together; that a new and further revelation should be given them and to the whole world, and that under this new dispensation Zion should be rebuilt, and the glory of God fill the whole earth as the waters cover the mighty deep. It should be as a sealed book unto them, which men deliver to one that is learned, saying, "Read this book," and he saith, "I cannot, for it is a sealed book." It is strange that a people once so favored of God, strengthened by His arm and counseled by His prophets and inspired men, should have wandered and become lost to all sense of duty to God! But so it was, until, as the prophet says, the Book that should come unto them spoke to them out of the ground - out of the dust of the earth; as a "familiar spirit, even out of the dust of the earth."

The Book that was to contain the Divine revelation of God was to come forth, written upon plates, in a language unknown to men. But a man unlearned, not by his own power, but by the power of God, by means of the Urim and Thummim, was to translate it into our language. And this record, in due time, came according to God's will. It was found deposited in the side of a mountain, or hill, called Cumorrah, written in the reformed Egyptian language, in Ontario County, in the State of New York. It was deposited in a stone box, put together with cement, air-tight. The soil about the box was worn away, until a corner of the box was visible. It was found by the Prophet Joseph, then an illiterate lad, or young man, who had been chosen of God as His instrument for making the same known to men.

65

The Prophet Joseph was a young man of moral character, belonging to no sect, but an earnest inquirer after truth. He was not permitted to remove the box for a period of two years after he found it. The angel of God that had the records in charge would not permit him to touch them. In attempting to do so, on one occasion, his strength was paralyzed, and the angel appeared before him and told him how that record contained the gospel of God and an historical account of the God of Joseph in this land; that through their transgressions the records were taken away from the people and hid in the earth, to come forth at the appointed time, when the Lord should set His heart, the second time, to recover the remnant of His people, scattered throughout all nations; that the remnant of His people should be united with the stick of Judah, in the hands of Ephraim, and they should become one stick in the hands of the Lord. This is the Bible, which is the stick of Judah, that contained the gospel and the records of the House of Israel, till the Messiah came. The angel further informed Joseph that when the ten tribes of Israel were scattered one branch went to the north; that prior to the birth of Jesus Christ the other branch left Jerusalem, taking the records with them, of which the Book of Mormon is a part. The branch of the ten tribes which went north doubtless have a record with them.

When these plates containing the Book of Mormon and God's will, as therein revealed, were removed from Ontario County, New York, they were taken to Professor Anthon, of New York City, for translation. He replied that he could not translate them, that they were written in "a sealed language, unknown to the present age." This was just as the Prophet Isaiah said it should be.

Do any of the present denominations counsel with the Lord? No, they deny Revelation, and seek to hide their ways from Him. Upon all such He pronounces woe. I do not wish to be considered as casting aspersions on any other sect. It is not my purpose to do so. The love that I have for truth and the salvation of the human family may cause me to offend, but if I do so it is because of my exceeding zeal to do good. Remember that the reproof of a friend is better than the smite of an enemy. Jesus said, "Woe unto you that are angry and offended because of the truth."

It is not policy on your part to be offended on account of the truth. If your systems will not stand the scrutiny of men, how can they stand the test of the great Judge of both the living and the dead? I place a greater value upon the salvation of my soul than I do upon all earthly considerations.

After my second discussion I began to baptize some of the leading members of the Campbellite Church. Among the first to be baptized were John Thompson and wife. Brother Thompson was sheriff of Rutherford County, and an influential man. Among others who were baptized were Wm. Pace and wife. Mrs. Pace was a sister of Parson Nichols, who assisted Parson Hall in his last discussion with me. Major D. M. Jarratt and wife, Mrs. Caroline Ghiliam, Major Miles Anderson, and others were also baptized and received into the Church.

My friend Webster, after being with me about a month, returned to visit and strengthen the branches of the Church established in Smith, Jackson, and Overton counties. I continued my labors on Stone River and Creple Creek about six months. During the most of this time I availed myself of the opportunity of studying grammar and other English branches. During my stay I lectured three times a week, Wednesdays, Saturdays, and Sunday afternoons.

Sabbath forenoon I attended the meetings of other denominations. During this time I held four public discussions in addition to those I had with Parson Hall. I held two discussions with the Rev. James Trott, who for fifteen years had been a missionary to the Cherokee Nation. I held a closing debate in that settlement with the Rev. Mr. Cantrall, of the Campbellite faith. He came from a distance, at the request of friends, to endeavor to save the flock.

After consultation with Parson Hall and other members of the flock they refused to submit to moderators or judges; neither were they willing to be confined to the Old and New Testaments for authority to disprove the doctrine that I defended. Their proposition was that Mr. Cantrall should speak first, bringing out any argument he chose; when he finished I was to conclude the debate, and the people were to judge for themselves who had the best of the argument.

My friends would not consent to this arrangement, but I told the opposition they might have it their own way. If the Rev. Cantrall wished to condescend to the platform of a blackguard, in a case of necessity I would meet him there, though I preferred honorable debate to slander and ridicule. This statement I made to the assembly prior to the gentleman's mounting the stand, with Parsons Hill, Crulee, Trott, and Nichols as prompters.

They had provided themselves with a roll of pamphlets and newspapers, containing many of the low, cunning, lying stories about the Prophet Joseph walking on the water, being a money digger, an impostor, and a thousand such tales. Mr. Cantrall read and emphasized each story, as his prompters handed them to him. He occupied two hours and a half in this manner, and about half an hour in trying to point out discrepancies in the Book of Mormon.

He spoke of the absurdities of the boat that the Nephites built in which to cross the ocean, from Asia to America, and said that it was built tight, excepting a little hole on top for air, and that it would shoot through the water like a fish, and ridiculed such an absurdity. He defied me to point to any such inconsistencies in the Holy Bible. He said the Bible was a book of common sense, written by men inspired of God. It was full of good works and pure characters, nothing like the impostor Joseph. He challenged me again to point to a single instance in the Bible which would compare with the stories in the Book of Mormon. The idea of apostles and prophets and supernatural gifts in the Church, as in the days of Christ, was absurd. He said the History of Nephi was absurd and a burlesque upon common sense; that he hoped none of the people would be led away by such nonsense and folly. I sat facing him during all his long harangue of abuse and ridicule.

When it was my turn to speak I asked the reverend gentleman to occupy my seat. I did not want more than thirty minutes to reply. I said to the assembly that a sense of duty to the truth, and the cause I had espoused, alone prompted me to make any reply to the long tirade of abuse and sarcasm they had been listening to. The gentleman and his prompters had gathered quite an angry-looking cloud of pamphlets and newspaper slang and abuse, without quoting a single passage of Scripture to disprove my position, or in support of their own. But on the contrary, he had become an accuser of the brethren, speaking evil of things he knew not. The spirit of persecution, hatred, and malice is not the spirit of the meek and lowly Saviour. The gentleman tells you that the day of perfection has arrived, that Satan is bound in the gospel chain, that we have no need of spiritual manifestations, that this is the reign of Christ. Now, I will say that if this is the millennial reign of Christ, and the devil is bound in the gospel chain, I pity the inhabitants of the earth when he gets loose again. After reading the description of the millennial reign, as it shall be, as described by the Prophet Isaiah, can anyone be so stupid as to believe that we are now living in that holy day? Shame on him who would deceive and tamper with the souls of men! The gentleman who told you this, doesn't believe it.

The gentleman has challenged me to produce anything from the Bible equaling in strangeness the building of a boat like a fish, in which the Nephites crossed the ocean from Asia to America. I call his attention to the first chapter of the Book of Jonah. Here a very strange craft was used for three days and nights, in which to send a missionary to Nineveh. This craft was constructed after the manner of the boat spoken of in the Book of Mormon. If the prophet was correct in the description of his craft, he too scooted through the water in the same way that the Nephites did in their boat. The Book of Mormon is nothing more or less than a book containing the history of a portion of the House of Israel, who left Jerusalem about the time of the reign of Zedekiah, King of Judah, and crossed the ocean to America; containing also the gospel which was preached to them on this continent, which is the same gospel as that preached by Christ and His Apostles at Jerusalem. The Bible and the Book of Mormon both contain a history of the different branches of the House of Israel, and each contains the gospel of Christ as it was preached unto them, the different branches of the house of Israel, and to all nations. Both testify of each other, and point with exactness to the dispensation of the fullness of time. The Book of Mormon does not contain a new gospel; it is the same gospel as that preached by Christ. It is a mysterious book, just what the prophet said it should be, "a marvelous work, a wonder." But my friend says that it is too mysterious, too wonderful, for human credence, and challenges me to point out anything told in the Bible that seems inconsistent with reason or experience. Now, which is the more reasonable, that Nephi built a boat after the pattern mentioned in the Mormon Bible, being directed by God how to build it, and then crossed the ocean to this continent, or that Jonah was in the whale's belly for three days and three nights, and then made a safe landing? Or would it sound any better if Nephi had said that when he and his company came to the great waters, the Lord had prepared whales, two or more, to receive them and their outfit, and set them over on this side?

Nothing is impossible with God. If He saw fit to send Jonah on his mission in a whale's belly, I have no fault to find with Him for so doing. He has the right to do His own will and pleasure; and if He instructed Nephi how to fashion his boat, or Noah to build an ark against the deluge, or caused Balaam's ass to speak and rebuke the madness of his master, or Moses to lead the children of

Israel through the Red Sea, without any boat at all, or the walls of Jericho to fall to the ground, and the people to become paralyzed through the tooting of rams' horns, or empowered Joshua to command the sun to stand still while he slaughtered his enemies, is any of these things more wonderful than the other?

Now one of these instances that I have selected from the Bible, if found in the Book of Mormon, would be sufficient to stamp it with absurdity and everlasting contempt, according to the gentlemen who oppose me; but when found in the Bible the story assumes another phase entirely. It is as the Saviour said of the Pharisees, "Ye strain at a gnat and swallow a camel." My opponent strains at a gnat, when found in the Book of Mormon, but if camels are discovered in the Bible he swallows them by the herd. I cannot see why a big story, told in the Bible, should be believed any more readily than one found in the Book of Mormon.

It is not my purpose to find discrepancies in the characters of the ancient prophets or inspired writers, but my opponent has challenged me to produce from the Bible a character of such disrepute as that of Joseph, the Mormon Prophet. Now I will say that of the characters I shall mention we have only their own history or account of what they did. Their enemies and contemporaries have long since passed away. But if their enemies could speak worse of them than they have of themselves, decency would blush to read their story. I will refer to only a few instances.

Moses, the meek, as he is called, murdered an Egyptian that strove with an Israelite, and had to run away from his country for the offense. He was afterwards sent by God to bring the Israelites out of bondage. Noah was a preacher of righteousness. He built the ark, and was saved through the deluge. His name has been handed down from posterity to posterity, in honorable remembrance, as one who feared God and worked righteousness. But we find him soon after the Flood getting drunk, exposing his nakedness, and cursing a portion of his own posterity. Lot, whose family was the only God-fearing family in Sodom and Gomorrah, rescued by the angel of God from the judgments that overwhelmed those cities, when only a short distance from Sodom became drunk and debauched his daughters. Think of the conduct of David with Uriah's wife - and David was, we are told, a man after God's own heart. Also Judah, Judge in Israel. Peter cursed and swore and denied his Master. The enemies of Christ said He was a gluttonous man and a wine bibber, a friend of the publicans and sinners; that after the people at the marriage feast were well drunken, He turned water into wine that they might have more to drink; that in the cornfield He plucked the ears of corn and ate them; that He saw an ass hitched, and without leave took it and rode into Jerusalem; that He went into the Temple and overset the tables of the money changers and took cords and whaled them out, telling them they had made His Father's house a den of thieves. I am aware that all Christians justify the acts of Christ, because He was the Son of God. But the people at that time did not believe Him to be the Son of God, any more than the gentleman believes that Joseph is the prophet of God. I have alluded to these instances merely in answer to the challenge imposed upon me by my opponent.

Few seem to comprehend that man, in and of himself, is frail, weak, needy, and dependent, although the Creator placed within his reach, as a free agent, good and evil, and instilled in the heart of every rational being a degree of light that makes us sensitive to, and teaches us right from, wrong. As the Saviour says:

"There is a light that lighteth every man that cometh into the world."

My argument as I relate it here has been abbreviated very much, lest I tire my readers. I had scarcely closed speaking before my reverend opponents were making for the door. They would have nothing more to do with the Mormons. Some were honest enough, however, to acknowledge that Mormonism had stood the test; that it could not be disproved from the Bible, and sooner or later all other creeds would have to give way to it, or deny the Bible, for the more it was investigated the more popular it would become, as it would expose the many weak points and inconsistencies of the different denominations. Others denounced it as an imposition, and warned their adherents to have nothing to do with it. This kind of talk from the pulpit served to give Mormonism a new impetus. I soon baptized many converts, and organized branches in that and adjoining counties of over one hundred members.

CHAPTER X
LEE CASTS OUT DEVILS

After holding the discussion mentioned, Brother Young, of Jackson County, Tennessee, wished me to go with him and join in a discussion with a couple of Campbellite preachers. At first I declined, as the distance was nearly one hundred miles, and my labors in the ministry where I was were pressing. I had more calls to preach than I could fill. However, I finally consented to go and attend the discussion. On our arrival at the place agreed upon I learned that all necessary arrangements had been made. The subject was:

"Is the Book of Mormon of Divine authenticity, and has it come forth in direct fulfillment of prophecy found in the Old and New Testaments; and is Joseph Smith Divinely inspired and called of God?"

There was a large concourse of people assembled. The discussion lasted two days. At the close of the debate the judge decided that the Mormons brought forth the strongest reasonings and Scriptural arguments, and that the other side had the best of the Mormons in sarcasm and abuse.

When I was about to leave, Brother Young exchanged horses with me, he keeping my pony, and giving me a fine blooded black mare. I was then built up, so far as a good outfit for traveling was concerned. Brother Young traveled with me as far as Indian Creek, Putnam County, twenty-five miles southeast, as report said that a couple of Mormons had been there. We concluded to visit the place and learn the facts.

This was about the 1st of March. It was Saturday when we arrived there. We rode at once to the Methodist chapel. Here we found several hundred people assembled - the most distressed and horrified worshipers my eyes had ever beheld. Their countenances and actions evinced an inward torture of agony. Some of them were lying in a swoon, apparently lifeless; others were barking like dogs; still singing, praying, and speaking in tongues - their eyes red and distorted with excitement.

The chapel was situated in a yard surrounded with trees. I was so overcome with amazement and surprise that I forgot I was on horseback. The first I remember was that a man had led my horse inside the gate and was pulling me off, saying:

"Come, get down, you are a Mormon preacher; we are having fine times."

Presently a chair was set for me by some rational person, and I leaned my head upon my hands and commenced praying. I was a stranger, both to the people and to their religious exercises. I was puzzled, not knowing what to do.

There was a young woman, about eighteen years of age, of handsome form and features, in her stocking feet, her beautiful black hair hanging down over her shoulders in a confused mass. She was preaching what she called Mormonism, and warning the multitude to repent and be baptized, and escape the wrath of God. In front of her stood a young Methodist minister, to whom she directed her remarks.

He smiled at her.

Of a sudden she changed her tack, and belted him right and left for making light of what she said.

The next moment she confronted me, and shouted:

"You are a preacher of the true Church, and I love you!"

Thus saying, she sprang at me with open arms. I stretched forth my hand and rebuked the evil spirit that was in her, and commanded it to depart in the name of the Lord Jesus, by virtue of the holy Priesthood in me vested. At this rebuke she quailed, and turned away from me like a whipped child, left the crowd, and went home, ashamed of her conduct. This gave me confidence in God, and in Him I put my trust still more than I had ever done before.

It was now about sunset, and we had had no refreshments since morning. I arose and informed the multitude that we would preach at that place on the morrow at ten o'clock. A merchant by the name of Marshbanks invited us home with him, some of the leading men accompanying us.

They informed us that a couple of men, brothers, from west Tennessee, named William and Alfred Young, formerly members of the Baptist Church, had joined the Mormons, and had been there and preached; that they enjoyed spiritual gifts as the apostles anciently did, and had baptized the people into that faith, and ordained John Young, who was Receiver of the Land Office there, a preacher; that he had been an intelligent, well-educated man, but was now a fanatic; that their leading men were ruined and business prostrated, and all through that impostor, Joe Smith. They said he ought to be hanged before he did any more harm; that their settlement was being ruined and all business stopped; that if anyone would give John Young, or Mark Young, his father, who

71

was formerly a Methodist class leader, his hand, or let either of them breathe in his face, he could not resist them, but would come under the influence and join them. I told them that I had been a member of this Church for a number of years and had never seen or heard of anything of this kind.

The next morning about daybreak those two fanatics, the Youngs, were at Marshbanks' house. They said they had had a glorious time through the night, and had made a number of converts. I began to reason with them from the Scriptures, but as soon as I came in contact with their folly they began to whistle and dance, and jumped on their horses and left.

Some time after, on our way to the chapel, my friend Marshbanks indulged in a great deal of abuse of the Prophet Joseph. He told me that I could not be heard among the fanatics at the chapel, and had better return to his house and hold a meeting there. I said to him:

"In the name of the Lord Jesus Christ, I will preach there to-day, and not a dog will raise his voice against me; you shall bear witness to it."

"Very well. I will go with you and try to keep order," he replied.

As we entered the chapel, the same scene of confusion prevailed that we observed the day before. Some were stretched on the floor, frothing at the mouth, apparently in the agonies of death. Others were prophesying, talking in tongues, singing, shouting, and praying. I walked into the pulpit as a man having authority, and said:

"In the name of Jesus Christ, and by virtue and authority of the holy Priesthood invested in me, I command these evil spirits that are tormenting you, to be still, while I lay before you the words of life and salvation."

As I spoke every eye was turned upon me, and silence reigned; the evil spirits were subdued and made powerless.

There were two Presbyterian ministers present who asked leave to take notes of my sermon, which I freely granted, telling them they were at liberty to correct me if, in anything, I spoke not according to the Law and Testimony of Christ. I preached a plain sermon on the first principles of the gospel of Christ, as taught by the apostles. I showed them that the house of God was a house of order, and not confusion; that the Spirit of God brings peace, joy, light, and complete harmony.

Before I dismissed the meeting I asked my Presbyterian friends if they wished to reply to me. They said they did not; that they were much pleased with my remarks, which were Scriptural and reasonable.

Now I concluded to return to the branch at Rutherford County and continue my labors there. A delegation came to me from the assembly and said:

"Mr. Lee, your discourse has turned us upside down. You have convinced many of us that we are going astray. Do not, for mercy's sake, leave us in this situation. We are persuaded that many are honest-hearted and will obey the truth." I replied:

"My mission is to preach the truth, to call erring children to repentance."

With that I appointed a meeting, and preached that evening at the house of David Young, a brother of Mark Young, the Methodist class leader, to a large body of inquiring minds.

72

The following day I preached by the side of a clear running brook. After the preaching many demanded to be baptized. I went down into the water and baptized twenty-eight persons, among whom were two well educated young men. One was a nephew of Gov. Carlin, of Illinois; the other was Brother McCullough, now a bishop at Alpine City, Utah.

Elder Samuel B. Frost had been laboring in DeKalb County, east Tennessee, where he baptized about thirty converts. As he was on his return to Nauvoo, I asked him to tarry with me a few days, and assist me, as Brother Young had returned home. Those of the people who had been under the power of the spirit of darkness had become alarmed, and dared not trust themselves away from us. We fasted and prayed three days and three nights, pleading with the Father, in the name of the Son, to give us power over those evil spirits.

And here I will say that up to the time of my witnessing what I have narrated I was skeptical on the subject of our power over evil spirits. I had heard of such manifestations, but had never seen them with my own eyes. My experience here impressed me with the fact that we could attain such power, and showed me the stern necessity of living near to God; for man, in and of himself, is nothing but a tool for the tempter to work with.

As I said, the people dared not trust themselves away from us. Once we were in a large room at Mark Young's house. I was sitting by a desk writing in my diary. Adolphus Young, the chairman of the delegation which had waited on me and requested me to remain with them and set them right, was walking to and fro across the room. As he came near me I noticed that his countenance changed, and as he turned he cast a fearful glance at me. I kept my eyes upon him as he walked away from me. When near the center of the room he wilted down and exclaimed:

"O God, have mercy on me!"

Without a word spoken, Elder Frost and I sprang to him. Laying my hands upon him I commanded the evil spirits, by virtue of the holy Priesthood, and in the name of Jesus Christ, to come out of him.

As I spoke these words I felt as if a thousand darts had penetrated my mouth, throat, and breast. My blood ran cold in my veins; my pulse stopped beating; in a word, I was terror- stricken. I saw a legion of evil spirits in the vision of my mind. And what was still more, they had fastened their fangs in me. I was about to give up the contest, when another influence came to my relief, and said to my spirit:

"Why yield to the powers of darkness? You hold the keys over evil spirits. They are subject to your bidding in the name of Jesus, through faith."

This last comforting assurance relieved my fears, strengthened my faith, and gave me power to overcome the evil spirits. I was only a minute or two in this situation, but during that time I endured more agony, torture, and pain than I ever did before or since. The man was restored, and bore witness to the power of God in his deliverance, and was to the day of his death an honorable, good citizen.

During my stay here I added to this branch of the Church until it was more than fifty members strong. My friend, Elder Frost, agreed to wait in Overton

County until I could revisit the branch in Rutherford County and set things in order there. Then I was to accompany him home to our families in Nauvoo, the City of Joseph. I ordained Brother William Pace in the office of the lesser Priesthood, to take charge of the Saints there. We also ordained Brother Adolphus Young to preside over the branch at Indian Creek, Putnam County.

After calling on Brother Young, I joined my friend, Elder Frost, and drove to Nauvoo for him six jacks and jennets to exchange for land, that on his coming he might have a place to dwell. We had a pleasant journey to Nauvoo, as the weather was fine. On arriving in the city I met my family, all in good health. I traded some of my stock with Hyrum Smith, the Prophet's brother, for land.

It was now June, 1842. In the summer and fall I built me a two- story brick house on Warsaw street, and made my family comfortable. I enclosed my ground and fixed things snug and nice. I then took a tour down through Illinois. H. B. Jacobs accompanied me as a fellow companion on the way. Jacobs was bragging about his wife, what a true, virtuous, lovely woman she was. He almost worshiped her. Little did he think that in his absence she was sealed to the Prophet Joseph.

We raised up a branch of the Church in Clinton County. Among others whom we baptized, were the Free sisters, Louisa and Emeline; also the Nelsons. Emeline Free was afterward sealed to Brigham, and her sister Louisa to myself.

In Randolph County, the home of my youthful days, I baptized my cousin Eliza Conners, with whom I had been raised. I also baptized Esther Hall, the sister of my old friend Samuel Hall, with whom I lived when I was first married. I was kindly received in my own county. Few, however, cared to investigate the principles of Mormonism, as the most of them were Catholics.

In all my travels I was agent for our paper, the Nauvoo Neighbor, and collected means, tithings, and donations for the building of the Temple. I returned home by steamboat.

Through the winter Joseph selected forty men for a city guard, from the old tried Danite veterans of the cause. I was the seventh man chosen. These men were to be the life guard of the Prophet and Patriarch and of the twelve apostles. My station as a guard was at the Prophet's mansion. After his death my post was changed to the residence of Brigham, he being the acknowledged successor of the Prophet. From the time I was appointed until we started across the plains, when at home I stood guard every night; and much of the time in the open air, one-half of the night at a time, in rain, hail, snow, wind, and cold.

CHAPTER XI
HOT FOR LEE IN TENNESSEE

During the winter of 1841 a letter was sent I the Prophet from the leading men and members of the branch church on Stone River, Tennessee, and Creple Creek, Rutherford County, Tennessee, desiring him to send me back to labor in that country, as it was a wide field for preaching. They stated that I had so ingratiated myself among the people that no other man could command the same influence and respect among them.

This was enough. In the latter part of February I took leave of my family and entered upon my mission. To refuse to comply with the call of the Prophet is a bad omen. One so doing is looked upon with distrust, renders himself unpopular, and is considered a man not to be depended upon.

At the time I started the river was blocked with ice. I traveled on foot, without purse or scrip, like the apostles of old, carrying out the motto of the Church, the bee of the desert, "Leave the hive empty-handed and return laden." In this way I, as well as many other elders, brought in money - thousands of dollars yearly - to the Church; and I might say hundreds of thousands, as the people among whom I traveled were mostly wealthy, and when they received the love of the truth their purses as well as their hearts were opened, and they would pour out their treasures into the lap of the bishop. All were taught that a liberal man deviseth liberal things, and by his liberality shall he live, and that he that soweth liberally shall reap bountifully.

As I passed along my way I strengthened the brethren of the various branches, reminding them of their duties, especially of the necessity of building the Temple. That duty was more important than all others, for in that alone, when completed, they could attain to the highest exaltation of the Priesthood, with all the spiritual gifts that belong thereunto.

When I arrived at my old home, the place of my childhood days, I there found Elder John Twist, who was waiting my coming. We stayed in that neighborhood a few days, and then started on. My uncle was going our way with a wagon for about one hundred miles, and we accompanied him. I passed through Kaskaskia, where I was born, but did not preach there, for my uncle was in a hurry to reach the point of his destination in Jackson County, where he was establishing a woodyard on the Mississippi River. Here we intended to take steamer for Nashville, but no steamer would receive us on board at the landing, as it was a bad one for boats.

While staying at that place we preached to the people, and made our home with Mr. V. Hutcheson, and his sister Sarah, where we were treated very kindly. Finally a flatboat came in sight. We hailed it and went aboard. We were soon on good terms with the captain and crew, and went with them to Memphis, Tennessee. At this place the captain of the flatboat sold out his cargo, and then offered to pay our fare on a steamer from Memphis to Nashville. While we were in Memphis Gen. William Henry Harrison, then a candidate for

President, arrived, and a great political meeting of the Whig party was held in the open air.

After my friend Wm. Springer, the captain of the flatboat, had sold his cargo and received his money, he invited Brother Twist and myself to go with him to a saloon. There were quite a number of men in the saloon, fiddling, eating, drinking, and otherwise enjoying themselves. Capt. Springer was not used to drinking. He soon got mellow, felt rich, and commenced throwing his money around in a careless manner.

The saloon keeper was a man with an eye to business, and became particularly interested in friend Springer. He treated him often and insisted on his drinking. I tried to get Springer to his boat, and took him by the arm and started off with him, when one of the crowd told me not to be so officious, that the man knew his own business and was capable of attending to it. I said nothing in reply, but I sent Brother Twist in haste to the boat with word for the crew to come at once before Springer was robbed of his money. They came, but not any too soon for his benefit, as a row had commenced, with the design of going through him while it was on.

When the crew came I started for the boat with Springer, the crew keeping back the crowd of drunken robbers. By acting in this way we saved him and his money too. Brother Twist and myself refused all kinds of drinks that night. We were therefore sober and in condition to protect the man who had favored us and been our friend. Next morning Springer wished to reward us, but we refused to let him do so. I told him we had done nothing but our duty.

We parted with him and his crew, and took passage in a new steamer that was owned in Nashville, and making its first trip from Nashville to New Orleans. The boat got into a race with the Eclipse, another fast boat. The captain was a fine man. The crew were all negroes. One of the firemen on our boat took sick, and was unable to do his work. I saw that the Eclipse was crowding us closely. I threw off my coat and took the negro's place as fireman. There was a barrel of resin near by; I broke the head with an ax and piled the resin on the fire. This had its effect, and our boat soon left the Eclipse far in the rear. The steamers parted at the mouth of the Ohio. The captain was so well pleased with my work that he gave Elder Twist and myself a free passage.

When we reached Nashville. Elder Twist became homesick, and returned to Nauvoo. I gave him ten dollars to pay his way home. I was thus left alone once more. I found the branch at Nashville in a healthy condition, and much pleased to have me with them. I visited the branch in Putnam County, and preached to them, advising all to go to Nauvoo. I added several new members to the Church. By the next spring that entire branch had gone to Nauvoo.

The branch on Stone River also went to Nauvoo soon after I returned home. A delegation, headed by Capt. John H. Redd, invited me to preach in the settlement where Capt. Redd lived. They said I could not preach publicly, for my life would be in danger, as many of the citizens were hostile to the Mormons and had run one man out of the neighborhood for practicing Mormonism, and that Randolph Alexander had been run off for preaching Mormonism.

Capt. Redd was formerly a sea captain; he was a native of South Carolina. I told the delegation I would preach if they gave general publicity to my appointment. They were startled at the proposal, and said my life would not be safe if I undertook to preach in public. I told them to trust that to God.

They returned home and gave general notice of when and where I would preach. At the appointed time I started for the place of meeting, which was twenty miles from Murfreesborough. I was met by a guard of ten men, headed by Capt. Redd, who came to meet and protect me.

The next day I preached to a large number of people. I spoke two hours to them, upon the subject of our free institutions and the constitutional rights of American citizens. I told them who I was and what I was; that I was a free American citizen; that I claimed the right of free speech as a free man; that I held myself open for investigation; that if the people wished me to set forth the tenets of our faith I would do so, otherwise I would leave; that if they did not desire to hear the truth they could make it manifest and I would quit their country. The vote was unanimous for me to tarry and preach to them. I preached there twice.

My first sermon was upon the apostasy of the Churches of the day and the necessity of a purer gospel, proving what I said by the Scriptures. I followed with the origin and authenticity of the Book of Mormon. I was induced to continue my sermons. I stayed there to do my Master's will.

After the fourth sermon I commenced to baptize members. The first one that I baptized at that place was Parson John Holt, of the Christian faith. Then I baptized seven of the members of his Church; then Capt. Redd and his family. This unexpected success of the gospel created great excitement in that section of country.

About ten miles from where I preached lived two men, formerly lieutenants in the militia company of Capt. Bogardus, of Missouri infamy and disgrace. These men had strayed into this section of the country, and were employed by two wealthy farmers as overseers.

They circulated fearful stories about the Mormons in Missouri, and gathered up a mob of about twenty-five men and came with them, determined to tar and feather me if I preached again. Word reached the settlement of what was intended. The people flocked to me and asked what they should do. I told them to wait and let me manage the affair.

The next day, Sunday, while I was preaching one of the ruffians by the name of Dickey made his appearance with ten men. He informed me of his design, and said that I must quit preaching and leave for other parts of the country.

"Not just yet," said I.

At this he and his men made a rush for me. As they started, the sisters next to the stand formed a circle around me. While thus surrounded I continued my sermon. I refuted the absurd stories of Dickey and his crew. I then told the people what had been done at Far West by Lieut. Dickey and the members of Capt. Bogardus' company. The mob tore down my stand, but could not get at me because of the sisters. Then they retired to consult.

Capt. Redd appointed a meeting to be held at his place that afternoon, and he told the people that he did not want any person to come into his yard unless he came intending to behave; that if any violence was used there someone would get hurt. I preached at his house that afternoon. A fearful storm raged during most of the time, but this was fortunate, for it kept the mob away.

While I was preaching a drunken man interrupted me and called me a liar. Capt. Redd was sitting near me with two large pistols, which he called his peacemakers. The insult was no more than out of the fellow's mouth when Capt. Redd caught him by the neck and rushed him from the house into the rain. The coward begged hard for himself, but he was forced to go out and sit under a porch during the rest of the sermon. Capt. Redd was a kind-hearted, generous man, but would not stand abuse.

The next Sunday was a cloudy day, so the meeting was held within doors. Dickey had by this time raised his mob to fifty men, and made every arrangement to give me a warm reception. Two ruffians who were intoxicated had been selected to start the disturbance, or "open the ball," as they called it. I had just commenced speaking when one of these men began to swear and use indecent language, and made a rush for me with his fist drawn. I made a Masonic sign of distress, when, to my relief and yet to my surprise, a planter pushed to my aid. He was the man who employed Dickey. He took the drunken men and led them out of the crowd, and then sat by me during the rest of my sermon, thus giving me full protection. That man was a stranger to me, but he was a good man and a true Mason. His action put an end to mob rule at that place. After the meeting I baptized ten converts.

Soon afterwards I was sent for by Col. Tucker to come a distance of thirty miles. I attended, and delivered three lectures, which were well received by all, the Colonel in particular. He was a wealthy Virginian, and he pressed me warmly to make his house my home. His wife and family were very favorably impressed. They were of the Presbyterian order, and two of Mrs. Tucker's brothers were ministers of that faith. I remained a few days, and made an appointment to preach on the following Saturday and Sunday. Before leaving I let the Colonel's lady have books on our faith, and then went to fill some appointments that I had made at Capt. Redd's. At the appointed time I returned to preach, as I had promised, on Buckskin River.

Within half a mile of Col. Tucker's house was a Methodist chapel. At this place lived a New Light preacher, an old man, who invited me to stop with him. He informed me that Col. Tucker had become bitter against the Mormons because his wife believed in them; and that she wanted to be baptized. She had left word with him, requesting me not to leave without baptizing her.

This was something I wished to avoid, so to prevent trouble I concluded not to go to Col. Tucker's at all. I filled my appointments, and returned to my Christian friend's house for refreshments, intending to make my way over the mountains that night, and thus avoid meeting Mrs. Tucker.

This, however, was not to be. I had just finished supper, and stepped to the door to start back when I met Mrs. Tucker. She upbraided me for not calling to see her. I said that it was contrary to the rules of our faith for an elder to interfere in any man's family against the wish or will of the husband or parents; that she must keep quiet and the Lord would take the will for the deed. The more I tried to reconcile her, the more determined she grew to be baptized.

While I was talking with her a young man came to us and reported that Col. Tucker had ambushed himself, with a double-barreled shotgun, near the place of baptizing, swearing vengeance against the man that attempted to baptize his wife. I tried to persuade her to return, but in vain. She said to me:

"You have declared that your mission is from Heaven, that you are a servant of God; and I believe it. Now I demand baptism at your hands. If you are a servant of God, don't shrink from your duty."

I looked at her for a moment, and said: "Sister, if you have faith enough to be baptized under these circumstances, I have faith enough to try it."

Some personal friends who lived in the little village accompanied us to the water, a short distance above the usual place of baptizing, and were present during the performance of the ordinance. They advised her to return home immediately, with her two servants, and never let on that anything had happened.

For myself, I started for the house of my friend, carrying my boots in my hand. It was now dark. As I got to the top of a high fence and cast my eyes about me, I luckily saw a man with a double-barreled shotgun in his hands, or what I supposed was such. He was within ten steps of me, or nearer. I recognized Col. Tucker.

Having heard of his threats, I was induced not to tempt him too far. I placed my hands on the fence and leaped over it, alighting on the other side, near a cross fence which separated the garden from a field of corn. As quick as thought I got among the corn, which was at full height. I was within twenty feet of Tucker and could hear all that was said. I heard him rave, and demand with oaths what my friends, who came up, were doing there. Had they been baptizing his wife? I recognized the voice of the parson's lady with whom I was stopping. She had the wet clothes of Mrs. Tucker.

"Tell me," said Tucker, "if my wife has been baptized, or I will blow your brains out." The reply was: "She has been baptized."

"Where is that infernal Mormon preacher?" demanded the Colonel; "I will put a load of shot through him."

"He is in that cornfield," was the reply.

The Colonel raved the more. Finally some of his friends persuaded him to return home, and not disgrace himself. He pretended to do so, but it was only a feint to get me out.

After waiting until all was quiet I returned to the house of my friend, and passing through the door went out on the porch. I sat down and was slipping off my socks, to put on dry ones, when I heard a rustling in the room behind me. The next moment Col. Tucker had his gun leveled on me, but it flashed in the pan. He then whirled up the butt of it to fell me to the earth.

Seeing my danger I sprang and caught him around the waist, with one of his arms in my grasp, which left him only one arm loose.

"I have you now where I want you," he cried.

He was a strong, muscular man, and, no doubt, supposed I would be no match for him. I ordered a young man who stood near to take his gun. I then gripped him with an iron hug, and sent him back into the room.

The old gentleman with whom I was stopping ordered him out of the house unless he would behave himself. He said he had invited me to his house, and felt it his duty to protect me. The Colonel replied that he would go if he could; he never knew before that when he was in the hands of a Mormon he was in a bear's clutches. I said:

"I will take you out if it will accommodate you."

Thus saying, I stepped out on the porch with him. I saw that he was willing to go. This gave me new courage.

"Let me go, or I will blow your brains out when I get loose," he said.

"There is one condition on which I will let you go, which is that you will go home and be quiet and trouble me no more," I replied.

"I will settle with you for all this," was his answer.

It was in the month of July, and very warm. I had hugged him closely, and he was growing weak. As I was in the act of dashing him to the ground he begged of me, saying that if I would set him loose he would go and trouble me no more. I let him fall to the ground, handed him his gun, and let him live. When he got a little distance away he began threatening me, and said he would be revenged. When all had quieted down I retired to rest in the upper story of my friend's house.

About one o'clock in the morning I was awakened by a voice which I recognized as the voice of Mrs. Tucker. She informed me that her husband was bent on my destruction, and he and ten men were then waylaying my road, and advised me not to start in that direction. Her husband had accused her of wetting the loads in his gun to save my life; but she told me to be of good cheer and put my trust in God, and that she had not regretted the steps she had taken. I thanked her for her kindness, and begged her to return home and not see me any more; that I was in the hands of God, and He would protect me and deliver me safe; that her visits would only make her husband more enraged at her.

At four o'clock I awoke, dressed myself, and ordered the servant to saddle my horse. As the servant hitched my horse to the post Tucker and several men appeared upon the ground. Tucker told the servant that he would shoot him in two if he saddled my horse. I spoke to Tucker, saluting him with the time of day. His reply was:

"I have got you now."

Thus saying, he ordered his nephew to bring Esquire Walls immediately.

After washing, I took my seat on the porch, and got out my Bible to read. Tucker stood about ten steps from me to guard me and my horse.

While this was the situation my old friend, the New Light preacher with whom I was lodging, had a fine horse saddled and hitched on the south side of the cornfield. He advised me in a whisper to pass down through the cornfield while I could do so without being detected, take the horse, and thus get out of the county before a warrant had been issued for my arrest.

Deliverance was very tempting, yet I did not like the name of running away from trouble. It would convey the impression of fear, if not of guilt. So I chose to face the music and abide the consequences. A little after sunrise I saw Justice Walls coming, and some men with him. At this my heart leaped for joy. Among so many I was satisfied all were not against me, as some of them had attended lectures and were favorably impressed.

After a short interview with Col. Tucker, Justice Walls informed me that Col. Tucker demanded from him a warrant for my arrest for having baptized his wife without his consent. I asked Col. Tucker if he ever forbid me to baptize his wife; whether he had not invited me to his house and asked me to stop there when I returned. I told him I had not seen him, after this conversation, until his wife was baptized; that I had not urged her to be baptized - she had come to me and demanded to be baptized. I told the Justice that I had violated no law of Tennessee. The law allows a wife much greater privileges than being baptized without the consent of her husband; she could sell one-third of his real estate, and her deed would be good. The Justice said I was right, and told the Colonel it would be useless to issue a warrant without lawful cause.

The Colonel then demanded a warrant for my arrest on the charge of assault and battery. He said I had abused his person, and that he was sore and scarcely able to walk. The Justice told the Colonel that it seemed to him that he was the one who made the assault; for he snapped a loaded gun at me and attempted to take my life, while what I had done was in self-defense. He told Col. Tucker he would talk with him again. He then beckoned me to follow him, and I did so. We went into a room by ourselves, when he said to me,

"Parson Lee, you have warm friends here. I have been much interested in your lectures. I believe you to be honest and firm in your faith, and will do all I can for your benefit. Col. Tucker is a desperate man when aroused. As a matter of policy, to humor him, I will give him a writ; but I will manage to delay the time, so as to enable you to get out of the county. I will send for my law books, with instructions to delay in getting them here, and will argue with the Colonel that I must have my books to examine the law. It is only four miles to the county line, where you will be all right. Take the trail over the mountain, and they will not know which way you have gone. When you get into your own county, remember me on election day. This county and Rutherford County send three members to the Legislature. I am a candidate, and the vote of your friends in these counties will secure my election. When I send for my books appear and bid us good-by, as though you were not afraid of any man. Col. Tucker has promised that he will use no violence if I give him a writ."

The Justice then gave me a token of the Brotherhood, and walked out to confer with Col. Tucker. He sent his nephew back for his books, instructing him in whispers to delay in getting them, so as to give me time to get out of the county before an officer could overtake me.

After the boy started, the Justice told the Colonel to keep cool and he would soon have a writ for me. I went into the dining-room and sat down to breakfast, and ate a little as a blind. Then taking up my saddlebags, I bade them all good-by. I walked to my horse, that stood hitched where the servant had left him.

As I left the house Justice Walls followed me as though he was much surprised, and said:

"Parson Lee, I hope you will tarry until this matter can be settled amicably."

Again I told him that I had violated no law; that my ministerial engagements compelled me to leave, and I should have done so before had not this unpleasant affair detained me; that I chose to serve God rather than fear the ire of man.

Thus saying, I placed my saddle upon my horse. Col. Tucker leveled his gun on me, and said:

"I knew you would run."

At this I turned and eyed him and told him to put up his gun; that I had borne all I intended to from him; that if he attempted violence he would never trouble another man. At the same time the Justice exhorted him to be careful, saying that he had made himself liable already. I mounted my horse and turned to the Colonel and told him he might guard that woodpile until the day of judgment, for all I cared. He again raised his gun, but was prevented by the by-standers from shooting. I rode off leisurely, and when about seventy-five yards away I stopped and watered my horse. Tucker again drew his gun on me, and I expected him to shoot every moment, but I dared not show fear.

My road lay along the mountain for two miles. When I passed a house I would walk my horse, and sing and seem to be wholly unconcerned; but when I was out of sight I put my horse on the keen jump, and was soon out of Marshall County. Finding an out- of-the-way place, with good blue grass and plenty of shade, I swung down from my horse and returned thanks to my Father in heaven for my deliverance.

In the afternoon I arrived at the house of Capt. Redd, where, when in that county, I generally made my home. The brethren all came to welcome me back, and I related to them my experience and deliverance. A short time after this James K. Polk and Col. Jones, both candidates for the office of Governor of Tennessee, and the candidates for the Legislature, including my friend Walls, met at Murfreesborough and held a political meeting. Walls gave me the sequel of what happened with Col. Tucker.

When Justice Walls' nephew went for the law books he permitted his horse to run away, and it was nearly ruined in the brush and grapevines. Col. Tucker did not blame the Justice at all, but rather sympathized with him in his misfortune. Mrs. Tucker to the end remained firm in her faith.

The kindness of Justice Walls in my hour of peril was not forgotten. I spoke of it in all my meetings, and to my friends in private. And to this act of justice and humanity he owed his election, as he was elected by a majority of only five votes.

Next I visited the branch on Stone River and made arrangements to return to my family at Nauvoo, the City of Joseph. The two branches now numbered about sixty members. I organized a branch west of Murfreesborough, and ordained Brother John Holt to the office of Elder. I baptized a young girl at Readysville, by the name of Sarah C. Williams, of rich parentage. I lectured at Murfreesborough for ten days, and about the beginning of October, 1843, I took the steamer at Nashville for my home in Nauvoo, arriving there on the 14th of October.

CHAPTER XII
OF PECULIAR INTEREST IN NAUVOO

Upon my return home I found my family well. Work on the Temple was progressing finely, every effort being made to push it ahead. About this time a man named Bennett came on a visit to the Prophet, and soon after joined the Church. At that time he wielded quite an influence in government affairs. He grew in the graces of the Prophet and became his right-hand man. He endeavored in connection with Stephen A. Douglass to obtain a charter for the city of Nauvoo.

Bennett organized the Nauvoo Legion, and was elected Major General. Through his influence, backed by Douglass, arms were obtained for the Legion from the government. A Free Mason's lodge, and the privileges of Masonry, were extended to the Legion. Judge Cleveland, of Springfield, was very friendly, and frequently visited the Prophet. A fine Masonic lodge was built in Nauvoo, and many were admitted as members. The Prophet Joseph and Hyrum Smith held high positions in the brotherhood.

The institution flourished during our stay in Nauvoo, and was frequently visited by the Grand Worshipful Master from Springfield; lectures were given and a library established. I was librarian of the order. I was also Wharf Master of the city, and held the position of Major in the Nauvoo Legion; also, I commanded the escort in the Fifth Infantry. I was made the general clerk and reader for the Seventies, and issued the laws to that body. I held the office of a Seventy, and was collector of the delinquent military tax.

The same fall I was appointed on a committee, with Brigham as counselor, to build a hall for the Seventies, the upper story to be used for the Priesthood and the Council of Fifty. Previous to my being appointed on the committee two committees had been named, but accomplished nothing. We commenced without a dollar. My plan was to build it by shares, of the value of five dollars each.

Hyrum Smith, the Patriarch, told me that he would give the Patriarchal Blessing to any that labored on the foundation of the building. The Seventies numbered about four hundred and ninety men. I was to create the material. That is, when I could get a contract to take lumber from the river, as rafts would land at the city, I would take common laboring men, and the portion of the lumber that we got for our pay we piled up for the building. In this way we got all the lumber needed. The bricks we made ourselves, and boated the wood to burn them and our lime from the island.

In the month of March, 1844, we had the building up on the west side nearly two stories high. One day when the wall was built up nine feet high and forty-five feet long, and was, of course, green, a tornado blew the wall down, breaking columns and joists below, doing a damage of several thousand dollars. I was inclined to be down in the lip, but Brigham laughed at me, and said it was the best omen in the world; it showed that the devil was mad, knowing that the Seventy would receive the blessings of God in that house; since they were to be special witnesses to the nations of the earth, they would make his kingdom quake and tremble. Brigham reminded me that when Noah was building the ark he was mobbed three times; but he persevered, and finally his tormentors said:

"Let the old fool alone, and see what he will accomplish."

"Just so with you," concluded Brigham. "Double your diligence and put her up again. If you do not you will lose many a blessing."

After that I went to work with as many men as could labor to advantage. We threw the wall down flat, and commenced a new one, another brick thicker than the former. I borrowed fifty thousand brick, and made them and returned them when the weather was fine. By the 1st of May we had the Hall closed in.

During the winter Joseph the Prophet set a man by the name of Sidney Hay Jacobs to select from the Old Bible such scriptures as pertained to polygamy, or celestial marriage, with instructions to write it in pamphlet form. This he did as a feeler among the people, to pave the way for celestial marriage. Like all other novelties, it met with opposition, though a few favored it.

The excitement among the people became so great that the subject was laid before the Prophet. No one was more opposed to it than was his brother Hyrum, who condemned it as from beneath. Joseph saw that it would break up the Church should he sanction it, so he denounced the pamphlet through the Wasp, a newspaper published at Nauvoo, as a bundle of nonsense and trash. He said that if he had known its contents he would never have permitted it to be published.

At the same time other leading men were advocating it on their own responsibility. The advocacy of polygamy by these leaders pleased the Prophet Joseph, albeit for policy's sake he pretended otherwise. Joseph said on the stand that, should he reveal the will of God concerning them, they - pointing to President W. Marks, P. P. Pratt, and others - would shed his blood. In this way he worked upon the feelings and minds of the people, until they feared that the anger of the Lord would be kindled against them, and they insisted upon knowing the will of Heaven concerning plural wives.

The Prophet Joseph anxiously desired polygamy, but he dared not proclaim it, so it was taught confidentially to such as were strong enough in the faith to take the forward step. About the same time the doctrine of "sealing" for an eternal state was introduced. Also the Saints were given to understand that their marriage relations with each other were not valid, and that those who had solemnized the rites of matrimony had no authority of God to do so. The true priesthood had been taken from the earth with the death of the apostles and inspired men of God. Since then people were married to each other only by their own covenants, and if their marriage had not been productive of blessings and peace, and they felt it oppressive to remain together, they were at liberty to make a new choice, as much as if they had not been married. The Prophet taught that it was a sin for people to live together and beget children in alienation from each other. There should exist an affinity between the sexes, not a lustful one, as the latter can never cement the love and affection that should exist between man and wife.

Perhaps I should mention that Orson Hyde and W. W. Phelps turned against Joseph in Missouri, and forsook him in time of peril and danger and testified against him in the courts. After the troubles were over, and Joseph was again in place in the midst of the Saints, they both wished to be restored to fellowship and standing in the Church, confessing their faults. Joseph laid the case before the Church, and said that if God could forgive them he ought to, and would do so, and give them another chance. With tears he moved that we forgive and receive them back into fellowship. He then sent Elder Hyde to the land of Palestine, to dedicate that land for the gathering of the Jews. Also Hyde's wife, with his consent, was sealed to Joseph for an eternal state. Brigham's wife was likewise sealed to Joseph. Shortly before the death of Joseph Brigham told me that Joseph's time on earth was short, and that the Lord allowed him privileges that we could not have.

There was trouble between Joseph and Brother Law, his second counselor, on account of Law's wife. Law said that the Prophet purposed making her his wife, and she so reported to her husband. Law loved his wife and was devoted to her, as she was an amiable and handsome woman, and he did not feel like giving her up to another man. He exposed the Prophet, and from that time became his enemy.

His brother, Wilson Law, sided with him. They were Canadians, and wealthy and influential men. They, in connection with Foster and Higbee, who were on the wane in the faith, established a paper at Nauvoo, called the Expositor. They set the Prophet up without mercy. They soon got after Brigham for trying to influence Martha Brotherton to be sealed to Joseph. Her father found it out and helped to expose them, which made it rather hot for them. The next move of the Prophet and his friends was to get the City Council to pass an ordinance declaring the Expositor to be a nuisance, unless the proprietors would close it up.

When I moved to Nauvoo I had one wife and one child. Soon after I got there I was appointed as the Seventh Danite. I had superiors in office, and was sworn to secrecy, to obey the orders of my superiors, and not let my left hand know what my right hand did. It was my duty to do as I was ordered, and not to ask questions. I was instructed in the secrets of the Priesthood, and taught that it was my duty, and the duty of all men, to obey the leaders of the Church, and that no one could commit sin so long as he acted as directed by his Church superiors.

One day the Danite Chief came to me and said that I must take two more Danites whom he named and watch the house of a widow woman named

Clawson. I was informed that a man went there nearly every night about ten o'clock, and left about daylight. I was to station myself and my men near the house, and when the man came out knock him down and mutilate him; it would not be inquired into if we killed him.

It was my duty to report unusual orders that I received from my superiors to the Prophet, Joseph Smith, or in his absence, Hyrum. I went to the house of the Prophet to report, but he was not at home. I then called for Hyrum, and he gave me an interview. I told him the orders I had received from the Chief, and asked him if I should obey or not. He said to me:

"Brother Lee, you have acted wisely in listening to the voice of the Spirit. It was the influence of God's Spirit that sent you here. You would have been guilty of a great crime if you had obeyed your Chief's orders."

Hyrum then told me that the man I was ordered to attack had been sealed to Mrs. Clawson, and their marriage was a most holy one; that it was in accordance with a revelation which the Prophet had recently received direct from God. He explained to me fully the doctrines of polygamy, wherein it was permitted, and why it was right. I was greatly interested in the doctrine. It accorded exactly with my views of the Scripture, and I at once accepted and believed in the doctrine as taught by the revelations received by Joseph the Prophet. As a matter of course I did not carry out the orders of the Chief. I had him instructed in his duty, and Mrs. Clawson's husband was never bothered by the Danites. A few months after, I was sealed to my second wife. I was sealed to her by Brigham, then one of the twelve.

In less than one year after I first learned the will of God concerning marriage among the Saints, as made known by Him in a revelation to Joseph, I was the husband of nine wives. I took my wives in the following order: First, Agathe Ann Woolsey; second, Nancy Berry; third, Louisa Free; fourth, Sarah C. Williams; fifth, old Mrs. Woolsey (she was the mother of Agathe Ann and Rachel A. - I married her for her soul's sake, for her salvation in the eternal state); sixth, Rachel A. Woolsey (I was sealed to her at the same time that I was to her mother); seventh, Andora Woolsey (a sister of Rachel); eighth, Polly Ann Workman; ninth, Martha Berry; tenth, Delithea Morris.

In 1847, while at Council Bluffs, Brigham sealed me to three women in one night, viz., eleventh, Nancy Armstrong (she was what we called a widow, that is, she had left her first husband in Tennessee, in order to be with the Mormon people); twelfth, Polly V. Young; thirteenth, Louisa Young (these two were sisters). Next, I was sealed to my fourteenth wife, Emeline Vaughn. In 1851 I was sealed to my fifteenth wife, Mary Lear Groves. In 1856 I was sealed to my sixteenth wife, Mary Ann Williams. In 1858 Brigham gave me my seventeenth wife, Emma Batchelder. I was sealed to her while a member of the Territorial Legislature. In 1859 I was sealed to my eighteenth wife, Teressa Morse. I was sealed to her by order of Brigham. Amasa Lyman officiated at the ceremony. The last wife I got was Ann Gordges. Brigham gave her to me, and I was sealed to her in Salt Lake by Heber C. Kimball. She was my nineteenth, but, as I was married to old Mrs. Woolsey only for her soul's sake, and she was near sixty years old when I married her, I never considered her really as a wife. After 1861

I never asked Brigham for another wife. By my eighteen real wives I have been the father of sixty-four children. Ten of my children are dead and fifty-four are living.

To return to Nauvoo: The Prophet Joseph had written a letter to Martin Van Buren, wishing to know his views in regard to the grievances and wrongs of the Mormon people, and what would be his action should he be elected President. He replied that he believed their cause was just, and Congress had no right to interfere; that it was a State matter, and must be left to the Executive.

The Prophet addressed another letter to Wm. H. Harrison, on the same subject. His answer was but little more satisfactory.

Joseph then drew up a statement of his own, of the power and policy of the Government. A convention was called, and the Prophet nominated as a candidate for the Presidency. He set forth his views in the Nauvoo Neighbor, formerly the Wasp. He stated that if the people would elect him President it would be the salvation of the nation; otherwise, the Union would soon be severed. The two political parties would continue to influence the people until it would end in civil war, in which all nations would take part, and this nation be broken up. At this convention the elders were assigned missions to different States. I was sent to stump the State of Kentucky, with ten elders to assist me.

"You had better shut up the Seventies' Hall and obey the last call of the Prophet," Brigham said to me.

Things looked squally before I left, with little prospect of growing better. I left Nauvoo on the 4th of May, 1844, with greater reluctance than I had on any previous mission. It was hard enough to preach the gospel without purse or scrip; but it was as nothing compared to offering the Prophet Joseph to the people as a candidate for the highest gift of the nation. I would a thousand times rather have been shut up in jail than to have taken the trip, but I dared not refuse.

About one hundred of us took the steamer Ospray for St. Louis. Our mission was understood by all the passengers on board. I was not long kept waiting before the subject was brought up. I had made up my mind to banish fear and overcome timidity. I made the people believe that I felt highly honored by my mission to electioneer for a prophet of God. It was a privilege few men enjoyed in these days. I endeavored to make myself agreeable by mixing with the passengers on the steamer. I told them that the Prophet would lead both candidates from the start.

There was a large crowd on the boat, and an election was proposed. Judges and clerks were appointed and a vote taken. The Prophet received a majority of seventy-five, out of one hundred and twenty-five votes polled. This created a tremendous laugh, and we kept it up till we got to St. Louis. Here the most of us took the steamer Mermaid.

The change of steamers afforded me a new field of labor. I met a brother of Gen. Atchison, one of the commanders of the militia that served against the Church at Far West. He became interested in me, and when we parted at Smithland he invited me to go home with him and preach in his neighborhood.

My destination being Frankfort, I could not accept his invitation. I started for Lexington, by way of Georgetown, lecturing as I went. I finally got to the capital, put up at a hotel, and endeavored to hire the State House to speak in, but found it engaged.

My funds were low, and my hotel bill was four dollars per day. After three days' trial I hired the Court House. The people said that no Mormon had ever been able to get a hearing, though several had attempted to do so.

When evening came I had to light up the house and ring the bell. Elder Frost assisted me. Soon the hall was filled with juveniles, from ten to fifteen years of age. I understood the trick. The people supposed I would leave, but to their surprise I arose and said I was glad to see the young ones out in such numbers; that I knew they had good parents, or they would not be there; that if they would take seats and be quiet we would sing them our Mormon songs.

Elder Frost was a charming singer. We sang two or three songs. Our juvenile hearers seemed delighted. I then knelt down and prayed. By this time the hall was crowded with grown men, and I begged them not to crowd out my little friends. I then spoke an hour and a half upon the constitutional rights of American citizens. I spoke of the character of the Southern people; how they were noted for their generous treatment of strangers; but I feared from the treatment I had received, I had missed my way in Kentucky. My sires were of Southern birth; my father was a relative of the Revolutionary Lee, of Virginia; my uncle was from Lexington, Kentucky, I had come a stranger into their midst, but I felt confident the right of speech would be extended to us, who were ministers of the gospel, dependent upon the generosity of the people for food and raiment. Nor did we preach for hire. If they wished, we would remain there and lecture, and if it met the approbation of the people they could have the gospel preached to them without money and without price.

The first man that spoke up was a saddler. He said he was a poor man, but we were welcome to his house, giving the street and number. About twenty more responded in like manner, among them the most wealthy men of the county. We went home with a rich farmer, and continued our labors, having more calls than we could fill.

We were sent for by a rich planter who lived about twenty miles away. I was anxious to extend our labors as much as was advisable. On our way to the planter's we found it difficult to obtain dinner. The orthodox people did not like to associate with Mormons. I finally asked them to direct me to where some infidel or gambler lived. They wanted to know what on earth I wanted of such. I replied:

"To get something to eat. Infidels and gamblers are too liberal- minded to turn a stranger away from their door. The Saviour ate with publicans and sinners - for the very reason that we do, for the Scribes and Pharisees would not feed Him."

They pointed us to the next house, where we were kindly received and entertained. The gentleman informed us that he belonged to no Church, but had an interest in a church, and said we were welcome to preach there. He made an appointment for us to preach.

We preached, and were received with kindness. I soon began to baptize, and calls came in from every side, when one day the papers brought us the news of the assassination of the Prophet Joseph and his brother Hyrum.

We returned immediately to Frankfort, as I expected the elders there, to learn what to do. We all retired to Maple Grove, on the Kentucky River, and kneeled in prayer and asked the Lord to show us whether or not these reports were true. I was the mouth-in- prayer, but received nothing definite in answer to my prayer. I told the elders to follow their own impressions, and if they wished to do so to return to Nauvoo. Each of them made his way back. I spent the evening with a Mr. Snow. He claimed to be a cousin of Brother Erastus Snow, and was favorable to us. We spent the evening talking over the reported deed.

The next morning about ten o'clock my mind was drawn out in prayer. I felt as though the solemnity of eternity was resting with me. A heavenly, hallowed influence fell upon me, and continued to increase until I was electrified from head to foot. I saw a large personage enter the door and stand before me. His apparel was as white as the driven snow and his countenance as bright as the noonday sun. I felt paralyzed, and was speechless and motionless. He remained with me but a moment, then receded through the door.

This bright being's influence drew me from my chair and led me south about three hundred yards, into a plot of clover and blue grass, and under a persimmon tree, which afforded a pleasant shade. I fell prostrate upon my face. While here I saw Joseph the Prophet and Hyrum the Patriarch, and the wounds by which they had been assassinated.

This personage spoke to me in a soft, low voice, and said that the Prophet and Patriarch had scaled their testimony with their blood. Our mission was like that of the apostles, and our garments were clear of the blood of the nation; I should return to Nauvoo and wait until power was granted us from on High; as the mantle of priesthood fell upon the Apostle Peter, so should it rest with the twelve apostles of the Church for the present. Thus the vision closed, and I gradually returned to my native element.

Rising up I looked at my watch and saw that I had been there an hour and a quarter. Returning to the house my friend Snow asked me if I was ill. I replied in the negative. He said I was very pale, and that he saw my countenance change while I sat in my chair; that when I went out of doors it was as though every drop of blood had left me, or been changed. I then told him that the reports in the papers were true, and the two Saints, the Prophet and the Patriarch, were no more. I asked him to take me to the landing; I wished to get the evening packet, as my labors were done in that country. He importuned so hard that I told him what I had seen.

He saddled a horse for me and one for himself, and we started, in company with several others, for the landing. When we were about to embark on the steamer Mr. Steele, a brother of the captain, introduced me to the captain. About eight persons demanded baptism; I could not stop, but advised them to come to Nauvoo. Among them was my friend Snow. I had a cabin passage free. When I reached Nauvoo I found excitement at highest point.

CHAPTER XIII
DEATH OF JOSEPH SMITH

Joseph the Prophet and Hyrum, his brother, were assassinated on the 24th day of June, 1844, at Carthage, about twenty miles from Nauvoo, while under the pledged faith of Governor Ford, of Illinois. Governor Ford had promised them protection if they would stand trial and submit to the judgment of the court. By his orders the Nauvoo Grays were to guard the jail while the prisoners awaited trial. The mob was headed by Williams and Sharp, editors of the Nauvoo Signal. When they approached the jail the guard made no resistance, but fell back.

Brother Stephen Markham, who had been to visit the prisoners an hour or so before they were killed, gave Joseph an Allen revolver. A part of the mob rushed upstairs, to the inner door of the prison and burst it open. Brother Richards parried the bayonets with his heavy cane. Joseph reached out his hand and fired his six shots at the crowd, and wounded several mortally. Hyrum, who was trying to brace against the door, received a shot in the face near the nose.

"I am a dead man," he cried, and fell.

Brother John Taylor received a shot, but fortunately it struck his watch, which saved his life. These four were in the prison. Brother Taylor, however, received another shot and fell. Joseph left the door, and sprang through the window, crying:

"O Lord, my God, is there no help for the widow's son!"

He fell pierced with several balls. The crowd then left the door and ran around to the windows.

Brother Richards covered Brother Taylor with a straw bed. Several shots were fired at the bed, some of which cut his leg. Richards looked from the window on the scene, and several balls passed through his clothing, but he received no injury.

After Joseph fell he was set up against the well-curb and shot again. A man named Boggs rolled up his sleeves, and with a knife attempted to cut off his head. At this instant a flash of light encircled the Prophet, and the man who was advancing to cut off his head fell back. They were frightened, and fled.

Governor Ford was terror-stricken, as it endangered his life, he being without a guard, and at the mercy of the Mormons, had they chosen to take advantage of him while he was in Nauvoo. Governor Ford promised that he would see the murderers prosecuted. He gave the Mormons a company of troops to bring their dead friends to Nauvoo.

The dead were placed in rough oak boxes and brought to the city. There were lamentation and mourning among the people. Joseph was a man dearly loved by the Saints, and blessed with direct revelation from God, and was an honorable, generous, high-minded man.

The remains of the Prophet and his brother were laid in a sepulcher made of stone. The oak boards which had enclosed them were sawed in pieces and distributed among their friends, many of whom had canes made of the pieces, with locks of the hair of the Prophet set in the top of them, and those canes are kept as sacred relics to this day. But I must go back and speak of the cause of their arrest.

While I was in Kentucky the printing press of Higbee & Foster was declared a nuisance, and ordered destroyed. The owners refused to comply with the decision of the City Council, and the Mayor directed that the press and type be destroyed, which was done. The owner of the grocery where the press was, employed John Eagle, a professional bully, and others to defend it. As the Danites entered, or attempted to enter, Eagle stood in the door and knocked three of them down. As the third fell the Prophet struck Eagle under the ear and brought him sprawling to the ground. He then crossed Eagle's hands and ordered them tied, saying that he could not see his men knocked down while in the line of their duty without protecting them.

This raised the ire of Higbee, Foster, and others, and they got out writs for the arrest of Joseph, and laid their grievances before the Governor. Joseph, knowing the consequences of such a move, concluded to leave for the Rocky Mountains and lay out a country where the Saints would not be molested. He crossed over into Iowa with a few faithful friends. These friends begged him to return and stand his trial; saying that the Lord had always delivered him, and would again. He told them that if he returned he would be killed, but if he went away he would save his life and the Church would not be hurt; that he would look out a new country for them. The Governor had advised him to do this.

Those old grannies then accused him of cowardice, and told him that Christ had said he would never leave his brethren in trouble. He then asked them if his Emma wished him to return. They answered:

"Yes."

Joseph then said it was all light before him, and darkness behind him, but he would return, though he felt as a sheep led to the slaughter.

The following day he crossed the river into Illinois. He kissed his mother, and told her that his time had come, and that he must seal his testimony with his blood. He advised his brother Hyrum not to go with him, saying that he would be a comfort to the Church when he, the Prophet, was no more. Hyrum said:

"No, my brother; I have been with you in life, and will be with you in death!"

The Prophet then called Brother Dunham and had some private talk with him, and then started for the jail at Carthage. Dunham said that the Prophet requested him to take his Danites and ambush them in a grove near Carthage, and watch the movements of the crowd; but Dunham dared not go contrary to the orders of the Governor.

About this time the settlements on Bear Creek and at Great Plains had a difficulty with the Gentiles, and the settlements were broken up and the settlers driven to Nauvoo. The Mormons sought redress under the law. The sheriff tried to suppress the riot by a posse, but since he could not get a posse from the Gentiles, he was obliged to summon them from the Mormons. This made him unpopular, endangered his life, and rendered him powerless.

91

Governor Ford sought to bring to justice those who had assaulted the Prophet and Hyrum, but public opinion was against him, and the mass of the people objecting, nothing was done. Certain leaders in the horrid deed were members of the Legislature, and though the disturbance was partially quelled, still the feeling of enmity continued to exist until the final breaking up of the Church.

Before proceeding further, we must learn who was to be the successor of the Prophet and lead the Church. It had been understood among the Saints that young Joseph was to succeed his father. Joseph the Prophet had bestowed that right upon him by ordination, but he was too young at that time to fill the office and discharge its solemn duties. Someone must fill the place until he had grown to more mature age.

Sidney Rigdon set up his claim, he being the second counselor to the Prophet. Rigdon had a few backers. A man by the name of Strong, who had been writing for the Prophet, put up his claim to the office, by forging an appointment from Joseph. Time passed on until the whole twelve had returned from their missions, and a conference was held, at which the several claimants came forward with their demands.

Sidney Rigdon was the first who appeared upon the stand. He had been rather in the background for some time previous to the death of the Prophet. He made but a weak claim. Strong did not file any.

Just then Brigham arose and roared like a young lion, imitating the style and voice of Joseph the Prophet. Many of the brethren declared that they saw the mantle of Joseph fall upon him. I myself saw and heard a strong resemblance to the Prophet in him, and felt that he was the man to lead us until Joseph's legal successor should grow up to manhood.

As soon as Brigham got the reins of government in his hands he swore that he would never suffer an officer to serve a writ on or arrest him, as they had Joseph; that he would send them the dark and gloomy road over which no traveler ever returned. He wished me to remove near to him, as I was one of the Danites assigned to guard him. I had a good brick house and lot, all in fine order, on Warsaw street. He told me to let him have my property on Warsaw street and he would buy me a house on the flat, nearer his own. I did so, and he bought out Brother Frost, and sent him on a mission to Kentucky, where I had been laboring. He had a nice little frame house. I moved into it and had it finished on the inside and made comfortable.

Brigham at that time was living in a log house, but was preparing to build a brick house. I renewed my labors on the Hall of the Seventies, and finished it in grand style. It was then dedicated, and the different quorums had picnic parties in it, beginning with the first quorum, consisting of seventy-seven men to each quorum. Brigham said this hall would be a building creditable to London. He called upon me to organize the young men into quorums of Seventy, and keep the records for them. He appointed me General Clerk and Recorder of the Seventies, and through me were to be issued the licenses of the quorums. This was to be a compensation for my services.

Joseph Young was the senior president over all the quorums. My burdens increased daily. I was offered the position of senior president, I to select my six counselors and my Quorum of Seventy, but I declined, as I did not want the responsibility. I held then all the offices I could fill. Having finished the hall, I was offered, or rather given a mission, to build Joseph Young, the head president of the Seventies, a neat brick dwelling. Calling upon the Seventies to assist me, I soon mustered what help was necessary, and made brick enough to build me a large dwelling house. Including my other buildings, it was ninety feet front, two and a half stories, high, with a good cellar. By the middle of July, 1845, I had both houses, the one for Joseph Young and the one for myself, finished, ready for painting.

During the winter of 1844-5 a man by the name of Stanley took up a school, teaching the use of the broadsword. At the expiration of his term I opened three schools, of fifty scholars each, in the same exercise. I gave thirteen lessons in each school, receiving two dollars from each scholar. This made me six hundred dollars. I received twenty-five cents for each license that I issued. With these means I purchased paints and oils to finish my dwelling house. I became popular among the Saints, and many of them donated labor and materials for my dwelling house. I had a handsome enclosure, with fine orchard, well of water, house finished and grained from top to bottom, and everything in finest order. I was young, strong, and athletic. I could drive ahead and work all day and stand guard half the night, through all kinds of weather.

My pay for doing the latter was the trust reposed in me. To guard the President and leading men of the Church was considered a mighty thing, and would not have been exchanged by those holding that office for ten dollars a night. It was considered that this would qualify ones performing the duty for any position of honor or worth.

In 1845 I was present when two young men named Hodges were tried for murdering an old man and his wife. The Hodges said that Brigham had sent them to rob the old people of their money, of which they were supposed to have a large amount. When they went to the house they found the inmates ready for them, and one of them was wounded. Thinking then that they would be detected, they killed the old people.

One of the party became alarmed and reported on the two Hodges boys. Their older brother, Erwin Hodges, said that Brigham had gotten his brothers into this scrape, and must get them out of it; that if he did not do so his (Brigham's) blood would atone for it.

That evening, as Erwin was returning home, a little after dark, he was met by two Danites who had been waiting for him to come along. After some little conversation, as Erwin was turning he was struck on the head with a club, and then stabbed four times over the heart. The Danites left, supposing him to be dead. He was, however, only stunned, and the bleeding revived him. He crawled about one hundred and fifty yards, and fell near Brigham's gate. He called for water, and for Brigham to lay his hands upon him.

Some persons asked him who had done the deed. He replied that they were his friends, and expired without finishing the sentence. A neighbor came running to my house, knowing that Brigham was there, as he often came there to keep away from suspicious persons. I started home with Brigham, and while on the way remarked that it was a shocking affair. He replied that it was not worse for Hodges to be killed than it would have been for him (Brigham) to have had his blood shed. This answer recalled the threat that Erwin had made during the day, at the trial of his brothers.

Those men who had turned away from the Church were the most bitter enemies to Brigham, and sought every opportunity to entrap him. They tried to ensnare him, and find an occasion to arrest him with a warrant. This caused Brigham to lie hidden as much as possible.

In the meantime his Destroying Angels were diligently on the watch, and every suspicious man was closely tracked up, and no strategy neglected to find out his business. If they suspected that any man wanted to serve a writ on Brigham they never let that man escape. Sometimes they would treat him with great kindness, and in that way decoy him to some out-of-the-way place, and there "save" him, as it was called. The Danites were not only on the track of officers, but all suspected characters who might come to spy out what was going on. I knew of many men who were put out of the way.

If any Danite was caught in a scrape, it was the duty of the rest to unite and swear him out. It was shown that the Gentiles had no right to administer an oath. The Danites might swear a house full of lies to save one of the brethren.

Whatever the Danites were ordered to do, they were to do and ask no questions. Whether it was right or wrong mattered not to them, they were responsible only to their leaders, amenable only to God. I was one among them, into the secret of all they did; and they looked for me to speak a good word for them with Brigham, as they were ambitious to please him and obtain his blessing. The captain of the Danites never asked me to do anything he knew I was averse to doing. Under Brigham, Hosea Stout was Chief.

The Danites buried a man in a lot near the Masonic Hall. They got him tight and some were joking with him while others digged his grave. They asked him to go with them into a field of corn, saying it was fully grown. They told him they had a jug of whisky cached out there. They led him to his grave, and told him if he would get down into it, hand up the jug, he should have the first drink. As he bent over to get down, Roswell Stevens struck him on the back of the head and dropped him. They tightened a cord around his neck to shut off his wind, and then covered him up and set the hill of corn back on his grave to cover any tracks that might lead to discovery.

Another man they took in a boat, about two o'clock at night, for a ride. When out in the channel of the river the Danite who sat behind him struck him upon the head and stunned him. They tied a rope around his neck and a stone to the other end of the rope, and sent him to the bottom of the Mississippi.

There was a man whose name I have forgotten, who was a great annoyance to the Saints at Nauvoo. He generally brought a party with him when he came to the city, and would threaten them with the law; but he always managed to get away safely. They (the Saints) finally concluded to entrust his case to Howard Egan, a Danite who was thought to be long-headed. He took a party of

Destroying Angels and went to La Harp, a town near the residence of this man, and watched for an opportunity when he would pass along. They "saved" him, and buried him in a washout at night. A short time afterwards a thunder storm washed the earth away and exposed the remains.

The Danites also made an attempt to kill an old man and his son over on Bear River. Ebenezer Richardson, an old tried Danite had charge of this mission. Four Danites went to the residence of the old folks. Two of them asked for lodgings and refreshments. The old gentleman told them he was not prepared to entertain them, and directed them to a neighbor who lived a mile away. They insisted upon stopping, and said they were weary and would lie down upon their blankets. The old man was suspicious of them and utterly refused to keep them.

They then went away and counseled over the matter, and concluded to wait until the family were asleep, then burst in the door before they could have time to resist. The old man and his son, being sure that the Danites had come for the purpose of "saving" them, were waiting their return. Each of them had a gun.

Brother Richardson and his party waited until about midnight, when they slipped carefully to the house and listened. All was still. Then Richardson and another burst in the door. As the Danites were in the act of entering the house the old man and his son fired. Richardson's arm was broken below the elbow; another Danite received a slight wound. The reception was overhot and they backed water, glad to get away. Richardson later wore a cloak to conceal his broken arm.

These matters were kept a profound secret. I was in Brigham's office about this time. His brother Joseph and quite a number of the others were present, when Brigham raised his hand and said:

"I swear by the eternal Heavens, and all good Mormons will do the same, that I have unsheathed my sword, and will never return it until the blood of the Prophet Joseph, and Hyrum, and those who were slain in Missouri, is avenged. This whole nation is guilty of shedding their blood, by assenting to the deed and holding its peace. Now," said he, "betray me, any who dare do so!"

Everyone who passed through his endowments in the Temple was placed under the most sacred obligations to avenge the blood of the Prophet, whenever opportunity offered, and teach their children to do the same.

Once I heard Mother Smith, the mother of Joseph the Prophet, plead with Brigham, with tears, not to rob young Joseph, her grandchild, of his birthright, which his father, the Prophet, bestowed upon him previous to his death. Young Joseph should have succeeded his father as the leader of the Church; it was his right in the line of the Priesthood.

"I know it," replied Brigham; "don't worry or take any trouble, Mother Smith; by so doing you are only laying the knife to the throat of the child. If it be known that he is the rightful successor of his father the enemies of the Priesthood will seek his life. He is too young to lead his people now, but when he arrives at mature age he shall have his place. No one shall rob him of it."

Brigham sought to establish himself as the leader of the Church. Many years, however, passed away before he dared assume or claim to be the rightful successor of Joseph, the Seer, Prophet, and Revelator to the Church. When the time arrived, according to Brigham's own words, for Joseph to receive his own, Joseph came, but Brigham received him not. He said that Joseph lacked the true spirit. Joseph's mother had married a Gentile lawyer, and had infused the Gentile spirit into him. Joseph denied the doctrine of celestial marriage.

Brigham barred young Joseph from preaching in the Tabernacle, and raised a storm against him. He took Joseph's cousin, George A. Smith, as his first counselor. This he did as a matter of policy to prevent George A. from using his influence in favor of Joseph as the leader of the people, which he otherwise would have done. He also ordained John Smith, the son of Hyrum the Patriarch, to the office of Patriarch, and his brother, Joseph F. Smith, to the office of one of the twelve apostles, thus securing their influence, telling them also that had young Joseph been willing to act in harmony with them, the heads of the Church, he could have had his place, but that he was too much of a Gentile to lead this people. Brigham said he had hopes that David, a brother of young Joseph, when he became older, might occupy the place of his father, but Joseph never would.

CHAPTER XIV
THE DOCTRINE OF SEALING

In the winter of 1845 meetings were held all over the city of Nauvoo, and the spirit of Elijah was taught in the different families as a foundation to the order of celestial marriage, as well as the law of adoption. Many families entered into covenants with each other - the man to stand by his wife and the woman to cleave unto her husband, and the children to be adopted to the parents. I was one of those who entered into covenants to stand by my family, to cleave to them through time and eternity. I have kept my obligations sacred and inviolate to this day.

Others refused to enter into these obligations, but separated from each other, dividing their substance, and mutually dissolving their former relations on friendly terms. Some agreed to exchange wives by virtue and authority of the holy Priesthood. One of Brigham's brothers, Lorenzo Young, now a bishop, made an exchange of wives with Brother Decker.

All people are aliens to the commonwealth of Israel until adopted into the Kingdom by baptism, and their children born unto them before the baptism of the parents must be adopted to the parents, and become heirs to the Kingdom only through the law of adoption. The children that are born to parents after the baptism of the parents are legal heirs to the Kingdom.

This doctrine extends further. All persons must be adopted by some of the leading men of the Church. In this, however, they have the right of choice, thus forming the links of the chain of Priesthood back to the father, Adam, and to the second coming of the Messiah. Time will not allow me to enter into the full details of this subject.

The ordinance of celestial marriage was practiced by men and women who had covenanted to live together, and plural marriages are stepping-stones to celestial exaltation. Without plural marriage a man cannot attain to the fullness of the holy Priesthood and be made equal to our Saviour. Without it he can only attain to the position of the angels, who are servants and messengers to those who attain to the Godhead. These inducements cause every true believer to exert himself to attain that exalted position - both men and women. In many cases the women do the "sparking," through the assistance of the first wife.

My second wife, Nancy Bean, was the daughter of a wealthy farmer who lived near Quincy, Illinois. She saw me on a mission and heard me preach at her father's house. She came to Nauvoo and stayed at my house three months, and grew in favor and was sealed to me in the winter of 1845. My third and fourth wives were sealed to me soon afterward in my own house. My third wife, Louisa, was then a young lady, gentle and beautiful, and we never had an angry word while she lived with me. She and her sister Emeline were both under promise to be sealed to me.

One day Brigham saw Emeline and fell in love with her. He asked me to resign my claims in his favor, which I did, though it caused a struggle in my mind to do so, for I loved her dearly. I made known to Emeline Brigham's wish, and went to her father's house and used my influence with her to induce her to become a member of Brigham's family. The two girls did not want to separate from each other; however, they both met at my house at an appointed time, and Emeline was sealed to Brigham, and Louisa was sealed to me. Brother Amasa Lyman officiated at the ceremony.

At the same time Sarah C. Williams, the girl that I baptized in Tennessee when but a child, at the house of Brother William Pace, and who later came to Nauvoo, stood up and claimed a place in my family. She is yet with me and is the mother of twelve children. She has been a kind wife, mother, and companion.

By Louisa I had one son born, who died at the age of twelve. She only lived with me one year after her babe was born. She then told me that her parents were not satisfied to have a daughter sealed to the one highest in authority and the other below her. Their teasing caused us to separate, not as enemies, however. Our friendship was never broken.

After we got to Salt Lake she offered to come back to me, but Brigham would not consent. Her sister became a favorite with Brigham, and remained so until he met Sister Folsom, who captivated him to such a degree that he neglected Emeline, and she died broken-hearted.

Plural marriages at first were not made public; they had to be kept still. A young man did not know when he was talking to a single woman. As far as Brigham was concerned, he had no wives at his house, except his first wife, or the one that he said was his first wife. Many a night have I gone with him, arm in arm, and guarded him while he spent an hour or two with his young brides, then guarded him home, and guarded his house until one o'clock, when I was relieved. He used to meet his beloved Emeline at my house.

In the spring of 1845 Rachel Andora was sealed to me - the woman who has stood by me in all my troubles. A truer woman was never born. She has been to me as true as I have been to Brigham, and always tried to make my will her pleasure. I raised her in my family from five years of age. She was a sister of my first wife. Her mother, Abigail Sheffer, was sealed to me for an eternal state. The old lady has long since passed away, and entered into endless rest and joy.

But to resume the narrative of events at Nauvoo. In the year 1845 the building of the Temple was progressing. Through the summer trouble was brewing among the Saints, both in Illinois and Iowa. Many of my friends from Tennessee, and some from Kentucky, joined us during the summer and fall, as well as numbers from other places. An effort was made to complete the Nauvoo House, if possible, but finding the storm approaching too fast the work on the House was abandoned and all hands put to work on the Temple. We were anxious to complete the Temple, in order that we might receive our promised blessings in it before we commenced our pilgrimage across the plains in search of a home, we knew not where.

Our time was limited, and our Gentile friends who surrounded us, and whose ire had been aroused to the highest pitch, were not likely to allow us to remain longer than the appointed space. The killing of the Prophet Joseph and Hyrum had led to other acts of violence, and many Mormons whose houses were burned and property destroyed, and who had come to Nauvoo for protection and shelter, retaliated by driving in Gentile stock from the range to subsist upon. No doubt the stock of many an innocent Gentile was driven away, and this served to brew trouble. Thus things went from bad to worse while the saints remained at Nauvoo.

Much of the trouble that came upon the Church was brought down through the folly of the Saints. A company was organized called the "Whittlers." They had long knives, and when a stranger came to town they would gather around him and whittle, none of them saying a word, no matter what question was asked. They would watch any stranger, gathering close to him, until they ran him out of town.

During the fall of 1845 companies were formed to make wagons for the contemplated move, as many of the Saints were poor and had neither wagons nor teams. Teams - with Gentile horses loose on the range - were more easily obtained than wagons. People traded off their lots and personal property for outfits. Many of the wagons had wooden hoops in place of tires, though iron and everything else was at the lowest price. Common labor was only twenty-five cents per day, but money was hard to get.

About the 1st of December, 1845, we commenced filling up the Temple rooms for giving endowments. I assisted in putting up the stoves, curtains, and other things. It was about fifteen days before we got everything ready. I must mention that when the doctrine of baptizing for the dead was first introduced the families met together, down by the riverside, and one of their number, of the order of the Melchisedek Priesthood, officiated. They were baptized in behalf of all the dead friends they could remember, the men for men, and the women for women. But when the fount was ready in the Temple, which rested on the twelve carved oxen, they went and were baptized in it, after the same order, except that a clerk must make a record of it, and two witnesses must be present, and the name of the person baptized and for whom he or she was baptized, and the date of baptism, together with the name of the officiating elder and those of the clerk and witnesses must be entered in the record. All who are baptized must also be confirmed. Men and women alike pass through the same ceremony, and the fact is entered in the record kept for that purpose.

This is done for all who have died without the knowledge of the gospel. As Jesus, while His body lay in the tomb, preached to the spirits in the spirit world the doctrine of his gospel to all who had died before hearing it since the days of Noah, so through baptism for the dead can our friends, and those who have gone before us, be made partakers of this new and last gospel sent to us, and receive its blessings and eternal reward.

No person, however, is allowed the privilege of this baptismal fount, or his washings or anointings, unless he has paid his tithings and has a certificate to that effect. In many cases, also, where men require it, just debts must be settled before one is permitted to be baptized, washed, or anointed.

In the Endowment a list is made out the day previous, of those who are to take their endowments. Every person is required to wash himself clean, from head to foot. Also to prepare and bring a good supply of food, of the best quality, for themselves and those who labor in the house of the Lord. About twenty-five persons are required in the different departments to attend to the washing, anointing, blessing, ordaining, and sealing. From twenty-five to fifty persons are passed through in twenty-four hours. I was among the first to receive my washings and anointings, and even received my second anointing, which made me an equal of the Priesthood, with right and authority to build up the Kingdom in all the earth and power to fill any vacancy that might occur. I have officiated in all the different branches, from the highest to the lowest.

There were about forty men who attained to that rank in the Priesthood, including the twelve apostles and Brigham, and to them was intrusted the keeping of the records. I was the head clerk; Brother Richards was my assistant clerk. My office was in room number one, of Brigham's apartments. I kept a record of the sealings, anointings, marriages, and adoptions.

Also, I was the second son adopted of Brigham. I should have been his first adopted son, being the first who proposed it to him, but, ever ready to give preference to those in authority, I placed Brother Rockwood's name first on the list. I had also had my children adopted to me in the Temple. Brigham had his children adopted to himself, and we were the only ones, to my knowledge, that had our children so adopted in the Temple of Nauvoo.

Officers were on the alert to arrest Brigham. He often hid in the different apartments of the Temple. One day about sunset an officer, knowing that he was in the Temple, waited for him to come out. Brigham's carriage was standing at the door.

Brigham threw his cloak around Brother Miller, who resembled Brigham in build and stature, and sent him to the carriage with Grant, his driver. As they got to the carriage Grant said to Miller:

"Brother Young, are you ready to go?" As he spoke to him, the officer said:

"Mr. Young, I have a writ for you. I want you to go with me to Carthage, twenty miles distant."

"Shall I take my carriage?" Miller rejoined.

"You may, if you choose, and I will pay the bill," the officer answered.

Grant then drove Miller to Carthage, and the marshal took him to the hotel and supplied him with refreshments. After supper an apostate Mormon called to see him. When he beheld Miller he said to the marshal:

"By heavens! you are sold this time. That is not Brigham; that is Miller."

The marshal was a deal nettled, and, turning, he said to Miller:

"I am much obliged to you."

"You are quite welcome. I hope you will pay my bill as you agreed to do."

"Why did you deceive me?"

"I did not," replied Miller; "you deceived yourself. I said nothing to deceive you."

"All right," replied the marshal, "I will settle your bill, and you may return in the morning, if you choose."

This gave Brigham to understand that it was time for him to get away; many such tricks would not be wholesome.

In the Temple I took three wives - Martha Berry, Polly Ann Workman, and Delithea Morris, and had my family sealed to me over the altar in the Temple, and six of them received their second anointings - that is, the first six wives did, but the last three there was not time to attend to.

On the 10th of February, 1846, Brigham and a small company crossed the Mississippi River, on the ice, into Iowa, and formed an encampment on a stream called Sugar Creek. I crossed, with two wagons, with the first company. Brigham did this in order to elude the officers, and aimed to wait there until all who could fit themselves out should join him. Such as were in danger of being arrested were helped away first.

Our Danites crossed over to guard Brigham. Those who were not liable to be arrested remained behind and sent their teams forward. I took one of Brigham's wives, Emeline, in the first of the wagons, with Louisa, her sister, as far as Rainsville. All of Brigham's wives, except the first, were taken by the brethren, as he did not at that time have the teams or the means to convey his family across the plains, but was dependent on the brethren for help, though he had used every means in his power to raise an outfit.

Brigham called a council of the leading men. Among them was Brother Joseph L. Heywood and myself. Heywood was a merchant at Quincy, Illinois, doing a fair business before he joined the Mormon Church, and was considered an honorable man. When the Mormons were driven from Missouri many had occasion to bless him for his kindness to them in their hour of trouble.

At the council, after some conversation upon our present move, Brigham proposed to appoint a committee of men, against whom no charges could be brought, to return to Nauvoo and attend to selling the property of the Saints, and see to fitting out the people and starting them forward. He proposed that I, with Brothers Babbitt, Heywood, and Fulmer be that committee. Brother Heywood was asked to turn over his whole stock of goods to fit out Brigham and the apostles for their journey.

This to Brother Heywood was a stunner. He replied that he was indebted to honorable men in the East for the most of his goods, and that he did not dare defraud them; that he had been taught from childhood to deal honorably with all men. He was told by Brigham that he might take the money to pay his Eastern creditors from the sales of the Mormon property at Nauvoo. This Brother Heywood thought a doubtful method, as the property of the deserted city would not be very valuable.

Brigham then said that this was a case of emergency, and they must have the goods; that Brother Heywood could write to his creditors and tell them that, owing to the trouble among the people, business had fallen off, and he was not able to pay them then, but would in the future. Brigham told him if he failed to raise money from the sale of city property, as soon as the Church was established he (Brigham) would raise the money for him to satisfy his creditors, and this would give him more influence than ever among the outside world. They finally persuaded Brother Heywood to turn over his goods.

For my services to the leading men I never received a dollar. I have managed, however, to maintain my family in good style, to pay my tithing and live independently of help from the Church. I was called a shrewd trader, a keen financier, and had plenty. I always had money on hand. These were considered by Brigham noble traits in my character.

CHAPTER XV
THE SAINTS TURN WESTWARD

Only a few words in regard to the Prophet Joseph. He was tried twenty-one times for different offenses, and acquitted each time. Once when he was visiting in Peoria he was captured by four men from Missouri, who started with him in a wagon to take him to that State. Two sat beside him with cocked pistols, punching him in the side occasionally, and telling him that if he opened his mouth they would blow his brains out. He was not arrested by any process of law, but they were trying to kidnap him. Brother Markham, an old friend of Joseph, ran ahead to the town of Peoria, employed a lawyer, got out a writ of habeas corpus, and had him set at liberty.

When the news reached Nauvoo the Saints were in the wildest state of excitement. The Mormon steamer was crowded with Danites, and sent full steam ahead to Peoria to rescue the Prophet. When the Danites arrived they found him at liberty. This was in 1843.

The same winter Joseph organized what was called the "Council of Fifty." This was a confidential organition. A man by the name of Jackson belonged to it, though he did not belong to the Church. This Council was designated as a law-making department, but no records were kept of its doings, or if kept, were burned at the close of each meeting. Whenever anything of importance was on foot this Council was called to deliberate upon it. The Council was named the "Living Constitution." Joseph said that no legislature could enact laws that would meet every case or attain the ends of justice in all respects.

As a man, Joseph tried to be a law-abiding citizen, but he had to manage those who were constantly doing something to bring trouble upon themselves. He often reproved them and some he dis- fellowshipped. But being of a forgiving disposition, when they came back to him and begged forgiveness his humane heart could not refuse them. He was often basely imposed upon.

Joseph's sympathies were quick. Once I was standing with him, watching a couple of men who were crossing the river in a canoe. The river was full of ice, running swiftly. As they neared the shore the canoe upset, throwing them into the river. One of them got on a cake of ice, but the other made several attempts before he could do so. Joseph sent a runner to them with a bottle of whisky, saying:

"Those poor boys must be nearly frozen."

Joseph also had a sharp tongue. On one occasion, the 4th of July, 1843, at a celebration, a number of toasts had been offered when someone said:

"Brother Joseph, suppose you give us a toast."

Raising his glass, with water in it in the place of spirits, he said:

"Here is wishing that all the mobocrats of the nineteenth century were in the middle of the sea, in a stone canoe, with an iron paddle; that a shark might swallow the canoe, and the shark be thrust into the nethermost pit of hell, the door locked, the key lost, and a blind man hunting for it."

To return to our expedition across the plains. The snow lay about eight inches deep when the first company crossed the river. The plan was this: We must leave Nauvoo, whether ready or not. All covenanted to help each other, until every one was away that wanted to go. The teams and wagons sent to help others away were to return as soon as a suitable place was found at which to make a settlement, and leave the poor, or rather those who had no teams to go on with. I was unwilling to start with a part of my family, leaving the rest behind, and thought that now was the time to get them out before worse trouble commenced. I went into Brigham's tent and told him what I thought of the matter, and that I could fit up teams in a few days and bring them all away. He replied that he had been thinking of the same thing. Said he:

"Go; I will give you five days in which to sell out and cross the river again, and bring me one hundred dollars in gold."

My first wife was still at Nauvoo. I had the confidence of my family, as I never undertook anything that I did not carry out. I started back on foot and crossed the river on the ice. I fell in with acquaintances about La Harpe, who were in trouble over a number of wagons and teams which they had purchased in the State. The devil was to pay generally. Some of the Gentiles who had lost cattle laid it to the Mormons in Nauvoo, and were determined to take cattle from the Mormons until they got even. I had a brick house and lot on Parley street that I sold for three hundred dollars in teams. I told the purchaser that I would take seven wagons and teams, and before I went to sleep that night I had my entire outfit of teams.

For my large house, costing eight thousand dollars (in Salt Lake City it would have been worth fifty thousand dollars), I was offered eight hundred dollars. My fanaticism would not allow me to take so meager a sum for it. I locked it up, selling only one stove out of it, for which I received eight yards of cloth. The building, with its twenty-seven rooms, I turned over to the committee, to be sold to help the poor away. The committee afterwards parted with the house for twelve dollars and fifty cents.

One day I was sitting with my family, telling them that I ought to get five hundred dollars in some way, but the Lord had opened no way by which I could get it, and I had but five days to get out of Nauvoo. In an adjoining room was an old gentleman and his daughter who rented the room of me. They were from Pennsylvania, and the old gentleman was wealthy. The daughter stepped into her father's room, and soon returned, saying that he wished to see me. I went into his room. He gave me a seat and said:

"You did me a kindness that I have not repaid. Do you remember meeting me, when coming from the Temple? I had been there with my wife and only child to get my washings and anointings. I was not admitted, because I was a stranger, and no one to vouch for me. I was returning with a heavy heart, when I met you. You returned with me and used your influence, vouched for us and procured our admittance. I obtained our endowments. I had a cancer on my breast at that time that was considered incurable. From the hour I received my endowments it has never pained me and is healing up. I am thankful I have it in my power to do you a little favor in return."

So saying, he lifted the lid of a box and counted out five hundred dollars in gold coin, saying that if it would help me I was welcome to it. I offered him a team, but he said he had money enough to buy his outfit and support him while he lived, and that he felt grateful for an opportunity of returning my favor. This was to me an unexpected blessing from an honest heart. I wept with joyful gratitude; I had the means that I desired in my hands.

The next morning I received my teams and wagons. All had to be fitted up for the journey. My family went to work making tents and articles needful for the journey. I sent my wagons to the Mormon wagonshop and told the men to work night and day, and put them in order within three days, and I would give them fifty dollars in gold, which was five dollars for a day and night's work, quite a difference from fifty cents, the usual price. They went to work in earnest, and as fast as a wagon was rolled out finished I had it loaded.

In the meantime Brother Babbitt was urging me to cross the river, as there was an officer in town looking for me. On the third day I started one of my ox teams across the river on the ice, and came near losing the whole outfit, by its breaking through. I crossed no more teams that way. I got a large wood boat, with twenty-five men to help me, and cut through the ice across the river, so that the boat could be towed over. On the fourth day I had all of my effects at the riverside.

The day before, when I crossed the team that broke through the ice, I met the officer, to whom I was unknown, at the riverside looking for me. He purposed to arrest me on the charge of having more wives than one. I told him I had seen Mr. Lee crossing the river the day before, and that one of his oxen broke through; I added that it was a pity Mr. Lee had not broken through also. I stepped into a saloon with the officer and we took a drink together. I then went with him into the wagonshop, and, stepping ahead of him and tipping the wink to the men there, said:

"Have any of you seen Mr. Lee to-day? Here is an officer looking for him."

They replied that he had crossed the river the day before. This satisfied the officer, and he went away. I bought oils and paints for my wagons, and five gallons of whisky with which to treat the boys who had helped me over the river.

As we left the river a heavy storm came up. It was so dark I could see nothing. I had four mule teams, and let them follow the road. We halted about a mile beyond the town of Montrose, and a man who lived there, named Hickenlooper, took us in and attended to the animals. I went to sleep and did not wake until ten o'clock the next morning. This man had all the supplies we needed, - flour, bacon, etc., - and I purchased my store of supplies from him. I learned that the company had moved on, and was camped at a place called Richardson Point, forty-five miles from Montrose.

Before reaching the encampment I was met by Brigham, H. C. Kimball, and Dr. William Richards in their carriages, who bade me welcome. After we reached camp a council was held, and I reported my success, and gave ah account of my mission. When I had finished Brigham asked me if I had brought him the hundred dollars. I replied that I had, and handed it to him. He counted it, and then said:

"What shall I do with it?"

"Feed and help the poor," I replied.

Brigham then prophesied, saying I should be blessed, and means come unto me from an unexpected source; that in time of need friends would be sent to my assistance.

The roads were in bad condition, and we lay quiet a few days, during which time I painted and numbered my wagons. Myself, Geo. S. Clark, Levi Stewart, and another man were appointed hunters, as there was much game in the country we had to pass through - turkey, deer, and some elk.

From here we traveled to the Raccoon Fork of Grand River, about seventy-five miles. At the three forks of the Grand River we came to a halt. In fact, the rain had made the country impassable, and our provisions were running short. Here we found some wild hogs, and the men killed several. Brigham said they were some of our hogs that had become scattered when we were driven out of Missouri. This was license for us to kill anything we could find.

104

While we lay here two men came to our camp, named Allen Miller and Mr. Clancy. They were traders to the Potowatomie Indians. Allen Miller later married one of my wives. They informed me that we could get everything we needed fifty miles from there, near Grand River. We unloaded seventeen wagons and selected such articles as we could spare. I was appointed Commissary, to do the purchasing for the companies. This was in April, 1846.

We started with the seventeen wagons, and drove to Miller's and made that place headquarters, as he had provisions in abundance. The grass was like a meadow. I had some horses and harness to exchange for oxen and cows. When we had turned out our stock for the day at Miller's Mr. Clancy invited me home with him.

On entering his house I found his partner, Patrick Dorsey, an Irishman, sick. Mr. Dorsey had been tormented with a pain in his eyes, insomuch that he had rested neither day nor night, and was losing his sight. I asked him if he was a Catholic. He answered that he was. I knew their faith, as I was raised a Catholic and once believed in their doctrines. I asked him if he wished me to pray for him. He inquired if I was a minister, to which I replied that I was.

"Do pray with me, for I am in great distress," he then said.

With that I laid my hands upon his head, and asked the Father, in the name of the Son, and by virtue of the holy Priesthood in me vested, to stay his sufferings and heal him. The pain left him instantly. He took his hat and walked with me to Miller's house. They were astonished to see him without pain, and asked him what I had done for him. He answered:

"I was in distress; a stranger laid hands upon my head and prayed and made me whole; but who he is, or whence he came, I know not. But this I know, that I was almost blind, and now I see; I was sick, but am well."

This occurrence created an excitement in the settlement, and nothing would do but I must preach the next evening.

During the day I made several trades. Evening came, and I preached at my friend Miller's. When I had closed my sermon they made me up a purse of five dollars, and offered to load one of our wagons with provisions.

We remained about a week and did finely in trading. On Sunday a large attendance, for a new country, turned out to hear me preach. I was weary and did not feel like preaching. However, I talked about an hour and a half. At the close of the service they made up ten dollars for me, and Mr. Scott, a wealthy farmer, said that if I would drive my wagons to his establishment he would fill them with flour, bacon, and potatoes. I had the use of my friend Miller's store to warehouse our traps, as I had more than we could take away. The people were anxious for me to remain and take up a farm, make my home with them, and preach and build up a church. I told them I was bound for the Rocky Mountains.

As for Mr. Dorsey, he offered me all he had, and wanted to know what to do to be saved. He gave me a history of his life. He told me that he led a company of men from Carroll County, Missouri, when we were driven from the State. I reflected a little, and gave him a list of city property at Nauvoo that I would turn over to him at one-fourth its value for what property he would turn out to me.

He said he had twelve yoke of oxen and twenty-five cows, besides other stock; four bee stands, three wagons, six to eight hundred dollars' worth of bacon, flour, meal, soap, powder, lead, blankets, thirty rifles, guns, knives, tobacco, calicos, spades, hoes, plows, and harrows; also twelve feather beds, and all of his improvements. He said he only wanted his carriage and a span of black horses to take himself, wife, and partner to Nauvoo. And all the above property he would turn over to me, and I might give him deeds to property in Nauvoo.

Brigham commenced making a settlement at the place where he was camped. He called the place Garden Grove. We returned to camp, laden with all that our teams could haul, besides the three wagons I had from Dorsey. There was a deal that we could not move away. I took a forty-gallon cask of honey and a quantity of whisky and brandy from Dorsey. The bee stands, improvements, and farming utensils I turned over for the use of what settlers remained behind at Garden Grove. I also made arrangements for the labor needed by the company that was left, so that they might be planting crops and raising supplies while building houses to live in.

All the borrowed teams were returned to Nauvoo to bring others forward, while those who had teams of their own pushed on and made another settlement called Pisgah, and then went forward to Council Bluffs - afterwards called Kanesville, in honor of Col. Thomas L. Kane. From this point I took a cargo of traps, consisting of feather beds, fine counterpanes, quilts, and such goods, and went down to Missouri, with a number of wagons, to obtain supplies, together with beef cattle and cows.

During my absence a call was made on the Mormons for five hundred men to go to Mexico and defend the American flag. Col. Ethan Allen and Thos. L. Kane began to raise the required number of men. An express was sent to Pisgah and Garden Grove asking them to furnish their number. The ranks were nearly full before I reached camp. Upon my arrival Dr. Richards said to me:

"I am glad you have returned. We want you for one of the captains."

"All right," I answered.

Brigham called me and said he could not spare me; that there were men enough to fill the bill without me. The battalion was filled, and Col. Allen, a United States officer, marched with them to Fort Leavenworth, Kansas.

From Council Bluffs I returned to Missouri, to buy a drove of cattle for Brigham, Dr. Richards, and others, they having received money from England. I loaded twenty wagons with provisions and articles for trade and exchange. I exchanged horses for oxen, as the latter were low and the former high in price. About the middle of August I returned with over five hundred head of cattle.

While I was gone the camp moved across the Missouri River, to a place called Cutler's Park. The cattle swam the river, but the provision train was still on the Iowa side. Grant and some of Brigham's men, teamsters and waiters, crossed back for a couple of loads of provisions for Brigham. Without saying a word to me they took from my train their supply of provisions.

When I heard of it I was ruffled, as this train was in my charge and I was responsible for it. I went to Grant, who seemed to be the leader, and told him he had not acted the gentleman in interfering with what did not belong to him.

We had warm words, and had not others interfered would have come to blows. He justified himself by saying that Brigham sent him. I told him I did not care who sent him - there was a right way and a wrong way of doing things. The feeling grew bitter between us, and he accused me of doing wrongful acts in my office.

Finally Brigham called us together in the presence of the twelve apostles, and we made our statements. My accusers said what they had to say, and then I replied. When Brigham had heard our statements he scolded my accusers sharply, and approved of what I had done. He then said that we must not have ill-feeling, and directed us to shake hands and be friends. I was the first that arose to comply. We shook hands; still, though we agreed to drop the matter, the old spirit lingered, even after we had crossed the plains.

CHAPTER XVI
LEE GOES TO SANTA FE

We got into camp the next day. After striking camp I noticed that a tire was gone from one of the wagons. A few days afterwards the mother of my first wife went down to a stream near by and caught a number of fine fish; on her way back to the camp she found the missing tire. It had rolled nearly three hundred yards from the road, and was lying where it stopped.

The people began cutting hay and stacking it, so as to be prepared for feeding our stock during the winter.

One night, in the latter part of September, I dreamed that Lieut. James Pace, of Company E, Mormon Battalion, then on its way to New Mexico, stood at my tent door, and said Col. Allen, commanding the Mormon battalion, was dead. I saw him plainly in my dream; after he gave the information he started back to his camp, and later a man, who always kept his back towards me, went from our encampment with him. I saw him and his companion, and all they did on their way back to Santa Fe, their dangers from the Indians, and all that took place. From first to last in my vision the comrade of Pace kept his back my way. Pace's companion, as affairs turned out, was myself.

The next evening I went, as was usual, with Brigham and Dr. Willard Richardson, the Church historian, to attend a Council at Heber C Kimball's camp. After the meeting was over and we were going back to our tents I said to Brigham:

"We will find Lieut. Pace at my tent when we get there."

"How do you know that?" said he. I then told him my dream, and we walked on.

When we got in sight of the tent there stood Lieut. James Pace, just as I had seen him in my dream. This did not surprise me, for I knew he would come. Brigham said:

"What on earth has brought you back?" He replied:

"Col. Allen is dead. The battalion is without a commander, and I have returned by order of the officers to report to you, and ask you who shall now lead us."

"Why did you not elect one of your captains?" said Brigham.

"The officers prefer to let Col. Smith, of the United States army, lead us, if you will consent to it. But some of our men object, so I came for orders from you."

The matter was taken under advisement by Brigham until next morning. In the morning he came to me in my tent and said:

"John, how would you like to go back with Brother Pace and get the remittances of the soldiers?" I said:

"My family is large, I have no houses for them; they are without provisions, and I have no means to shelter them from the winter storms. I have not hay cut to feed my stock through the winter. I must attend to keeping my stock in order or I will have nothing left to take me and my family over the plains next spring. But," said I, "there is no one more willing to sacrifice himself and his own interests for the benefit of the Church than I am."

Brigham waited and heard me through; then he said:

"Thus sayeth the Lord. You shall go, my son. Prosperity shall attend you during your absence, and you shall return in safety; not a hair of your head shall be hurt."

"It is enough to know your will; I will go. But who will take care of my family in my absence?"

"I will see to your family, and attend to all you are interested in during your absence," said Brigham.

At that, I was satisfied, and proceeded to carry out Brigham's will. I had cut considerable hay in company with the brethren, but as it had to be divided, I felt sure I would not have much to my share, especially after I had divided with the lazy poor. I never went much on this copartnership system of labor. There are always a number who will not work, and yet they are always present when there is a division to be made of the proceeds of the labor.

Joseph the Prophet classed the poor into three divisions. He said:

"There are three kinds of poor. The Lord's poor, the devil's poor, and the poor devils." I never objected to share with the Lord's poor, but when it came to dividing with the devil's poor and the poor devils, it was more than I desired; it took away the profits.

My outfit for the intended journey to Santa Fe consisted of a snug light wagon, a span of good mules, a spyglass, and such guns and traps as a man needs on the plains. I also took Dr. Willard's dog with me to watch while I was asleep. I was ordered to keep my business secret from everyone, for fear of being robbed on my return home. I was not allowed to even tell my wives where

108

I was going, or how long I would be gone. I went to St. Joseph, Missouri, and put up at John Green's, and stayed while fitting out for the trip.

While there I met Luke Johnson, one of the witnesses to the Book of Mormon. I had a curiosity to talk with him concerning the same. We took a walk on the river bank. I asked him if the statement he had signed as to seeing the angel and the plates was true, and whether he did see the plates from which the Book of Mormon was printed or translated. He declared it to be true. I then said:

"How is it you have left the Church? If the angel appeared to you, and you saw the plates, how can you live out of the Church? I understand that you were one of the twelve apostles at the first organization of the Church?"

"I was of the twelve," said he; "I have not denied the truth of the Book of Mormon. I and several others were overtaken in a fault at Kirtland, Ohio - Wm. Smith, Oliver Cowdrey, one or two others, and myself. We were brought up for the offense before the Church authorities. Sidney Rigdon and Wm. Smith were excused, and the matter hushed up. But Cowdrey and myself were proceeded against and our choice given us between making a public confession or being dropped from the Church. I refused to make the public confession unless Rigdon and Smith did the same. The authorities said that that would not do, for Rigdon was counselor to the Prophet, and Wm. Smith the brother of the Prophet, and also one of the twelve; but that if Cowdrey and I confessed, it would be a cloak for the other two. I considered this unjust and unfair. I left the Church for that reason. But I have reflected much since that time, and have come to the conclusion that each man is accountable for his own sins; also that the course I have been pursuing injures me alone, and I intend to visit the Saints and again ask to be admitted into the Church. Rigdon has gone to destruction, and Wm. Smith is not much better off to-day than I am."

This conversation was a comfort to me.

We went to Fort Leavenworth, where we learned that Col. Smith had taken command of the battalion and marched away with it. Lieut. Pace got another good horse here, and what oats and provisions we needed. We then struck out after the command.

We overtook the battalion on the Arkansas River about fifty miles below Bent's Fort. Our brethren were rejoiced to see us. Many had grievances to relate, and all had much to tell and inquire about. That morning they had buried one of the battalion named Phelps. The men said his death was caused by arsenic which the doctor had forced him to take. They claimed that Colonel Smith was a tyrant - that he was not the man that Col. Allen had been. The command was on the march when we came up with it. There was a fifty-mile desert before us, and little water on the route.

Col. Allen had allowed the men to pray with and for each other when sick and had not compelled them to take medicine when they did not want it. But Col. Smith deprived them of their religious rights and made them obey the doctor's orders at all times. The doctor examined the sick every morning and made them take medicine. When they refused to take it they were compelled to walk; if unable to walk and keep up with the others they were tied to the wagons like animals. The doctor was called "Death"; he was known to all by that name.

While traveling along, Capt. Hunt, of Company A, introduced Col. Smith to me. I invited them to ride in my wagon. They got in, and I soon brought up the subject of the treatment of the troops adopted by Col. Allen, and spoke of its good influence over them. I said the men loved Col. Allen, and would have died for him, because he respected their religious rights. I said they were volunteers, and not regular troops; that they were not used to military discipline, and felt that they were oppressed. They had lost confidence in their officers. I referred to the ill- treatment of the men, and talked freely.

Capt. Hunt got angry and jumped from the wagon. He said that I talked like an insane man rather than a man of sense. The Colonel said that he was willing to give up the command to the choice of the battalion. I said he had better keep it until we arrived at Santa Fe, but for his own sake to ease up on the boys.

That evening Capt. Hunt sent a delegation to inform me that I was inciting the command to mutiny, and must stop or he would have me under arrest. I asked where he was going to find his men to put me under guard - that he could not locate them in that command, and if he doubted my word he had better try. The Captain knew I was right, and the matter ended. I told the Colonel I would encourage the men to obedience until we reached Santa Fe. The troops were better treated after that.

On the march water was scarce; I saw a man offer sixteen dollars for a coffeepot of water on the desert. I walked most of the time, and let the sick ride in my wagon. When we reached the Spanish settlements we got water, pepper, onions, corn, sheep, goats, and other articles of food.

We reached Santa Fe in the midst of a snow storm. All the Mormons were pleased to find that honest Missourian, Col. Doniphan, in command at that place. He had a humane nature. The sick and disabled men of the battalion were sent to a Spanish town called Taos, under charge of Capt. Brant, for care and rest.

Soon after reaching Santa Fe Col. Philip St. John Cook took command of the battalion. The soldiers were paid off, and Howard Egan, who had accompanied me, was given one-half the checks and money donated by the soldiers for Brigham and Heber C. Kimball, and the remainder was given to me to carry back to winter quarters. I remained in camp ten days to recruit my mules, because I could not purchase any there. The army had taken everything.

Lieut. Gully desired to return with me, and it was necessary to obtain permission for him to resign before he could do so. I went to the commander, stated the situation to him, and asked that Lieut. Gully be permitted to resign. The commander granted my request. The Lieutenant had been acting Commissary of Subsistence, and had to make up his papers before he could start. I waited until he was ready to go with me. I also took Russell Stevens with me, as he had been discharged on account of ill health.

While thus waiting I was troubled with Egan, for he got drunk every day, and I feared he would be robbed. I had Stevens watch him most of the time. By closely guarding him I kept him and the money safe. Col. Doniphan said I should have a guard to protect us through the Indian country, but animals could not be procured. I took the necessary trouble and got as good a team as I could to start back with. With the consent of the commander I bought a large mule, which after much trouble was able to work with one of my own.

While we were in camp at Santa Fe the doctor was robbed. His trunk was stolen, carried out of camp, and broken open. Two gold watches and some money were taken from it. Two mules were also stolen the same night. I knew nothing of this, nor who did it, until long afterwards. After we had started for home, Stevens suddenly brought in the mules. He brought them to camp and said they were his. Stevens and Egan robbed the doctor, but they never acknowledged it to me.

About the 11th of October, 1846, we started for home over a wilderness twelve hundred miles wide, every foot of it infested with Indians. We camped in the mountains at Gold Springs, where little particles of gold can be seen on the bottom of the streams. Egan and Stevens did not join us until we were fifty miles from Santa Fe. They had the doctor's mules and a Spanish horse with them when they came up.

When we had traveled ninety miles I discovered that my mules were failing. The little flesh that was on them was soft and would not last, for we had not fed them any grain. It is difficult to recruit mules on the desert grass, for it is very short generally, and the immense herds of buffalo ranging over the country keep the grass short. At the last Spanish town we passed through I sent Egan to buy a span of mules. That night Egan and Stevens came to camp with two miserable little beasts. I said:

"What on earth have you brought those poor brutes for?"

"We cabbaged them; it was the best we could do," said Egan.

Then I told him that I was on a mission of duty, and trusted in God, and I would not permit him to bring stolen animals to the camp. I sent him back with the mules at once.

"My trust is in God, and not in the devil. We shall go on, while you take back the mules, and leave them where you got them."

At Moro Station, on the Las Animas, the last camp we would find until we reached the eastern edge of the plains, we found a large, fat mule that belonged to the Government. Lieut. Gully gave the station keeper, a young man, a receipt for the mule, and we took it with us, as we were, in one sense, in Government employ. We were carrying a mail, and on general business for the Government. This was a fine, gentle mule. I called her Friendship. When the other animals grew weak I fastened the doubletree to the axle, and thus Friendship alone hauled the wagon fully three hundred miles.

At the Cimmaron Springs we met a company of traders from St. Louis, with a train of thirty-eight wagons. One of their wagons was loaded with pitch-pine wood for cooking purposes. It was raining, and a regular plains storm was coming on. These storms are sometimes tremendously destructive. A train had been overtaken at this same place the year before, and nearly all of the animals perished. I counted one hundred and ninety skeletons of mules that had died in that storm. Many of the men also died. The storm took place ten days earlier in the season than did the one which then threatened us.

We were invited to his camp by the captain; the others went, but I stayed in my wagon to write up an account of the trip, which I was obliged to keep by order of Brigham. Capt. Smith came to my wagon and gave me a drink of fine brandy. He invited us to take supper and breakfast with him, which we did. He asked me if I was not afraid to travel with so small a company, and said the Indians were on the warpath, committing depredations all along the road; that he had a large train, yet did not consider himself safe. I answered:

"My trust is in God, not in numbers."

This led to a conversation on religious subjects. When I told him who I was, and stated my belief to him, he was much interested in the Mormon doctrine. At supper he gave us everything to eat that could be desired. The Captain put up a large tent over my wagon to protect it from the storm and wind.

The next morning the storm was over and we made an early start. The Captain gave me a cheese, a sack of butter crackers, sardines, and many other matters which were of value to us on our journey over the plains. He also gave me his name, age, and place of residence in St. Louis, writing it in a little blank book which he presented me. He then gave me five dollars in gold, shook hands, and said:

"Remember me in coming days," and we parted.

At the Cimmaron crossing of the Arkansas River we met several companies of Missouri troops. They informed us that Capt. Mann, with three companies, had been attacked by a body of Southern Pawnee and Cheyenne Indians; that the troops were defeated and lost seven killed, with a number wounded; that three of the men had come for help; that Capt. Mann had lost all of his animals except the three that the messengers escaped with; that the men only had a small supply of ammunition, and shot it all away before they retreated. Reinforcements had gone to their assistance and would bring in the command.

They insisted that we stop with them, saying it was madness to attempt to go on. I told them that my trust was in God, my business urgent, and we could not stop. We went forward twelve miles, when we met the troops bringing in the wounded and the remnant of the men who had been engaged with Capt. Mann in the late Indian fight; they also insisted that we return with them. They said there were eight hundred mounted Indians not more than two miles back, following up the rearguard, and that we would be massacred unless we returned with them. I admit that the prospect looked dark. Still I felt impressed to push on.

Along this river, while it runs in nearly a level country and with no timber within a hundred miles, there are many washes and gullies that sometimes run out perhaps a mile from the river. Often these washes, which are quite deep, caused the road to twist round them, thus forcing one to travel a couple of miles to gain two hundred yards in distance. It was near one of these washes that we met the last of the troops.

We stopped at the point where the road turned back to the river. My comrades were in doubt what to do. I felt that the danger was great. While

112

debating the matter in my mind, my dream that I had the night when I saw Lieut. Pace at my tent door came fresh before me. I saw the whole situation.

While studying upon this matter I heard a voice - an audible voice - say:

"John, leave the road and follow me,"

The voice appeared to be about twenty feet in front of me, and the same distance from the earth. I was startled, for no human being was there who could have spoken thus to me. I said to Lieut. Gully:

"Did you hear that voice?"

"No," said he.

"What shall we do?" I asked.

"You are intrusted with this mission; follow your impressions and all will be right," he said.

From that moment I felt an invisible power which led me out upon the plains, away from roads or trails.

We went about half a mile, when we came to a low basin, which entirely hid us from the road. This basin contained about one acre of ground, and was covered with good grass. I felt impelled to stop there, and did so. It was then about 1 o'clock, p. m.

Soon after halting we saw a cloud of dust made by a large herd of buffaloes running from the river where they had gone for water and had been frightened by Indians. We did not see the Indians, for we were protected by our position. We stayed there and let our animals eat grass for about one hour and a half. We then drove on, following my invisible guide, in an easterly direction, over a country entirely strange to me. We traveled until after dark, when we came to a wash which my spirit guide directed me to follow to the river. I did so, and came to the very spot where the Indians had attacked Capt. Mann that morning. Fragments of the train lay scattered over the plain.

Our mules were frightened at the smell of the blood. We watered our animals, and filled our canteens. The night was still and the least noise echoed and re-echoed through the river canyons, until it made the place more than fearful for people in our situation. We traveled until near midnight, when we turned out our animals, tied the dog to the wagon tongue, to give us a guard, and then lay down and slept until daylight.

We never camped near watering places, nor near the trail. Our reasons for camping away from water, and at least half a mile from the trail, were to avoid the Indians. We never had a fire at night.

The next day we found a fat young mule, with all its harness on. It had been frightened during the battle and broken way from the command. It was fully forty miles from the battleground. I was in need of fresh animals, for mine were nearly worn out. The finding of this mule gave me renewed confidence in God, and strengthened my belief that He was leading us.

The next day we moved in the same direction. The heavy rains had made the grass good. Buffalo were constantly in sight. We followed our course three days, when we struck the trail at a stream called Walnut Creek.

Here we found an Indian encampment; the Indians were on a buffalo hunt. We crossed the creek and camped, concluding to cook our supper and let our animals eat and rest. It was no use trying to escape from the Indians; they had seen us and could capture us if they wished to do so. I felt that the best plan was to appear easy and without fear.

Soon after camping, a band of over fifty warriors surrounded us. I offered to shake hands, but they refused. I offered them pins and needles and some calico that I had purchased to trade with the Spaniards. They took my proffered gifts and dashed them on the ground. I began to feel that, although we had been delivered from former dangers, our time had come. I remarked to Lieut. Gully, who was a true and faithful man:

"Pray in your heart to God, and ask Him to turn away the ire of these people. They have been abused by white men and soldiers. They think we are of that class, and only friendly because we are in their power; if they knew who we are, and that we have been sent to preach the gospel to them, and teach them its truths through the Book of Mormon, they would die sooner than see us hurt."

An elderly Indian turned to a noble young buck. They talked some time, and would occasionally point to me. Then they dismounted and came nearer us. The old man raised his voice and talked in a loud tone and rapid manner to his men for five or ten minutes. The young buck then spoke to me in English, much to our surprise. He said:

"Young man, this is my father. He is Hard Robe, the war chief of the Osage Indians. I have been educated in the East. We came here with the intention of scalping you all. This tribe has been abused by what my father calls the palefaces, though he wishes to be friendly with them. When a small part of this nation comes in contact with a larger force of palefaces, they are shot and abused; but when the Indians have the advantage, the palefaces want to be friends. We thought you were of that class, but now my father is satisfied you are good men. I have read the Book of Mormon to him and to our tribe. I got the book from a preacher who was in the Cherokee Nation. My father wishes me to say to you that you shall not be hurt. If you need dried buffalo meat you can have all you want. Do not be afraid, we will not harm you, but you must remain here until morning, otherwise you might fall in with some of my father's braves, who, not knowing who you are, would attack you. If you stay until morning I shall go with you until you are out of danger."

To this I replied that we must go on; that we had letters from the Mormon Battalion to their friends at home, and must go at once. The young man told the chief what I said. The chief replied through the young warrior:

"If you cannot stay, I will send word to the other chiefs not to hurt you. They may not see you, as they are away from the trail, but I will send runners to tell them to let you pass in peace."

We thanked him, and I told him I was raised among the Delawares and Cherokees; that when a child I used to play with them before they were removed to this country, and was still their friend.

The chief then asked if we wanted any dried meat. I told him no, that I preferred fresh meat. I saw a buffalo near by, and asked them to kill it, and bring me some of the meat. One of the Indians rode for the buffalo at full speed of his pony. The well-trained beast stopped when near the buffalo, and the

114

Indian shot it down; then he jumped from his saddle and cut out a piece of the hump, and returned with it before we were ready to start. I gave the Indians what trinkets we had and started on again. It was now after sunset.

Here was another manifestation of Almighty God. I felt so grateful for our deliverance that I could not restrain my tears of gratitude. I care not what people may call me. I know there is a just God, and a Rewarder of those who diligently seek Him. I know that my Redeemer liveth and I shall see Him for myself and not for another. Though the day of my execution be now at hand - four days only are given me to continue this story of my life - my trust is in that Arm that cannot be broken. Though men may err, and cruelly betray each other unto death, nevertheless the hope of my calling in Christ Jesus, my Lord, is the same with me. I shall rest in peace. However, I must not destroy the thread of my narrative. I must continue, to the end that my story live when I am no more.

The next day two Indians came to us, but they could not talk English, and we could not speak their tongue, so we had no conversation. I am certain from the actions of the two Indians that the old chief had kept his word with us and notified his tribe to let us go in safety.

On reaching the Pawnee Fork, a tributary of the Arkansas, we found Capt. Bullard's train of thirty wagons. They lay by all day searching for eight mules that had been stampeded by the Indians, although picketed and closely guarded. The company could not find a trace of them.

The men were a rough, boisterous set, and, while our animals were weary, I concluded that it was best to go further before camping. It was raining, but that made traveling better, for the country was sandy.

We camped that night at Ash Creek. We now felt that we were over the worst of our dangers, but we still had enough of trials before us to keep the expedition from becoming a pleasure trip.

Next morning our riding animals were unable to travel. They refused to go on. I went to God in prayer and laid our case before Him, and asked that He open up the path for our deliverance. That night I dreamed that I was exceedingly hungry and had little to eat, when several ears of large, solid corn were handed me by an angel, who said:

"This will meet your needs until you are where there is plenty."

The ears of corn were of different colors; one ear was jet black, but perfectly sound; one was red, and one was yellow. I was much pleased with the corn and felt there was not much danger of suffering now. The next morning our animals still looked bad; only two of our riding animals could raise a trot. Lieut. Gully said that unless God soon sent us some fresh animals we would have to give up.

"We will not give up," said I. "God has protected us thus far and we will trust in Him - in the eleventh hour of our trouble He will aid us. We will find help to-day."

"I hope so," said he. "Have you been dreaming again?"

Thereupon I related my dream about the corn, and said that I thought the ears of corn meant mules.

After prayer (we always kneeled in prayer, night and morning) we started on our way. The mules could hardly travel.

115

We had gone about six miles when we saw fresh tracks made by shod animals, that appeared to be dragging long ropes and pins. The tracks were following the trail and going in the same direction that we were traveling. We had a long down grade before us. The plain was dotted here and there with herds of buffalo. I halted and with my spyglass took a careful survey of the country. My efforts were rewarded by the sight of mules feeding among the buffalo.

We went on until we arrived as close to them as we could go without leaving the trail. We called a halt, turned our mules loose, then spread out the oilcloth that I used to feed the mules on, and scattered a little of the grain we had left on the cloth. The strange mules saw it, and came running to get a feed of grain. We got hold of the ropes that were on the necks of four of the mules and tied them together.

There was a black mare mule that was quite shy, but I finally caught the rope that was on her neck. The mule at that came at me with her ears turned back and mouth open. She caught me by the arm and bit me severely, then turned and ran away. Lieut. Gully said:

"Let her go, she will kill some of us."

"No, we will not let her go," said I.

Again I caught her, and she made for me again, but I caught the rope near the end where it was fastened to an iron pin, and struck her a blow with the pin, which knocked her down. I then placed my knee on her neck, and caught her by the nose with my hands. I held her in this way until a bridle was put on her, after which we were able to manage her easily. I hitched this wild mule to the wagon by the side of Friendship. We now had fresh riding animals, and turned our jaded ones loose, and drove them before us.

At Kane Creek we lost the mule that I got from the soldiers in Santa Fe. It drank more of the alkali water than was good for it; we left it on the plains and went our way. We saw so many fresh Indian signs that we knew we had no time to stay and doctor sick mules. A few nights later I saw a large body of Indians among the cedars on a mountain, not far off, but our lucky star was guiding us, for soon we met three hundred soldiers, with whom we camped that night. The force was so strong that the Indians did not attack us. Next day we met soldiers frequently, and every few hours thereafter we encountered troops until we reached Fort Leavenworth.

It was storming hard when we got to St. Joseph, Missouri. We put up at a hotel, but before our animals were in a stable Eagan was gone. I could not find him that night, albeit we searched for him diligently. I was afraid he would be robbed; but he happened to meet honest men, as drunkards will, who put him in bed, and kept him and his money in safety until morning. After leaving St. Joseph, where we had purchased a lot of supplies, we started for winter quarters; we had to go through six feet of snow the whole distance.

We reached our friends. I had two hundred dollars, of which the soldiers had made me a present. I took three of the mules we had found on the way, and divided the others between my companions. We reached winter quarters, now called Florence, on the 15th day of December, 1846. The snow was deep, and

116

my family, all living in tents, were in a suffering condition. But I must report to Brigham, then attend to my family. My family received me as they always did, with open arms and thankful hearts.

CHAPTER XVII
LEE IS TREATED BADLY BY THE BRETHREN

With me I had brought home about all that my team could haul of supplies, clothing, and groceries, which soon made my family comfortable. I had met Brigham and shaken hands with him, but had not made my report or delivered the money to him. The next morning Brigham called to see me, and notified me that the Council would meet at nine o'clock at Dr. Richards', and for me to be there and make my report. He appeared ashamed of the manner in which my family had been treated.

"Brother Brigham, how does this compare with your promises to me, when I trusted all to you?" I said.

"Brother John," Brigham replied, "I am ashamed of the conduct of this people. Do not blame me, Brother John, for I have done the best I could." Then putting his hand on my shoulder, he said: "Don't feel bad about it. You will live through, and the day will come when we can look back and see what we have endured for the Kingdom of Heaven's sake. Lord bless you, Brother John."

Allow me to jump from 1847 to 1877, just thirty years. I have remained faithful to the end. I was adopted by Brigham, and was to seek his interests here, and in return he was to seek my salvation; I, being an heir of his family, was to share his blessings in common with his other heirs. True to my pledges, I have done his bidding. I have let him direct my energies in all things. And the time has come for me to receive my reward. An offering must be made; I must hew the wood and build the altar; then, as did Abraham of old with his son Isaac, I must be laid upon the altar as a sacrifice. I must meet my fate without murmuring or complaining; I must submit, true to the end. If I endure firm to the end, I will receive the martyr's crown.

After my return, my first duty was to build comfortable houses for my family. Soon afterwards I was sent to St. Joseph to cash the checks and purchase goods to supply the wants of the people. I was directed to purchase a lot of salt and potatoes from a Frenchman at Trading Point. I did so, and bought three hundred dollars' worth on credit, and sent it back to the settlement. I had to borrow the money from Mrs. Armstrong to pay the three hundred dollars. But she was afterwards sealed to me, and it was then all in the family. I never asked Brigham for it, and he never offered to pay it.

117

On that trip to St. Joseph I bought fifteen hundred dollars' worth of goods, such as were needed at the settlement. I advanced seven hundred dollars of my own money; the remainder was from the money sent home by the Mormon Battalion. I took the goods back and we opened a store at winter quarters. Brother Rockwood acted as chief clerk and salesman. We sold the goods at a great advance. What cost us seven cents in St. Joseph we sold at sixty- five cents. Everything was sold at a similar profit. I kept the stock up during the winter and did a good business. One drawback was this: many of the families of the men who were in the Mormon Battalion had no money, and we were obliged to let them have goods on credit. I had to stand the loss myself, for few of the men ever paid a dollar due me when they returned.

Andrew Little was in the battalion, and at the request of Brigham I let his family have two hundred and fifty-eight dollars' worth of goods. Brigham said I should have my money when Little returned, but I never got any of it. Little was also an adopted son of Brigham, and did about as he pleased. James Pace, Thomas Woolsey, and a few others of the soldiers paid me when they returned for what I had advanced their families, but the majority never paid.

When I returned from Santa Fe I found David Young, his wife, and two daughters lying sick and helpless - really in want. I took care of them and supplied them with food and such articles as they required until the death of the father, mother, and one son, which took place in a short time - a few months after my return home. I had baptized this family in Putnam County, Tennessee, and felt an interest in them. The two girls were sealed to me while we stayed at winter quarters, and became members of my family. They are both living. By them I have had three sons and three daughters. They were sealed to me in 1847. I was also sealed to Nancy Armstrong the same evening that I took the Young girls to wife. A few evenings afterwards I was sealed to Emeline Woolsey. She was my thirteenth wife.

Nancy Armstrong's maiden name was Gibbons. She was the wife of a wealthy merchant by the name of Armstrong, who owned a large establishment in Louisville, and another in Carlisle, Kentucky, at which places he did business as wholesale and retail dealer in dry goods. I became acquainted with the family at Carlisle, while preaching there.

The people of Carlisle were bitter enemies of the Mormon Church, and a mob threatened to tar and feather me one night, when Armstrong took me home with him and protected me. He was not a believer in any religion, but I always considered him a high- minded, honorable man. I afterwards often stopped at the house.

His wife and sister Sarah were believers in the Mormon faith, but as Mr. Armstrong was not, I advised his wife not to become a member of the Church, and refused to baptize her until her husband would consent to it. Elder Smoot afterwards baptized Sarah Gibbons and Nancy Armstrong.

Brother Smoot had taken his wife with him on the mission, and she laid the plan to get Sarah to go to Nauvoo. A wagon was sent to take Sarah Gibbons' goods to Nauvoo, and in it Mrs. Armstrong sent her valuable clothing and jewelry, amounting to more than two thousand dollars. She intended to join the Saints at the first chance.

Within a few months after Sarah had gone Mrs. Armstrong got the consent of her husband to pay a visit to her sister and the Church at Nauvoo; he fitted her up in fine style, sending two serving maids to wait on her.

Soon after she left home the friends of Armstrong advised him to stop his slaves at St. Louis, if he wanted to keep them, for his wife would never return to him. Armstrong stopped the slaves, and his wife went on to Nauvoo, where she stayed until the Saints left that place after the death of the Prophet. Elder Smoot had planned to get Mrs. Armstrong to Nauvoo, so he could be sealed to her and get her property. Sarah Gibbons was sealed to Elder Smoot, but Mrs. Armstrong would not consent to take him as her husband; but she lived in the family until she got disgusted with Smoot's treatment of her sister. She loaned him nearly all her money and he never paid it back; he wanted the rest, but she refused to let him have it; he then declined to take her with him across the plains. She told her griefs to my wife Rachel, and Rachel brought about the marriage between her and myself.

Mrs. Armstrong told Rachel that I was the first man on earth to bring the gospel to her, and she had always had a great regard for me, but I appeared to treat her coldly. Rachel told her that I always spoke kindly of her, and the reason I had not been more friendly was because I thought she wanted to become a member of Brother Smoot's family; that she had heard me speak of her in terms of praise many times.

Finally she came to my house and I asked her, in the presence of my wives, to become a member of my family. My wives advised me to be sealed to her, and, as the matter was agreeable all round, I was. Brigham sealed her and the Young girls to me. She was a true, affectionate woman. My whole family respected her. She was forty-eight years of age when she was sealed to me, and remained a true wife until her death.

In matters of this kind I tried to act from principle and not from passion. Yet I do not pretend to say that all such acts were directed by principle, for I know they were not. I am not blind to my own faults. I have been a proud man, and in my younger days I thought I was perfection. In those days, too, I expected perfection in all women. I know now that I was foolish in looking for that in anybody. I have, for slight offenses, turned away good-meaning young women who had been sealed to me; refused to hear their excuses, and sent them away heartbroken.

In this I did wrong. I have regretted the same in sorrow many years. Two of the young women so used still keep warm hearts for me, notwithstanding my conduct toward them. They were young and in the prime of life when I sent them from me. They have since married again, and are the mothers of families. They frequently send letters to comfort me in my troubles and afflictions, but their kind remembrances serve only to add to my self-reproach for my cruel treatment of them in past years. I banished them from me for lesser offenses than I myself had been guilty of.

Should my story ever fall into the hands of Emeline Woolsey or Polly Ann Workman, I wish them to know that, with my last breath, I asked God to pardon me for the wrong I did them, when I drove them from me - poor young girls as they were.

Brigham built a gristmill during the winter, and ground meal for the people, charging a toll for all that the mill ground. In the spring I was ordered to go out and preach, and raise thirty-three wagons with the mules and harness to draw them. I succeeded in getting thirty of the teams. Brigham told me to go again, that he had asked for thirty-three teams, not for thirty. I went again, and preached so that I soon had the other teams. I then turned the whole outfit over to Brigham, so he could send his pioneers to look up a new home for the Saints. I offered to go with the company, but Brigham said:

"I cannot spare you; I can spare others better than you."

Brigham directed me to take my family and a company and go and raise corn for the people. He said:

"I want you to take a company, with your family, and go up the river and open up a farm, and raise grain and vegetables to feed the needy and the soldiers' families. We cannot depend on hauling our substance from Missouri, to feed the many that we have on our hands. I want so much grain raised that all will be supplied next winter, for we must feed our animals grain if we wish to cross the plains next spring. There is an old military fort about eighteen miles above here, where the land was once farmed, and that land is in good condition for farming now. We will leave Father Morley in charge of the various settlements. Brother Heber C. Kimball will send some of his boys and make another farm this side of there." Then turning to Father Morley, he said: "I want John to take charge of the farming interests and the settlement at my place, and you must counsel and advise with him from time to time. I want you and all the brethren to understand that the land nearest the settlement is to be divided between John and his wives, for they are workers. The others are to go further for their land."

At this I said that such an arrangement would not give satisfaction to the people; there were several of his adopted sons already jealous of me, and I feared the consequences, and preferred to have the land divided more equally.

"Who is jealous of you?" he asked.

Then I named several persons to him. In reply he said, naming a man, that he would work all day under the shade of a tree. Another could work all day in a half-bushel. Then he said:

"Such men will do but little; let them go to some outside place for their land. I want those who will work to have the best land. Let each family have an acre near the settlement for a garden and truck patch. And now, Father Morley, I want you to see that John and his family have all the cleared land they can tend, for I know they will raise a good crop, and when it is raised we can all share with him. I want a company to follow Brother John, about the 1st of May, when the grass is good, made up of men that can fit themselves out comfortably. My brother, John Young, will lead them, and Jedde Grant will be their captain." Then he turned to me and said: "Brother John, I want you to fit my brother

John out. If he needs oxen, let him have them, and I will pay them back; see that he gets a good outfit. When he leaves here Father Morley will take charge of the Church. I want the brethren to do as Brother John tells them; he carries a good in- fluence wherever he goes; no evil reports follow him from his field of labor; all respect him, and that is evidence to me that he carries himself straight."

Now, I settled up my business at the winter quarters. Brigham was indebted to the firm two hundred and eighty-five dollars; he had not the money to settle the account, and he was just starting to look out a resting place for the Saints. His first adopted son, Brother Rockwood, our salesman, could not spare a dollar, so the loss of that money fell on me. I told Brigham he was welcome to the two hundred and eighty-five dollars. Before he left for the new land of promise he said to me:

"My son John, what shall I do for you?"

"Select me an inheritance when you find the resting-place," said I.

"I will remember you. May Heaven bless you. I bless you. Be a good boy. Keep an account of how each man under your charge occupies his time, while I am gone."

Brigham then said I was to have half the improvements that were made, and half the crop that was raised by the company I fitted out with teams, seeds, and provisions.

The pioneer company started April 1st, 1847. We moved to our new location, and called it Summer Quarters. We threw up a fort to protect us from the Indians, as they were troublesome. We then laid out our land. I found that if I obeyed orders it would require all the cleared land for my family, so I set off three acres to each family - there were thirty-seven families - for gardens, and took the balance.

Although I had given each family three times as much land, for a garden and truck patch, as Brigham ordered, the people found a great deal of fault with me. Mrs. Armstrong had some money left, and she told me to take it and send for supplies and seed corn. I did take it, and sent four teams to Missouri for corn and provisions, and then set all hands at work building the fort and putting the land in order for the crop.

About the beginning of May thirty-eight warriors of the Oto tribe came to our camp. They were in full paint, and on the warpath. They came in on the yell, and at full speed. It was just daylight; I was laying the foundation of a house when they came to me. I threw logs against them as if I did not see them, but most of the brethren kept out of sight.

The Indians began to build a fire in my garden, and one raised his gun to shoot one of my oxen which the boys were driving up. The majority of the Indians formed a half circle, holding their bows fully strung, and commenced a war dance. We had been told not to shoot Indians, but to take sticks and whale them when they commenced any depredations. As the Indian took the leather casing from his gun so that he could shoot, I rushed them with a heavy club, with the intention of knocking down as many as I could. I could speak their language some, and I told them I would kill them all if they shot my ox. They saw that I meant what I said. Then the two chiefs held out their hands, and yelled to the warrior not to shoot. He lowered his gun and returned to the crowd, but he was very angry. The other Indians seemed amazed, and stood as if paralyzed. Old man Knight followed me with a club, and stood by me all the time. Joseph Busby said:

"Hold on, Brother Lee, they outnumber us."

"For all that," said I, "there are not Indians enough in their nation to make me stand by and see them shoot down my oxen before my eyes."

Busby then ran into the house to load my gun, but he was so frightened he could not get the powder in it, and my wife Rachel loaded it for him. I looked around to see how things were, and saw seven of my wives standing with guns in their hands, ready to shoot if I was attacked. I succeeded in driving the Indians from the settlement.

Some time after the Indians had gone away an old chief returned and brought an ax that he said one of his bucks had stolen. I gave him a little ammunition and bread, and he left me as a friend.

My firm stand saved the settlement at that time and secured it from molestation in the future. The Indians never bothered us at Summer Quarters again. In the fall they made us a friendly visit, and called me a Sioux.

Near our settlement there was an abundance of wild game - deer, turkey, prairie chickens, ducks, geese, brant, and squirrels - which gave us much of our food during our stay. We worked diligently and raised a great crop of corn and vegetables. We built comfortable houses, and made the floors and roofs of basswood, which was plenty near by, and worked easily.

In July the people were all sick. The fever and ague were fairly a contagion. Other diseases were not uncommon. In August and September seventeen of our people died. During these months we had hardly a sufficient number of well people to attend to the sick. The most of my family were very sick. My little son, Heber John, the child of my first wife, Agathe Ann, died; also David Young, Sr., the father of my two wives, Polly and Louisa; also their brother, David Young, Jr. I lay at the point of death for some time. I was in a trance nearly one hour and a half.

While in this condition my wives Rachel and Nancy stood over me like guardian angels, and prayed for me. My spirit left the body and I was taken into another sphere, where I saw myriads of people - many of whom I was acquainted with and had known on earth. The atmosphere that they dwelt in was pure and hallowed. Pain and sorrow were unknown. All was joy and peace. Each spirit was blest with all the pleasure its ability enabled it to comprehend and enjoy. They had full knowledge of earthly doings and also of the sphere where they were so blest. The glory of God shone upon them, the power of Heaven over-shadowed them all, and was to them a shield from temptations and dangers. I was anxious to remain, but the spirits told me I must return to the body and remain in it until my appointed time for death - that my work on earth was not yet finished. I obeyed, but did so with reluctance, and once more entered the body, then apparently lifeless upon the bed of sickness.

After taking possession of the body again I lay some time in deep thought, contemplating the majesty of God's works. I then spoke to my faithful nurses, and told them of what I had done, heard, and witnessed. I recovered from my sickness, but my life was for some time a misery to me. I longed to join that angelic host I had so lately visited in their mansions of glory and pleasure, where I knew I was to go when I escaped from this body of earthly material.

This feeling of anxiety to go to my eternal rest was strengthened by the bitter, malignant actions of men who acted like demons toward me and mine. Every species of intrigue and meanness was resorted to by several of the brethren to injure and torment me. They were jealous of me and anxious to provoke me to violence. Everything that envy and hatred could suggest was tried to break up and scatter my family. Finally they reported to Father Morley that nothing but a change of rulers in the settlement would bring peace.

Father Morley came, with several elders, and called a meeting, at which he heard all the parties state their grievances against me. He then told them they had brought nothing against me that reflected upon me as presiding officer; that I had acted well and for the best interest of the entire people; that all the trouble arose from the wrong acts of the people.

One of the brethren, C. Kennedy, proposed a change. He wanted a High Priest to preside instead of a Seventy. I was tired of my position and consented to the change. A man by the name of Fuller was selected by Kennedy to rule over the people. Father Morley put the question to a vote of the people, and said that all who wished a change of rulers should hold up their hands. Only two hands were raised. Then he said that all who wished me to remain in charge should raise their hands, when every person present but two voted that I should still be the ruler at Summer Quarters.

Father Morley called upon the two brethren who had voted for a change to get up and tell what they had against me. They could give no good reason for wanting a change. They said they had never lived by a better neighbor or kinder man than I was, but that I was too kind. I let the people run over me; and they voted for a change believing it would tend to unite the people and satisfy those who had been raising a fuss and finding fault.

Father Morley told them it was wrong to vote against a good man for such reasons. He talked to the people on the principles of their religion for some time, and advised them to forsake their evil ways, for they were going in a road that led to hell. This ended my troubles for a time, but I soon found that my enemies had only let go their hold to spit on their hands and get a better one.

They asked to be allowed to organize a Danite force for the protection of the settlement. This was to be entirely apart from me. I granted their request. It was next decided to build an estray pound. A meeting was called and it was agreed that each man should build fence in proportion to the amount of stock he owned, and that the public corral should be used for the estray pound. But no stock was to be put into the pound until all the fencing was done and the gates set up. I at once completed my fencing, but the grumblers had no time to work; they were too busy finding fault. The whole thing was a subterfuge, and was meant to bother me. There was no need of a pound, as our cattle were herded in daytime and corralled at night. But I submitted, for I knew I could live by their laws as well as they.

One evening, as my cattle were being driven up for the night, one of the oxen broke through a brush fence and got into a patch of corn. The herdsman ran him out in a moment. Instead of holding the herder responsible for the damage, or coming to me to make a complaint and demand pay for the wrong, they took my ox out of the corral, and, contrary to the vote of the people, tied him up in Wm. Pace's private corral. I was the only man who had made his fence, as ordered by the meeting. I did not know that they had my ox tied up (for work had not been done to justify putting any stock in the pound).

Next morning I sent one of my boys to yoke up my oxen; he returned and informed me that one of my oxen was missing. I soon found the ox, and demanded its release. I was told I must pay twenty dollars before I could have the ox, and pay it in money. I saw this was done to worry me, and sent word that I would pay in any kind of property I had.

They refused everything but money or butter. I had neither to spare, and they well knew it. I was still weak from my recent sickness, but I walked over and had a talk with Wm. Pace and tried to reason with him, but to no purpose. I told him he ought to take pay for damage done by stock in the kind of property that the stock had injured, but no, I must pay money or butter, or lose my ox. I reflected a moment and concluded that forbearance had ceased to be a virtue; that unless I defended my rights I would soon be without anything worth protecting. I then walked into the yard, untied the ox, and told my boy to drive him home. Pace stood by the gate with a large cane, but made no resistance; in fact, he was not a bad man, but was being misled by evil company.

Kennedy, Busby, Dunn, and others were a little way off. They saw me, and came running up. Kennedy was the bully of the camp, and the leader of those against me. He came up and said:

"If I had been here you would not have turned that ox out. I would have switched you if you had tried it."

"Kennedy," I said, "I have lost property enough without your oppressing me any more."

He shoved his fist under my nose. I parried his blow, and told him that he would do well to keep at a proper distance from me. He again made a pass at me. I then threw down my hat and said:

"If you attempt that again you must take what follows."

He came at me the third time, and as he did so I aimed to spoil his face, but he dropped his head as I struck; the blow took effect on his eyebrow, and badly sprained my thumb. We were on a little knoll, full of stumps of small trees that had been cut down. Kennedy caught hold of me and commenced shoving me back.

I knew that my strength would not last long. I did not wish to risk having a tussle among the stumps, so I backed towards the cleared ground. I fastened my left hand in his long black hair to steady myself, and as I reached the flat ground I suddenly leaped back, breaking his hold by tearing my shirt. I then jerked him forward at an angle of forty-five degrees, and planted my fist in his face; stepping back, and drawing him after me, I kept feeding him in the face with my fist, the blood spurting over me.

The crowd saw their bully getting the worst of it, and ran in to help him. Brother Teeples caught me around the arms, to prevent me striking any more. My Rachel, who was standing by, called to her brother, James Woolsey, and he came and took hold of Kennedy and separated us. I was sorry that this fight took place, for I had severely punished the bully, and his face was badly bruised.

This suited the people; I had shown violence, and now they could lay a charge against me that they thought would stand. I was cited to appear before the High Council, and be dealt with according to the rules of the Church, for a breach of the peace and for unchristian conduct.

The whole people were not against me, only a few; but there were enough of them to keep up a constant broil. They began consecrating my property to their own use; killed my cattle, and ate them, and stole everything that was loose. They stole wheat from my graneries, had it ground, and ate it, and bragged about it.

Kennedy, by the evil influences he commanded, induced my young wife, Emeline, to leave me and go to his house, and she went with his family to the winter quarters. That was the reason that I turned her away and refused to take her back. She repented, and wished to come back, but I would not receive her.

Similar influences were brought to bear on all of my family, but without success. Such treatment was not calculated to bind me to such a people, whose only aim appeared to be to deprive me of every comfort and enjoyment that made life endurable. I was in great trouble; in place of friends I had found enemies. There was a struggle in my mind to decide what I should do. I looked upon those of my family that remained true and shared my persecutions, and knew that if I left the Church I could not keep or live with them; that if I left I must part with all but my first wife and her children, and to do so was worse than death. I did not know what to do. I finally appeared before the High Council to meet my accusers, who had formed a combination to destroy me. I had few friends to defend me, and they were in a measure powerless. They dared not speak their mind in my behalf.

Father Morley was true to the last, although he was becoming unpopular on account of having so long supported me. Lieut. Gully was another true friend of mine; he said he would never turn against me until I had done something wrong, even if Brigham should desire him to do so. This lost him his influence in the Council.

The most willful and damnable lies were brought up against me. Many things which had been said and done in moments of amusement and jocularity were remembered, as though I had said and done those things for wicked purposes. Everything that could be discovered or invented to injure me was laid to my charge. All who were against me had a full chance to talk.

Brother Johnson, who was there, but not as a member of the Council, was called upon to fill a vacancy occasioned by the absence of some member. He made a speech to the Council, and showed where I had acted well; he then voted for my acquittal. Brother Cummings, who had been a member of the Council when I was first tried in the summer, and who then took my part, now thought he would make himself popular with the people, so he volunteered his evidence and bore false witness against me. This man's action was wrong and uncharitable. I had been more than a brother to him in the past; I had supplied his family with food when they would have suffered but for the help I gave them.

The result of the trial was that I was ordered to confess I had been in fault; that I was alone to blame, and must ask the people to forgive me. If I refused I was to be cut off from the Church.

To a man in my situation it was equivalent to death to be cut off from the Church; my wives would be taken from me, my property consecrated to the Church, and I turned adrift, broken and disgraced, and liable to suffer death at the hand of any brother Danite who wished to take my life to save my soul. I replied that in justice to myself I could not make such confession, but, if nothing else would do, I would say as the Council commended me to say - that is, I would make the confession. I was told that this would not do; that no whipping of the devil around a stump would do them; my confession must be full and unconditional.

What the result would have been I cannot say, for just then a messenger returned, saying that Brigham was near at hand, on his return with the pioneers who had gone out with him to look for a resting place for the Saints. This stopped proceedings.

The majority of the people rushed forth to meet Brigham. I returned home, conscious of my innocence and willing that the people should have the first show to talk to Brigham and give him their side of the case. I did this so that I might see how much he could be stuffed.

The people told their story and misrepresented me in every way; they told Brigham how I had divided the land, and said that I and Father Morley both declared that he had ordered me and my family to take the cleared land.

Brigham sided against me.

After that there was nothing left undone by many of the people to irritate or injure me or my family.

My property was stolen, my fences broken down, and everything that vile men could imagine or work up by studying deviltry was done to make life a burden to me. I had raised over seven thousand bushels of corn, and everyone had a good crop. I had a large lot filled up in the husk, and I let my cattle run to it so as to keep them fat during the winter, that I might drive them over the plains in the spring. My enemies took advantage of my position, and drove my cattle from my own corn pile and put them into the estray pound. I offered to put all the corn I had into their hands as security, until I could have a meeting called to examine into the charge. I wanted my cows at home, for we needed the milk. I had a large family, and many little children that would suffer without milk. Half the men in the settlement offered to go my security, but to no purpose. I sent Lieut. Gully to Brigham with a statement of the case, but he paid no attention to it. Gully was well acquainted with Brigham, and a fine man too. He insisted on giving Brigham the story in full, and demanded that he should go in person and see to the matter. But Brigham was immovable.

Things stood this way until Emeline, one of Brigham's wives, took the matter to heart, and begged him to look into the affair. She asked him to bring her to my house, to visit her sister Louisa, then one of my wives. He came, but said little of the trouble, and soon left.

Two days afterwards I wrote Brigham a kind letter, and invited him to come to my house and eat a turkey dinner with me. I sent this by Brother Stewart. He met Brigham on his way to my house and gave him my letter. I did not expect he would come to see me, but he was there. He treated me most kindly. When supper time came he said to one of my wives:

"Sister, I have come for a bowl of good milk, but skim the cream off."

"We have no milk," she replied.

"How is that?" said he. "I thought Brother John always had milk." I then told him that the Danites had my cows in the pound.

"What on earth are they doing with your cows?" he asked.

Then I told him the whole story in a few words. He scarcely waited to hear me, but called to his carriage driver, Grant, and said:

"Come, George, I will go and see about this matter."

He soon returned, saying:

"Your cows will presently be here."

Brigham then asked me where my turkey was. I told him Kennedy had robbed me of all my turkeys, but perhaps I could borrow one from him. I then sent Brother Gully to ask Kennedy to loan me a couple of fat turkey's; that I had Brigham at my house and wanted them for his supper. He sent word that Brigham was welcome to all the turkeys he wanted, at his house. I then told Brigham I would go hunting and get him a nice one for dinner the next day. I went out that night with Gully and hunted some time, but the snow was a foot deep or more, and a crust had frozen, so that it was difficult hunting. At last we found a large flock of turkeys at roost in the tall Cottonwood timber. I shot two by starlight; one fell in the river, and we lost it, but the other fell dead at the roots of the tree. This was a large and fat turkey. I considered that it would do, and we returned home with it. We had been gone only a little over an hour.

Brigham stayed at my house. We sat by the fire and talked until midnight. I unbosomed myself to him. I told him of my ill treatment, and asked if I had failed in any respect to perform the duties of the mission he gave me before starting with the pioneers across the plains. I told him of the great crop we had raised; that we had it in abundance to feed the poor and for every purpose; so much, in fact, that there was no sale for it. He said:

"You have done well, and you shall be blessed for it."

To this I replied that I hoped my blessings would be different from those I had been receiving. He replied:

"Jesus has said, In this world you shall have tribulation, but in Me you shall have peace - that is, if you bear these things patiently, without murmuring."

CHAPTER XVIII
THE DANITE AND HIS DUTY

While my mind is running in that direction let me tell of certain of the doings of the Danites. These stories I relate will illustrate the purpose and uses of the Danite in the work of the Mormon Church, and show how the sword of Gideon was wielded in cases smaller than the affair at Mountain Meadows, still to be written down. What follows are instances of thousands of like kind.

In the fall of 1859 two young men on their way to California stopped at the Santa Clara fort to recruit their jaded animals. Expecting that while doing so they might be so fortunate as to meet with a train of people going to the same place, and have company to San Bernardino, the young men stayed at the fort over two months. Hamblin, one of the Danites, assured them that they could go alone through the country with perfect safety. At the same time he had his plans laid to take their lives as soon as they started. This was by direction of the Mormon leaders. The Indians around the fort wanted to kill the men at once, but Hamblin objected, and told the Indians to wait until the men got out in the desert.

At last these young men started from the fort. Hamblin told the Indians that the right time had come, and wanted the Indians to ambush themselves at a point agreed on near the desert, where the men could be safely killed. The Indians obeyed Hamblin's orders, and as the men approached the place of ambush fired upon them, killing one of the men. The other returned the fire, and shot one of Hamblin's pet Indians through the hand; this Indian's name was Queets, which means left-handed. By wounding this Indian he managed to escape, with the loss of the pack animals, provisions, and the riding animal of his partner, who lay dead upon the desert. The survivor stayed with Mr. Judd for a few days, when a company of emigrants came that way, and, departing with them, he succeeded in making his escape from the death that Hamblin still planned for him.

One day, this was in 1857, an emigrant train was passing through the Mormon settlements. Hamblin, the Danite at Santa Clara, made arrangements with Nephi Johnson, who was to act as their guide, how and where to relieve this company of the large herd of stock that belonged to the train. They had a number of horses and cattle, more than five hundred head in all. Several Indian interpreters were sent ahead of the train. One of these was Ira Hatch, a Danite. They were ordered by Hamblin to prepare the Indians for a raid upon the stock.

About 10 o'clock, a. m., just after the train had crossed the Muddy, and was a few miles beyond it on the desert, at the time and place settled on by Hamblin, over one hundred Indians made a dash on the train and drove off all the stock to the Muddy.

The emigrants fired at the Indians, but Nephi Johnson their guide, rushed out and told them that if they valued their own lives they must not fire again, for if they did he could not protect them from the cruelty of the savages - that the Indians would return and massacre them.

The acting of Johnson and the other Danites who were with him was so good that after a consultation the emigrants decided to follow his advice. The conclusion was that, as Johnson was friendly with the Indians, and could talk their language, he should go and see the Indians and try and get the stock back.

The emigrants waited in the desert, and Johnson went to the Indians, or pretended to do so. After a few hours he returned, and reported that the Indians were hostile, and threatened to attack the train at once; that he was afraid he could not prevent it, and the only chance for the emigrants lay in their instant departure; that while the emigrants were gaining a place of safety he would, at the risk of his life, make an effort to keep the Indians back and pacify them. Also that he would report to Hamblin as soon as possible, and raise a force of men at the fort and get back the stock, if it could be done, and write to the company, giving an account of his success. They were to get his letter at San Bernardino, and if he recovered the stock the emigrants could send back a party to receive it and drive it to California.

Under the circumstances the company adopted his plan, and he left them on the desert, with all their stock gone; but the danger was over, for the stock was what Hamblin and Johnson had been working for.

Johnson returned and ordered the Indians to drive the stock to the Clara. The Indians acted like good Mormons, and obeyed orders. Hamblin gave them a few head of cattle for their services in aiding him to capture the drove. The remainder of the cattle and horses Hamblin took charge of for the benefit of the Mission. As the cattle became fat enough for beef, they were sold or butchered for the use of the settlers. Some were traded to nearby settlements for sheep and other articles.

In the winter of 1857-8 John Weston, a Danite, took an Irishman who had been stopping with him as his guest on a hunt, and when he got him to the brush and timber four miles west of Cedar City he cut his throat and left the body unburied. He had received orders to kill the man, because Brother Haight considered him a spy.

Near the same time Philip Klingensmith, a Danite, laid in ambush to kill Robert Keyes (now a resident of Beaver City, Utah Territory), while Keyes was irrigating his field. Klingensmith decided to kill Keyes because Keyes refused to give testimony when requested to do so by Klingensmith, who was then a bishop of the Church. When Keyes came within a few feet of his hiding place Klingensmith raised his gun and took aim at Keyes' heart; but the cap burst without exploding the powder, and Keyes escaped.

After the Mountain Meadows massacre Haight reported that I was the big captain who had planned, led, and executed it; that the honor of such a deed for avenging of the blood of the Prophets would lead to honor, immortality, and eternal life in the Kingdom of God. In this way it became a settled fact that I was the leader in that affair. Year by year the story has gained ground and strength, until I am now held responsible, and am to die, to save the Church.

As I have stated in other places in my writings, the people in Utah who professed the Mormon religion were at and for some time before the Mountain Meadows massacre full of wildfire and zeal, anxious to do something to build up the Kingdom of God on earth and waste the enemies of the Mormon religion. At that time it was a common thing for small bands of people on their way from California to pass through Cedar City. Many of these people were killed. When a Gentile came into a town he was looked upon with suspicion, and most of the people considered every stranger a spy from the United States army. The killing of Gentiles was a means of grace and a virtuous deed. I remember an affair that took place at the old distillery in Cedar City, just before the massacre.

Three men came to Cedar City one evening; they were poor, and much worn by their long journey. They were on their way to California. The authorities believed they were dangerous men; that they were spies from Johnston's army; and ordered the Danites to devise a plan to put them out of the way decently and in order.

That the will of God might be done, these men were coaxed to go to the old distillery and take a drink. They went in company with Danites John M. Higbee, John Weston, James Haslem, and Wm. C. Stewart, and another man, whose name I have forgotten. The party drank considerable, and when the emigrants got under the influence of the whisky the brethren attacked them and knocked the brains out of two with the kingbolt of a wagon. The third man was powerful and muscular; he fought valiantly for his life, but after a struggle he was overcome and killed. They were buried near Cedar City.

Some time in the fall of 1857, not long after the Mountain Meadows massacre, it was decided by the authorities at Salt Lake City that Lieut. Tobin must be killed. Tobin had left a train in Salt Lake, joined the Church there, and afterwards married a daughter of Brother Charles C. Rich, one of the twelve apostles. Tobin was a smart man, and soon after his marriage he was sent to England on a mission.

While preaching in England, it was reported that he had committed adultery, and he was ordered home. On his arrival in Salt Lake he was cut off from the Church, and his wife taken from him by order of Brigham. He made several efforts to get out of the Territory.

Finally he joined a company and left Salt Lake, intending to go to California. After he had been gone a few days the Destroying Angels were put on his trail, with orders to kill him before they returned.

Two desperate Danites were selected, who knew nothing but to obey orders: Joel White and John Willis were the Danites. They started on the trail, determined to kill Tobin when they found him.

White and Willis overtook the company that Tobin was traveling with at a point near the crossing of the Magottsey. They found where he was sleeping, and, going to him as he lay on the ground rolled up in his blanket, they shot him several times. Although thinking him dead, they concluded to shoot him once more to make certain that he would not escape, so they put a pistol against his eye and fired; the ball put out his eye, but did not kill him. The Angels made their escape and returned to Salt Lake City, and reported that their orders were

130

obeyed. Severely wounded as he was, Tobin recovered, and was, when I last heard from him, in the Union army.

At Parowan, in 1855 or 1856, there was a man by the name of Robert Gillespie. He was a member of the Church, had one wife, and owned a fine property. Gillespie wanted to be sealed to his sister-in-law, but for some reason his request was denied. He had known of others obtaining wives by committing adultery and then being sealed to avoid scandal. So he tried it, and went to Apostle Smith, and again asked to be sealed to the woman. But Brother Smith refused to seal him or let him be sealed, giving as his reason for refusing, that Gillespie had exercised the rights of sealing without first obtaining orders to do so. A warrant was issued and Gillespie was arrested and placed under guard; he was also sued in the Probate Court, before James Lewis, Probate Judge, and a heavy judgment rendered against him, and all of his property was sold to pay the fine and costs. The money was put into the Church fund and Gillespie was broken up.

The fate of old man Braffett, of Parowan, was a peculiar one, and, as it afterwards led me into trouble, I will give the story briefly. Old man Braffett lived at Parowan, and in the fall of 1855 a man by the name of Woodward came to Braffett's house and stopped to recruit his teams before crossing the deserts. Woodward had two wives. He had lived in Nauvoo, and while there had been architect for the Nauvoo House. While Woodward and his family were stopping with Braffett, one of his wives concluded that she would be damned if she went to live in California, - leaving the land of the Saints, - and she asked to be divorced from Woodward and sealed to Braffett.

At first Braffett refused to take her, but she was a likely woman. She made love to the old man in earnest. Mrs. Braffett made a fuss about it. The authorities were informed of Braffett's transgressions, and he was arrested and taken before the Probate Judge and tried for the sin. He made a bill of sale of some of his property to me, for which I paid him before his trial.

After hearing the case, the Probate Judge fined him one thousand dollars, and ordered him to be imprisoned until fine and costs were paid. Ezra Curtis, the then marshal at Parowan, took all of Braffett's property that could be found and sold it for the purpose of paying the fine; but the large amount of property which was taken was sold for a small sum, for the brethren will not bid much for property taken from one who has broken his covenants.

Being unable to pay the fine, the old man was ordered to be taken to Salt Lake City, to be imprisoned in the prison there. I was selected to take him to Salt Lake. I took the old man there, and, after many days spent in working with Brigham, I succeeded in securing a pardon for him.

Braffett was put to work at Salt Lake by Brigham. He dared not return home at that time. His property was gone, and he was ruined. The part I took to befriend the old man made several of the brethren at Parowan angry with me, and they swore they would have revenge against me for interfering where I was not interested.

After Braffett's pardon I stayed in Salt Lake some time, and when I started home there were quite a number of people along. All the teams were heavily loaded; the roads were bad, and our teams weak. We all had to walk much of the time. After we had passed the Severe River the road was very bad. My team was the best in the whole company, and I frequently let some of the women who were in the party ride in my wagon.

One evening, just about dark, I was asked by a young woman named Alexander to let her ride, as she was very tired walking. I had her get into the wagon with my wife Rachel, and she rode there until we camped for the night. I got into the wagon after dark and drove the team. We had ridden in this way an hour or so, when Rachel said she was going to ride a while in the next wagon, which was driven by son-in-law Dalton.

Soon after Rachel got out of the wagon a couple of my enemies rode by. I spoke to them, and they rode on. As soon as these men reached the camp they reported that I had been taking privileges with Sister Alexander. I was told to consider myself under arrest, and that when we reached Parowan I would be tried by the Council for violating my covenants. I was surprised and grieved at the charge, for I was innocent, and the young woman was a virtuous woman. As God is soon to judge me, I declare that I never knew of her committing any sin.

When we reached Parowan there was a meeting called by the Priesthood to try me. This Council was composed of the President of that Stake of Zion and his two Counselors, the High Council, and the leading men of Parowan. It was a general meeting of the authorities, Church and civil.

The meeting was held in a chamber that was used for a prayer circle. It was called a circle room, because the people met there to hold prayer in a circle, which was done in this way: All the brethren would kneel in a circle around the room, near enough to each other for their arms to touch, so that the influence would be more powerful.

When the meeting was called to order, all the lights were put out; and I was taken into the darkened room and placed on trial. I could not see my hand before my face. The charge was stated to me and I was ordered to confess my guilt. I told them I was innocent; that I had committed no crime - in fact, had not thought of wrong. I told the truth, just as it was. I was then ordered to stand one side.

The young woman was then brought into the room, and as she came in a pistol was placed to my head and I was told to keep silent. She was questioned and threatened at length, but not all the threats they could use would induce her to tell a falsehood. She insisted that I was entirely innocent.

Next her father, an old man, was introduced and questioned. He told the Council that he had diligently inquired into the matter, and believed I was innocent. Neither the young woman nor her father knew who was in the room. All they knew was that they were being examined before the secret tribunal of Utah, and that a false oath in that place would insure their death.

When the evidence had been received, and the witnesses retired, the candles were again lighted. Then speeches were made by most of the men present, and every one but two spoke in favor of my conviction. Without taking a vote, the meeting adjourned, or rather left that place and went somewhere else to consult. I was left in the dark, the house locked and guards placed around the building. I was told that my fate would soon be decided, and I would then be informed. I knew so well the manner of dealing in such cases that I expected to be killed in the dark, but for some reason it was not done.

Next morning some food was brought to me, but I was still kept a prisoner and refused the liberty of consulting with friends or any of my family. Late that day I looked out of the window of the chamber where I was confined, and saw a man by the name of John Steel. He was first Counselor to the President of that Stake of Zion. I called to him and asked him to secure my freedom. After stating the case to him, he promised to see what could be done for me, and went away.

Through his exertions I was released. I was told to go home and hold myself subject to orders - that my case was not yet decided. I went home, but for months I expected death every day; for it is the usual course of the authorities to send an Angel after men who are charged with or suspected of having violated their covenants.

Nothing further was done about the case, but it was held over me as a means of forcing me to live in accordance with the wishes of the Priesthood and to prevent me from again interfering with the Church authorities when they saw fit to destroy a man, as they destroyed old man Braffett; and it did have the effect of making me more careful.

In 1854 (I think that was the year) there was a young man, a Gentile, working in Parowan. He was quiet and orderly, but was courting some of the girls. He was notified to quit, and let the girls alone, but he still kept going to see them. This was contrary to orders. No Gentile is allowed to keep company with or visit any Mormon girl or woman.

The authorities decided to have the young man killed, so they called two of Bishop Dames' Destroying Angels, Barney Carter and old man Gould, and told them to take that young Gentile "over the rim of the basin." That was a term used by the Danites when they killed a person. The Destroying Angels made some excuse to induce the young man to go with them on an excursion, and when they got close to Shirts' mill, near Harmony, they killed him and left his body in the brush.

The Indians found the body, and reported the facts to me soon afterwards. I was not at home that night, but Carter and Gould went to my house and stayed there all night. Rachel asked them where they had been. They told her they had been on a mission to take a young man, a Gentile, over the rim of the basin, and Carter showed her his sword, which was bloody, and said he used it to help the Gentile over the edge. Rachel knew what they meant when they spoke of sending him "over the rim of the basin." It was at that time a common thing to see Danites going out of Cedar City and Harmony, with suspected Gentiles, to send them "over the rim of the basin," and the Gentiles were always sent.

This practice was supported by the people, and everything of that kind was done by orders from the Council, or by orders from some of the Priesthood. When a Danite or a Destroying Angel was placed on a man's track, that man died, certain, unless some providential act saved him, as in Tobin's case.

The Mormons believe in blood atonement. It is taught by the leaders, and believed by the people, that the Priesthood are inspired and cannot give a wrong order. It is the belief of all that I ever heard talk of these things - and I have been with the Church since the dark days in Jackson County - that the authority that orders is the only responsible party and the Danite who does the killing only an instrument, and commits no wrong. In other words, if Brigham or any of his apostles, or any of the Priesthood, gives an order to a Danite, the act is the act of the one giving the order, and the Danite doing the act only an instrument of the person commanding - just as much an instrument as the knife used to cut the throat of the victim. This being the belief of all good Mormons, it is easily understood why the orders of the Priesthood are so blindly obeyed by the people.

In 1857 there was an emigrant, a Gentile, who worked a number of months for Captain Jacob Huffine, at Parowan. This man wanted his pay; it was not convenient to pay him; he insisted on being paid, but not getting his wages, determined to leave. He started for the settlement at Summit, about seven miles from Parowan. The Indians were sent for and ordered to overtake and kill the man. They did so, and shot him full of arrows. The man called to the Indians and told them he was a Mormon and that they must not kill him. The Indians replied by saying:

"We know you; you are no Mormon, you are a Mericat."

They beat his head with rocks, and cut his throat, and then went back to Parowan and reported what they had done.

Brother Laney had formed the acquaintance of the family of Aden while on a mission to Tennessee, and was saved by Mr. Aden from a mob that threatened his death because he was a Mormon preacher. When Fancher's train reached Parowan, Brother Laney met young Aden and recognized him as the son of the man who had saved his life. Aden told him he was hungry, and that he and his comrades had been unable to purchase supplies from the Mormons ever since they left Salt Lake City.

Brother Laney took young Aden to his house, gave him his supper, and let him sleep there that night. The next day Laney was accused by leading men of being unfaithful to his obligations. They said he had supported the enemies of the Church and given aid and comfort to one whose hands were still red with the blood of the Prophet. A few nights after that the Destroying Angels, doing the bidding of Bishop Dame, were ordered to kill Brother Laney to save him from his sins, he having violated his endowment oath and furnished food to a man who had been declared an outlaw by the Mormon Church.

The Angels were commanded by Barney Carter, a son-in-law of Bishop Dame. The Angels called Laney out of the house, saying that Bishop Dame wished to see him. As Laney passed through the gate into the street he was struck across the back of the head with a club by Barney Carter. His skull was fractured and for many months Laney lay at the point of death, and his mind still shows the effect of the injury he then received, for his brain has never quite settled since. I have frequently talked with Laney. He is still strong in the Mormon faith, and believes that Dame had the right to have him killed.

134

Punishment by death is the penalty for refusing to obey the orders of the Priesthood. About this time the Church was in the throes of a "reformation."

One of the objects of the reformation was to place the Priesthood in possession of every secret act and crime that had been committed by a member of the Church. These secrets were obtained in this way: a meeting would be called; some Church leader would make a speech, defining the duties that the people owed the Priesthood, and instructing the people why it was necessary that the Priesthood should control the acts of the people; it was preached that to keep back any fact from the knowledge of the Priesthood was an unpardonable sin.

After one or more such discourses the people were called upon by name, commanded to rise from their seats, and standing in the midst of the congregation publicly confess their sins. If the confession was not full and complete, it was made the duty of the members of the Church, or any one of them who knew that the party confessing had committed a crime which he or he had not divulged, to then make public the same.

Unless the party then confessed, a charge was preferred against him or her for a violation of covenants, and either full confession and repentance immediately followed, or the sinful member was slain for the remission of sins - it being taught by the leaders, and believed by the people, that the right thing to do when a sinner did not repent and obey the Council, was to take the life of the offending party and thus save his or her everlasting soul. This was called Blood Atonement. The members who fully confessed their sins were again admitted into the Church and rebaptized, taking new covenants to obey any and all orders of the Priesthood and refuse all manner of assistance, friendship, or communication with those who failed of strict obedience to the authorities of the Church. The most deadly sin among the people was adultery, and many men were killed by the Danites for that crime.

Brother Rosmos Anderson was a Danish man who had come to Utah with his family to receive the benefits arising from an association with the Latter-day Saints. He had married a widow lady somewhat older than himself; and she had a daughter who was fully grown. The girl was anxious to be sealed to her stepfather. Anderson was equally anxious to take her for a second wife, but Bishop Klingensmith had set his eye on her, and desired her for himself.

At one of the meetings Anderson and his stepdaughter confessed they had committed adultery, believing that if they did so that Brigham would allow them to marry when he learned the facts. Their confession being full, they were rebaptized and received into full membership. They were then placed under covenant that if they again committed adultery Anderson should suffer death.

Soon after this a charge was laid against Anderson before the Council, accusing him of adultery with his stepdaughter. This Council was composed of Bishop Klingensmith and his two counselors; it was the Bishop's Council. The Council voted that Anderson must die for violating his covenants. Bishop Klingensmith went to Anderson and told him the judgment was that he must die by having his throat cut, so that the running of his blood would atone for his sins.

135

Anderson, being a firm believer in the doctrine of Blood Atonement and the teachings of the Mormon Church, made no protest, but asked half a day to prepare for death. His request was granted. His wife was ordered to prepare a suit of clean clothing, in which to have her husband buried, and informed that he was to be killed for his sins, she being directed to tell those who inquired after her husband that he had gone to California.

Bishop Klingensmith and Danite James Haslem dug a grave in a field near Cedar City, and that night, about twelve o'clock, went to Anderson's house and told him to make ready to obey the Council. Anderson got up, dressed himself, bid his family good- by, and without remonstrance accompanied those he believed were carrying out the will of Almighty God. They went to the place where the grave was prepared, Anderson kneeling by the side of the grave and praying. Bishop Klingensmith then cut Anderson's throat and held him so that his blood ran into the grave.

As soon as he was dead they dressed him in his clean clothes, threw him into the grave and buried him. They then carried his bloody clothing back to his family, and gave them to his wife to wash, when she was again instructed to say that her husband was in California. She obeyed their orders.

No move of that kind was made in Cedar City unless by order of the Council or of the High Council. Anderson was killed just before the Mountain Meadows massacre. The killing of Anderson was a religious duty and a just act. It was justified by the people, for they were bound by the same covenants, and the least word of objection to thus treating the man who had broken his covenant would have brought the same fate upon the person wicked enough to raise his voice against the Church authorities.

Brigham knew that I was not a man who liked to take life. I was well known as one that stood high in the confidence of Brigham, and was close-mouthed and reliable. I knew of many men being killed in Nauvoo by the Danites. It was then the rule that all the enemies of the Prophet Joseph should be killed, and I know of many a man who was quietly put out of the way by the orders of Joseph and his apostles while the Church was there. It has always been a well understood doctrine of the Church that it is right and praiseworthy to kill every person who speaks evil of the Prophet. This doctrine was strictly lived up to in Utah, until the Gentiles arrived in such numbers that it became unsafe to follow the practice; but the doctrine is believed, and no year passes without one or more of those who have spoken evil of Brigham being killed, in a secret manner. Springfield, Utah, was one of the Church hotbeds, and more men were killed there, in proportion to population, than in any other part of Utah. In that settlement it was certain death to say a word against the authorities, high or low.

Brother Warren Snow was bishop of the Church at Manti, San Pete County, Utah. He had several wives, but there was a fair young woman in the town that Snow wanted for a wife. He made love to her with all his powers, went to parties where she was, visited her at her home, and proposed to make her his wife. She thanked him for the honor offered, but told him she was engaged to a young man, a member of the Church, and consequently could not marry the old priest.

136

This was no sufficient reason to Brother Snow. He told her it was the will of God that she should marry him, and she must do so; that the young man could be got rid of - sent on a mission or dealt with in some way so as to release her from her engagement; that, in fact, a promise made to the young man was not binding when she was informed that it was contrary to the wishes of the authorities.

The girl continued obstinate.

The "teachers" of the town visited her and advised her to marry Bishop Snow. Her parents, under the orders of the Counselors of the Bishop, also insisted that their daughter marry the old man.

She still refused.

Then the authorities called on the young man and directed him to give up the girl. This he steadfastly declined to do. He was promised Church preferment, celestial rewards, and everything that could be thought of - all to no purpose. He said he would die before he would surrender his intended wife.

This resistance of authority by the young people made Bishop Snow more anxious than ever to marry the girl. The young man was ordered on a mission to some distant locality. But the mission was refused.

It was then determined that the rebellious young man should be forced by harsh treatment to respect the advice and orders of the Priesthood. His fate was left to Bishop Snow.

It was decided to call a meeting of the people who lived true to counsel, to be held in the schoolhouse in Manti, at which the young man should be present, and dealt with according to Snow's will. The meeting was called. The young man was there, and was again requested to surrender the young woman to Snow, but he refused.

The lights were then put out. An attack was made on the young man. He was tied down with his back to a bench, when Bishop Snow took a bowie knife and slashed and mutilated him. They left the young man weltering in his blood. During the night he succeeded in releasing himself from his confinement, and dragged himself to some haystacks, where he lay until the next day, when he was discovered by friends. The young man has been an idiot or quiet lunatic ever since.

Bishop Snow took soon occasion to get up another meeting at the schoolhouse, so as to have the people of Manti and the young woman that he wanted to marry attend the meeting. When all had assembled the old man talked to the people about their duty to the Church, their obligation to obey counsel and the dangers of refusal; and called attention to the case of the young man. The young woman was sealed to Bishop Snow.

CHAPTER XIX
THE MOUNTAIN MEADOWS

My time I find is getting short. To continue as I have the story of the little details and what befell as we crossed the plains for the promised land of Utah would need more days than I have left me. I will go then direct to the story of the Mountain Meadows troubles for which I am to die, as I desire that the facts as they occurred should be known. As a duty to myself, I purpose to give a statement of all I know in that affair. I did not act alone; I had many to assist me at Mountain Meadows.

Those who were connected with the massacre, and took part in the transaction, were moved by a religious duty. All were acting under the orders and by command of their Church leaders. The immediate orders for the killing of the emigrants came from those in authority at Cedar City. I and those with me moved by virtue of positive orders from Brother Haight and his associates.

Before I started on my mission to the Mountain Meadows I was told by Brother Haight that his orders to me were the result of full consultation with Bishop Dame and all in authority. The massacre was decided on by the head men of the Church.

To approach this subject properly I must step backward several years. After the destruction of Nauvoo, when the Mormons were driven from the State of Illinois, I shared the fate of my brethren, and partook of the hardships and trials that befell them from that day until the time of the settlement of Salt Lake City, in the then wilderness. After reaching Salt Lake I stayed but a short time, when I went to live at Cottonwood, where the mines were afterwards discovered by General Connor and his men during the late war. I was just getting fixed to live there, when I was ordered to go into the interior and aid in forming new settlements and in opening up the country. I had no wish or desire, save to know and do the will of Brigham, since I had become his adopted son. I believed that Brigham spoke by direction of the God of Heaven, and I would have suffered death rather than disobey any request of his.

At the command of Brigham, I took one hundred and twenty-one men, went in a southern direction from Salt Lake City, and laid out and built up Parowan. George A. Smith was the leader and chief man in authority in that settlement. I acted under him as historian and clerk of the Iron County Mission, until January, 1851. I went with Brigham, acted as a committeeman, and located Provo, St. George, Fillmore, Parowan, and other towns, and managed the location of many of the settlements in southern Utah.

In 1852 I moved to Harmony, and built up that settlement. I remained there until the Indians declared war against the whites and drove the settlers into Cedar City and Parowan, for protection, in the year 1853. I removed my then numerous family to Cedar City, where I was appointed Captain of the Danites, and commander of Cedar City.

After I had commanded at Cedar City about one year I was ordered to return to Harmony and build the Harmony Fort. This order, like all other orders, came from Brigham. When I returned to Harmony and commenced building the fort, the orders were given by Brigham for the reorganization of the Danites at Cedar City. The old men were requested to resign and younger men were appointed in their places.

About the 7th of September, 1857, I went to Cedar City from my home in Harmony, by order of Brother Haight. I did not know what he wanted of me, but he had ordered me to visit him, and I obeyed. If I remember correctly, it was on Sunday evening that I went there.

When I got to Cedar City I met Haight on the public square of the town. Haight was then President of that Stake of Zion, and the highest man in the Mormon Priesthood, and next to Bishop Dame in southern Utah, and in the command of the Iron District. The word and command of Haight were the law in Cedar City at that time, and to disobey his orders was death; be they right or wrong, no Saint was to question them; it was obedience or death.

When I met Haight I asked him what he wanted with me. He said he must have a long talk with me on private and particular business. We took blankets and went over to the old Iron Works, and lay there that night, so that we could talk in safety.

After we got to the Iron Works Haight told me about the train of emigrants. He said that the emigrants were a rough and abusive set of men. That they had, while traveling through Utah, been abusive to the Mormons. That they had insulted many of the Mormon women. That the abuses heaped upon the people by the emigrants during their trip from Provo to Cedar City had been constant and shameful; that they had burned fences and destroyed growing crops; that they had poisoned the water, so that all people and stock that drank of the water became sick, and many had died from the effects of the poison. That these vile Gentiles publicly proclaimed that they had the very pistol with which the Prophet Joseph was murdered, and had threatened to kill Brigham and all of the apostles. That, when in Cedar City, they said they would hang Brigham by the neck until he was dead, before snow fell in the Territory. They also said that Johnston was coming with his army from the East, and they were going to return from California with soldiers, as soon as possible, and desolate the land and kill every Mormon man, woman, and child they could find in Utah. That they violated the ordinances of the town of Cedar, and had, by armed force, resisted the officers who tried to arrest them for violating the law. That after leaving Cedar City the emigrants camped in the company, or cooperative field just below Cedar City, and burned the fencing, leaving the crops open to the herds of stock. Also that they had given poisoned meat to the Corn Creek tribe of Indians, which had killed several of them, and that they and their Chief, Konosh, were on the trail of the emigrants, and would soon attack them. These things, and much more of like kind, Haight told me as we lay in the dark at the old Iron Works.

Brother Haight said that unless something was done to prevent it the emigrants would rob every one of the outlying settlements in the south, and that the whole Mormon people were liable to be butchered by the troops the emigrants would bring back with them from California. I was then told that the Council had held a meeting that day, to consider the matter, and it had been decided by the authorities to arm the Indians, give them provisions and ammunition, and send them after the emigrants. The Indians were to give them a brush, and if they killed part or all of them, so much the better.

"Brother Haight, who is your authority?" I said.

"It is the will of all in authority," he replied. "The emigrants have no pass to go through the country, and they are to be killed as common enemies, for the country is at war now. No man has a right to go through this country without a written pass."

We lay and talked much of the night, and during that time Haight gave me instructions as to what to do, and how to proceed in the affair. He said he had consulted with Bishop Dame, and everyone had agreed to let the Indians use up the whole train if they could. Haight then continued:

"I expect you to carry out your orders."

Then I knew I must obey, or die. I had no wish to disobey, for my superiors in the Church are the mouthpieces of Heaven, and it is an act of godliness to obey any and all orders given by them, without asking questions.

My orders were to go home to Harmony and see Carl Shirts, my son- in-law, an Indian interpreter, and send him to the Indians in the south, to notify them that the Mormons and Indians were at war with the "Mericats" (as the Indians called all whites that were not Mormons), and bring the southern Indians up and have them join with those from the north, so their force would be sufficient to make a successful attack on the emigrants.

It was agreed that Haight would send Nephi Johnson, another Indian interpreter, to stir up what other Indians he could find, so that we might have a large enough force to give the emigrants a good hush. In conclusion Haight said to me:

"These are the orders that have been agreed upon by the Council, and it is in accordance with the feelings of the entire people. Some of the Indians are now on the warpath, and all of them must be sent out; all must go, so as to make the thing a success."

It was then intended that the Indians should kill the emigrants, and make it an Indian massacre, and not have any whites interfere with them. No whites were to be known in the matter; it was to be done by the Indians, so that it could be laid to them, if questions were asked. We agreed upon the whole thing, how each should act, and left the Iron Works, and went to Haight's house and got breakfast. After breakfast I made ready to start, and Haight said to me:

"Go, Brother Lee, and see that the instructions of those in authority are obeyed; and as you are dutiful in this, so shall your reward be in the Kingdom of God, for God will bless those who willingly obey counsel, and make all things fit for the people in these last days."

At this time the Mormons were at war with the United States, and the orders to the Mormons were to kill and waste away our enemies, but lose none of our own people These emigrants were from the section of country most hostile to our people, and it was the will of every true Mormon that the enemies of the Church should be killed as fast as possible, and inasmuch as this lot had men among them that had helped kill the Prophets in the Carthage jail, the killing of them would be keeping our oaths and avenging the blood of the Prophets. I will give my talk with Brother George A. Smith.

In the latter part of the month of August, 1857, about ten days before the people of Capt. Fancher, who met their doom at Mountain Meadows, arrived at that place, Gen. George A. Smith called on me at one of my homes in Washington City, Washington County, Utah Territory, and wished me to take him round by Fort Clara, via Pinto Settlements, to Hamilton Fort and Cedar City. He said:

"I have been sent down here by Brigham, to instruct the brethren of the different settlements not to sell any of their grain to our enemies. And to tell them not to feed it to their animals, for it will all be needed by ourselves. I am also to instruct the brethren to prepare for a big fight, for the enemy is coming in force to attempt our destruction. But Johnston's army will not be allowed to approach our settlements from the east. God is on our side, and will fight our battles for us, and deliver our enemies into our hands. Brigham has received revelations from God, giving him the right and the power to call down the curse of God on all our enemies who attempt to invade our Territory. Our greatest danger lies in the people of California - a class of reckless miners who are strangers to God and His righteousness. They are likely to come upon us from the south and destroy the small settlements. But we will try and outwit them before we suffer much damage. The people of the United States who oppose our Church are a mob, from the President down, and as such it is impossible for their armies to prevail against the Saints who have gathered here in the mountains."

Gen. Smith held high rank as a military leader. He was one of the twelve apostles of the Church of Jesus Christ of Latter-day Saints, and an inspired man. His orders were sacred commands, which it was my duty to obey, without question or hesitation.

The day we left Fort Clara, then the headquarters of the Indian missionaries under the presidency of Jacob Hamblin, we stopped to noon at the Clara River. While there the Indians gathered around us in numbers, and were saucy and impudent. Their chiefs asked me where I was going and whom I had with me. I told them that he was a big captain.

"Is he a Mericat captain?"

"No," I said, "he is a Mormon."

The Indians then demanded to know more. They wanted to have a talk. The General told me to tell the Indians that the Mormons were their friends, and that the Americans were their enemies, and the enemies of the Mormons, too; that he wanted the Indians to remain the fast friends of the Mormons, for the Mormons were all friends to the Indians; that the Americans had a large army just east of the mountains, and intended to come over the mountains into Utah and kill all the Mormons and Indians in Utah Territory; that the Indians must get ready and remain ready for war against the Americans, keep friendly with the Mormons and do what the Mormons told them to do - that this was the will of the Great Spirit; that if the Indians were true to the Mormons and helped them against their enemies, the Mormons would keep them from want and sickness and give them guns and ammunition to hunt and kill game with, and also help the Indians against their enemies when they went into war.

This talk pleased the Indians, and they agreed to all that I asked them to do. I saw that Gen. Smith was nervous and fearful of the Indians, notwithstanding their promises of friendship. To relieve him of his anxiety I hitched up and started on our way as soon as I could do so without rousing the suspicions of the Indians. We had ridden along about a mile or so when Gen. Smith said:

"Those are savage fellows. I think they would make it lively for an emigrant train if one should come this way." Then the General fell to a deep study for some time, when he said: "Suppose an emigrant train should come along through this southern country, making threats against our people and bragging of the part they took in killing our Prophets, what do you think the brethren would do with them? Would they be permitted to go their way, or would the brethren pitch into them and give them a good drubbing?" I reflected a few moments, and then said:

"You know the brethren are now under the influence of the late reformation, and red-hot for the gospel. The brethren believe the Government wishes to destroy them. Any train of emigrants that may come through here will be attacked and destroyed. I am particularly sure they will be wiped out if they have been making threats against our people. Unless emigrants have a pass from Brigham, they will never get safely through this country."

My reply pleased him, and he laughed heartily, and then said:

"Do you believe the brethren would make it lively for such a train?"

"Yes, sir," I replied, "I know they will, unless protected by a pass, and I wish to tell you, and you must inform Brigham, that if he wants emigrants to pass without being molested he must send orders to that effect to Bishop Dame or Brother Haight, so that they can give passes to the emigrants; their passes will insure safety, but nothing else will, except the positive orders of Brigham, as the people are bitter against the Gentiles, full of religious zeal, and anxious to avenge the blood of the Prophets."

The only reply he made was to the effect that on his way down from Salt Lake he had had a long talk with Haight on the same subject, and that Haight had assured him, and given him to understand, that emigrants who came along without a pass from Brigham could not escape from the Territory. We then rode along in silence for some distance, when he again turned to me and said:

"Brother Lee, I am satisfied that the brethren are under the holy influence, and I believe they will do just as you say they will with the wicked emigrants that come through the country, making threats and abusing our people."

Thereupon I repeated my views to him, but at much greater length. I went into a statement of the wrongs of our people, and told him that the people were under the blaze of the reformation, full of wildfire, and that to shed the blood of those who would dare speak against the Mormon Church or its leaders would be doing the will of God, and the people would do it as cheerfully as they would any other duty. That the Apostle Paul was not more sincere than was every Mormon who lived in southern Utah. My words served to cheer up the General; he was delighted, and said:

"I am glad to hear so good an account of our people. God will bless them for all they do to build up His Kingdom in the last days."

On my way from Cedar City to my home in Harmony I came up with a band of Indians under Moquetas and Big Bill, two Cedar City chiefs; they were in their paint, and fully equipped for battle. They halted when I came up and said they had had a big talk with Haight, Higbee, and Klingensmith, and got orders from them to follow up the emigrants and kill them all, and take their property as a spoil.

These Indians wanted me to go with them and command their forces. I told them I could not go with them that evening; that I had orders from Haight, the Big Captain, to send other Indians on the warpath to help them kill the emigrants, and must attend to that first; that I wanted them to go where the emigrants were and camp until the other Indians joined them; that I would meet them the next day and lead them. This satisfied them, but they wanted me to send my little Indian boy, Clem, with them. After some time I consented to let Clem go with them, while I returned home.

When I got home I told Carl Shirts what the orders were that Haight had sent to him. Carl being naturally cowardly was not willing to go, but I told him the orders must be obeyed. He started that night, or early next morning, to stir up the Indians of the south, and lead them against the emigrants. The emigrants were then camped at Mountain Meadows.

The Indians did not obey my instructions. They met, several hundred strong, at the Meadows, and attacked the emigrants Tuesday morning, just before daylight, and at the first fire killed seven and wounded sixteen of the emigrants. The latter fought bravely, and repulsed the Indians, killing many of them and breaking the knees of two chiefs, who afterwards died.

The news of the battle was carried over the country by Indian runners, and the excitement was great in all the small settlements. I was notified of what had taken place early Tuesday morning, by an Indian who came to my house and gave me a full account of what had been done.

The Indian said it was the wish of the Indians that I lead them, and I must go back with him to the camp. I started at once, and taking the Indian trail over the mountain I reached the camp by going twelve miles. To go round by the wagon road would have been between forty and fifty miles.

When I reached the camp I found the Indians in a frenzy of excitement. They said they had been told that they could kill the emigrants without danger to themselves, but they had lost numbers of their bucks, and others were wounded, and unless they could kill all the "Mericats," as they called them, they would declare war against the Mormons and kill everyone in the settlements. I did as well as I could under the circumstances. My talk served to increase their excitement. I told them I would go south and meet their friends, and hurry them up to help them.

At first the Indians would not consent, but they finally said I might go and meet their friends. I then got on my horse and left the Meadows and went south. I had traveled about sixteen miles when I met Carl Shirts with one hundred Indians and a number of Mormons from the southern settlements. They were going to the scene of conflict. How they learned of the emigrants being at the Meadows I never knew, but they did know it, and were coming armed, and determined to obey orders.

Among those that I remember to have met there were Brothers Samuel Knight, Oscar Hamblin, William Young, Carl Shirts, Harrison Pearce, James Pearce, John W. Clark, William Slade, Sr., James Matthews, Dudley Leavitt, William Hawley, William Slade, Jr., George W. Adair, and John Hawley.

The Mormons camped that night with me, but most of the Indians rushed on to their friends at the camp on the Meadows. I reported to the brethren what had taken place at the Meadows, but none were surprised in the least. I spent much of the night in prayer. I wrestled with God for wisdom to guide me.

In the morning we agreed to go on to Mountain Meadows and camp there, and then send a messenger to Haight. We knew that the original plan had been for the Indians to do the work, and the Mormons to do nothing beyond plan for and encourage them. Now we saw the Indians could not do the work, and we were in a fix. I did not then know that a messenger had been sent to Brigham for instructions. Haight had not mentioned it to me; James Haslem, a Danite, was sent to Brigham.

We went to the Meadows and camped at the springs, about half a mile from the emigrant camp. There were a larger number of Indian there - fully three hundred, and I think as many as four hundred of them. The two chiefs who had been shot were in a bad way. The Indians had killed a number of the emigrants' horses, and about sixty or seventy head of cattle were lying dead on the Meadows, which the Indians had killed for spite and revenge.

Our company butchered a small beef for dinner, and after eating a hearty meal we held a council and decided to send a messenger to Brother Haight. The messenger started for Cedar City, from our camp on the Meadows, about 2 o'clock, p. m. We stayed on the field, and I tried to quiet and pacify the Indians, by telling them that I had sent to Haight, the Big Captain, for orders, and when he sent his order I would know what to do. This appeared to satisfy the Indians, for said they:

"The Big Captain will send you word to kill the Mericats."

Along toward evening the Indians again attacked the emigrants. This was Wednesday. I heard the report of their guns, and the screams of the women and children in the corral. I ran with Brothers William Young and John Mangum, to where the Indians were. While on the way to them they fired a volley, and three balls from their guns cut my clothing. One ball went through my hat and plowed through my hair. Another ball went through my shirt and leaded my shoulder, another cut my clothes across my bowels. I thought this was rather warm work, but I kept on until I reached the place where the Indians were in force.

CHAPTER XX
THE MUSTER OF THE DANITES

On Thursday, about noon, several Danites joined us from Cedar City. I cannot remember the order in which the brethren came to the Meadows, but I do recollect that at this time and in this company were Brothers Joel White, William C. Stewart, Benjamin Arthur, Alexander Wilden, Charles Hopkins, and James Tate. These men said little, but everyone seemed to know what he was there for. As our messenger had gone for further orders, we moved camp about four hundred yards further up the valley on to a hill, where we made a camp as long as we stayed there.

The emigrants' wagons were corralled after the Indians made the first attack. On the day following our arrival the emigrants drew their wagons closer together and chained the wheels one to the other. While they were doing this there was no shooting going on. Their camp was about one hundred yards above and north of the spring. They generally got water from the spring at night.

Thursday morning I saw two men start from the corral with buckets, and run to the spring and fill them with water, and go back again. The bullets flew around them thick and fast, but they got into their corral in safety.

The Indians made a determined attack on the train on Thursday morning about daylight. At this attack the Clara Indians had one buck killed and three wounded. This so enraged them that they left for home, driving a number of cattle with them. During the day I said to Brother John Mangum:

"I will cross the valley and go up on the other side, on the hills to the west of the corral, and take a look at the situation."

As I was crossing the valley I was observed by the emigrants, and as soon as they saw that I was a white man they ran up a white flag in the middle of their corral or camp. They then sent two little boys from the camp to talk to me, but I could not talk to them at that time, for I did not know what orders Brother Haight would send to me, and until I had his orders I would not know how to act. I hid, to keep away from the children. They came to the place where they had last seen me and hunted all around for me, but being unable to find me they turned and went back to the camp in safety. It is false what has been told about little girls being dressed in white and sent out to me. There was nothing of the kind done. I stayed on the west side of the valley for about two hours, looking down into the emigrant camp.

While I was standing on the hill looking into the corral I saw two men leave the corral and go outside to cut wood; the Indians and Mormons kept up a busy fire all the time, but the two paid no attention to danger, and stuck to their work until they had it done; then they went back to camp. The men acted so bravely that it was impossible to keep from respecting them. After staying there and looking down into the camp awhile I returned to my company.

On Thursday evening Higbee, Chief of the Iron Danites, and Klingensmith, Bishop of Cedar City, came to our camp with two or three wagons and a number of Danites all well armed. I can remember the following as a portion of those who came to take part in the work of death which was so soon to follow, viz.: Brothers John M. Higbee, Chief of the Iron Danites, and also first Counselor to Brother Haight; Philip Klingensmith, Bishop of Cedar City; Ira Allen, of the High Council; Robert Wiley, of the High Council; Richard Harrison, of Pinto, also a member of the High Council; Samuel McMurdy, one of the Counselors of Klingensmith; Charles Hopkins, of the Counselors of Cedar City; Samuel Pollock; Daniel McFarland, a son-in-law of Haight; John Ure, of the City Council; George Hunter, of the City Council; Samuel Jukes; Nephi Johnson, with a number of Indians under his command; Irvin Jacobs; John Jacobs; E. Curtis, a Captain of Ten; Thomas Cartwright, of the City and High councils; William Bateman, who afterwards carried the flag of truce into the emigrant camp; Anthony Stratton; A. Loveridge; Joseph Clews; Jabez Durfey; Columbus Freeman. There were others whose name have slipped me. I know that our total force was fifty-four Danites and three hundred Indians. As soon as these gathered around the camp I demanded of Brother Higbee what orders he had brought. I then told all that had happened at the Meadows, so that every person might understand the situation. Brother Higbee reported as follows:

"It is the orders that the emigrants be put out of the way. President Haight has counseled with Bishop Dame, and has orders from him to put the emigrants to death; none who is old enough to talk is to be spared."

Brother Higbee then said substantially that the emigrants had come through the country as our enemies, and as the enemies of the Church of Jesus Christ of Latter-day Saints. That they had no pass from anyone in authority permitting them to leave the Territory. That none but friends were permitted to leave the Territory, and as these were our sworn enemies they must be killed. That they were nothing but a portion of Johnston's army. That if they were allowed to go on to California they would raise the war cloud in the West and bring destruction upon all the settlements in Utah. That the only safety for the people was in the utter destruction of the whole rascally lot.

The Danites then in Council now knelt down in a prayer circle and prayed, invoking the Spirit of God to direct them how to act in the matter. After prayer Brother Higbee said:

"Here are the orders," and handed me a paper from Haight.

The paper read in substance that we were to decoy the emigrants from their position and kill all that could talk. This order was in writing. Brother Higbee handed it to me and I read it. The orders were that the emigrants should be decoyed from their stronghold, and exterminated, and no one left to tell the tale. Then the authorities could say it was done by Indians. Haight told me the next day that he got his orders from Bishop Dame.

After the Council I retired and bowed in prayer before God. Brother Hopkins, a man in whom I had great confidence, came to me from the Council, saying that he believed it was right, for the brethren and the Priesthood were united in the thing. At the solicitation of Brother Hopkins I returned with him to the Council. When I got back the Council again prayed for aid. The Council formed a prayer circle, and kneeling down, so that elbow touched elbow, the Danites prayed for Divine instructions. After prayer Brother Higbee said:

"I have the evidence of God's approval of our mission. It is God's will that we carry out our instructions to the letter." He then said to me: "Brother Lee, I am ordered by President Haight to inform you that you shall receive a crown of celestial glory for your faithfulness, and your eternal joy shall be complete." I was much shaken by this promise.

The meeting was then addressed by me. I spoke in about this language:

"Brethren, we have been sent to perform a duty. It is a duty that we owe God and our Church and people. The orders are that the emigrants must die. Our leaders speak with inspired tongues, and their words come from the God of Heaven. We have no right to question what they have commanded us to do; it is our duty to obey. On Wednesday night two of the emigrants got out of camp and started back to Cedar City for assistance to withstand the Indian attacks; they had reached Richards' Springs when they met Brothers William C. Stewart, Joel White, and Benjamin Arthur, three of our Danite brethren from Cedar City. The men stated their business to the brethren, and as their horses were drinking at the spring Brothers Stewart, feeling for the glory of God and the upbuilding of the Kingdom of God on earth, shot and killed one of the emigrants, a young man by the name of Aden. When Aden fell from his horse Brother Joel White shot and wounded the other Gentile; but he got away, and returned to his camp and reported that the Mormons were helping the Indians in all they were doing. Now the emigrants will report these facts in California if we let them go. We must kill them all, and our orders are to get them out by stratagem if no other thing can be done to put them in our power."

The plan of action had been agreed upon, and it was this: The emigrants were to be decoyed from their stronghold under a promise of protection. Brother Bateman was to carry a flag of truce and demand a parley, and then I was to go and arrange the terms of surrender. I was to demand that all the children who were so young they could not talk should be put into a wagon, and the wounded were likewise to be put into another. Then the arms and ammunition of the emigrants must be put into a third; I agreeing that the Mormons would protect the emigrants from the Indians and conduct them to Cedar City in safety, where they would be safe until an opportunity came for sending them to California.

It was understood that when I had made the treaty the wagons would start for Hamblin's Ranch with the arms, the wounded, and the children. The women were to march out on foot and follow the wagons in single file; the men were to follow the women, they also to march in single file.

Brother Higbee was to stand with his Danites about two hundred yards from the camp, double file, open order, with about twenty feet space between the files so that the wagons could pass between them. The drivers were to whip along, and not stop. The women were not to stop, but to follow the wagons. The Danites were to halt the men for a few minutes, until the women were some distance ahead and among the cedars, where the Indians were in ambush. Then the march was to be resumed, the troops to form in single file, each Danite to

147

walk by an emigrant, and on the right-hand side of his man, the Danite to carry his gun on his left arm, ready for instant use. The march was to continue until the wagons had passed beyond the ambush of the Indians, and the women were in their midst. Brother Higbee was then to give the order:

"Do Your Duty to God!"

At this the Danites were to shoot down the men; the Indians were to kill the women and larger children, and the drivers of the wagons and I were to kill the wounded and sick men that were in the wagons. Two men were to be placed on horses near by, to overtake and kill any of the emigrants that might escape the first assault. The Indians were to kill the women and large children, as we desired to make certain that no Mormon would be guilty of shedding innocent blood - if it should happen that innocent blood was in the company that were to die. Our leading men all said, however, there was no innocent blood in the whole company.

The Council broke up a little after daylight on Friday morning. All the horses, except two for the men detailed to overtake those who might escape, and one for Brother McFarland to ride, so that he could carry orders from one part of the field to another, were turned out on the range. Then breakfast was eaten, and the brethren prepared for the work in hand.

The Mormons were then at war with the United States, and we believed all Gentiles should be killed as a war measure, to the end that the Mormons, as God's chosen people, hold and inhabit the earth and rule and govern the globe.

Soon after breakfast Brother Higbee ordered the two Indian interpreters, Carl Shirts, and Nephi Johnson to inform the Indians of the plan of operations, and place them in ambush, so that they could not be seen by the emigrants until the work of judgment should commence. This was done in order to make the emigrants believe that we had sent the Indians away. The orders were obeyed, and in five minutes not an Indian could be seen on the Meadows. They secreted themselves and lay still as logs of wood, until the order was given them to rush out and kill the women.

Brother Higbee called the people to order and directed me to explain the plan to them. I did so, explaining how every person was expected to act during the whole performance. Brother Higbee then gave the order for his men to advance. They marched to the spot agreed upon, and halted there. Brother William Bateman was then selected to carry a flag of truce to the emigrants and demand their surrender; I was to go and make the treaty after someone had replied to our flag of truce. The emigrants had kept a white flag flying in their camp ever since they saw me cross the valley.

Brother Bateman took a white flag and started for the emigrant camp. When he got about halfway to the corral he was met by one of the emigrants. The two talked some time, but I never knew what was said between them.

Brother Bateman returned to the command and said that the emigrants would accept our terms, and surrender as we required them to do. I then started for the corral to negotiate the treaty and superintend the business. I was to make certain and get the arms and ammunition into the wagons. Also to put the children and the sick and wounded in the wagons, as agreed upon in Council. Brother Higbee said to me:

"Brother Lee, we expect you to faithfully carry out the instructions that have been given you by our Council."

Two Danites, Samuel McMurdy and Samuel Knight, were then ordered to take their teams and follow me into the corral to haul off the children and arms. The troops formed in two lines, as had been planned, and were standing in that way, with arms at rest, when I left them. I walked ahead of the wagons to the corral. When I reached it I met Mr. Hamilton, one of the emigrant leaders on the outside of their camp.

CHAPTER XXI
THE BLOOD FEAST OF THE DANITES

It was then noon, or a little after. I found the emigrants strongly fortified; their wagons were chained to each other in a circle. In the center was a rifle-pit, large enough to hold the entire company. This had served to shield them from the constant fire which had been poured into them from both sides of the valley and a rocky range that served as a breastwork for their assailants.

The valley at this point is not more than five hundred yards wide, and the emigrants had their camp near the center of the valley. On the east and west there is a low range of rugged, rocky mountains; it afforded a splendid place for the protection of the Indians and Danites, leaving them in comparative safety while they fired upon the emigrants. The valley at this place runs nearly due north and south.

When I entered the corral I found the emigrants engaged in burying two men of note among them, who had died but a short time before from the effect of wounds received from the Indians at the time of the first attack on Tuesday morning. They wrapped the bodies in buffalo robes, and buried them in a grave inside the corral. I was told by some of the men that seven men had been killed and seventeen wounded in the first attack made by the Indians, and that three of the wounded men had since died, making ten of their number killed during the siege.

As I entered the fortifications men, women, and children gathered around me in wild consternation. Some felt that the time of their happy deliverance had come, while others, though in deep distress, and all in tears, looked upon me with doubt, distrust, and terror. I told the people they must put their arms into the wagon, so as not to arouse the animosity of the Indians. I ordered the children and wounded, some clothing, and the arms to be put into the wagons. Their guns were mostly Kentucky rifles of the muzzle-loading style. Their ammunition was about all gone - I do not think there were twenty rounds left in their whole camp. If the emigrants had had a good supply of ammunition they never would have surrendered, and I do not think we could have captured them without great loss, for they were brave men, very resolute and determined.

Just as the wagons were loaded Brother McFarland came riding into the corral and said that Brother Higbee had ordered haste to be made, as he was afraid the Indians would return and renew the attack before he could get the emigrants to a place of safety. I hurried the people, and started the wagons off towards Cedar City. As we went out of the corral I ordered the wagons to turn to the left, so as to leave the Danites on the right.

Brother McFarland rode before the women and led them out to the Danites, where they still stood in open order as I had left them. The women and larger children were walking ahead, as directed, the men following them. The foremost man was about fifty yards behind the last woman.

The women and children were hurried on by the Danites. When the men came up they cheered the Danites. Brother Higbee then gave orders for his men to form in single file and take each his place at the right hand of an emigrant. I saw that much, then our wagons passed out of sight of the troops, over the hill.

It was my duty, with the two drivers, to kill the sick and wounded who were in the wagons, and do so when we heard the guns. I was walking between the wagons; the horses were going at a fast walk, and we were fully a half mile from Brother Higbee and his men when we heard the firing. As we heard the guns I ordered a halt and we proceeded to do our part. I here pause and ask myself the question: Am I not a traitor to my people, to my friends and comrades who were with me on that holy day when the work of the Church was carried on in God's name?

Heretofore I have said that the small children were put into the wagons; that was wrong, for one little child, about six months old, was carried in its father's arms. It was killed by the same bullet that entered its father's breast. It was shot through the head. I was told by Brother Haight afterwards that the child was killed by accident. I saw it lying dead when I returned to the place of judgment.

When we had got out of sight, as I said before, and just as we were coming into the main road, I heard a volley of guns at the place where I knew the Danites and emigrants to be. Our teams were then going at a brisk walk. I first heard one gun; then a volley followed.

Brothers McMurdy and Knight stopped their teams at once, for they were to help kill the sick and wounded who were in the wagons, and do it as soon as they heard the guns of the Danites. Brother McMurdy was in front; his wagon was mostly loaded with the arms and small children. Brothers McMurdy and Knight got out of their wagons; each one had a rifle. Brother McMurdy went up to Brother Knight's wagon, where the sick and wounded were, and raising his rifle to his shoulder, said:

"O Lord, my God, receive their spirits; it is for Thy Kingdom I do this."

He then shot a man who was lying with his head on another man's breast; the ball killed both men.

150

Then I went up to the wagon to do my part of the killing. I drew my pistol and cocked it, but it went off prematurely, and shot Brother McMurdy across the thigh, my pistol ball cutting his buckskin trousers. Brother McMurdy turned to me and said:

"Brother Lee, keep cool. Keep cool, there is no reason for being excited."

Brother Knight then shot a man with his rifle; he shot the man in the head. He also brained a boy that was about fourteen years old. The boy came running up to our wagons, and Brother Knight struck him on the head with the butt end of his gun and crushed his skull.

By this time many Indians had reached our wagons, and the rest of the sick and wounded were killed almost instantly. I saw an Indian from Cedar City, called Joe, run up to the wagon and catch a man by the hair, raise his head up and look into his face; the man shut his eyes, and Joe shot him in the head. The Indians then examined the wounded in the wagons, and all of the bodies, to see if any were alive, and any that showed signs of life was shot through the head.

Just after the wounded were killed I saw a girl, some ten or eleven years old, running towards us from the place where the Danites had attacked the main body of emigrants; she was covered with blood. An Indian shot her before she got within sixty yards of us.

After all were dead I ordered Brother Knight to drive one side and throw out the dead bodies. He did so, and threw them out of his wagon at a place about one hundred yards from the road, and then came back to where I was standing. I then told Brothers Knight and McMurdy to take the children that were saved alive (sixteen was the number), and drive to Hamblin's ranch. They did as I ordered them to do.

Before the wagons started Nephi Johnson came up in company with the Indians that were under his command, and Carl Shirts I think came up too. I then considered Carl Shirts a coward, and afterwards made him suffer for being a coward. Several Danites joined me, but I cannot tell their names, as I have forgotten who they were.

After the wagons with the children had started for Hamblin's ranch, I turned and walked back to where the brethren were. While returning to the brethren I passed the bodies of several women. In one place I saw six or seven bodies near each other; they were stripped naked. I walked along the line where the emigrants had been killed, and saw many bodies dead and naked on the field. I saw ten children; they had been killed close to each other; they were from ten to sixteen years of age. The bodies of the women and children were scattered about the ground for quite a distance. Then I came to where the men were killed. I do not know how many were killed, but I thought then that there were fifteen women, ten children, and forty men killed, but the statement of others with whom I have since talked about the massacre makes me believe there were fully one hundred and ten justified that day on the Mountain Meadows. The ten who had died in the corral, and young Aden killed by Brother Stewart at Richards' Springs, would make the total number one hundred and twenty-one.

When I reached the place where the dead men lay, I was told how the orders had been obeyed. Brother Higbee said:

151

"The boys have acted admirably; they took good aim; and all of the Gentiles but three fell at the first fire."

Brother Higbee said that three or four got away some distance, but the men on horses soon overtook them and cut their throats. He said the Indians did their part of the work well, that it did not take over a minute to finish up when they got fairly started. Three of the emigrants did get away, but the Indians were put on their trail and overtook and killed them before they reached the settlements in California. I found Brothers Higbee, Klingensmith, and most of the brethren standing where the largest number of the dead men lay. Brother Higbee said:

"We must now examine the bodies for valuables."

The bodies were searched by Brothers Higbee, Klingensmith, and Stewart. The search resulted in a little money and a few watches, but there was not much money.

After the dead were searched the brethren were called up, and Brothers Higbee and Klingensmith, as well as myself, made speeches, and ordered the Danites to keep the matter a secret from the entire world. They were not to tell their wives, or most intimate friends, and we pledged ourselves to keep everything relating to the affair hidden during life. We also took the most binding oaths to stand by each other, and to always insist that the massacre was committed by Indians alone. This was the advice of Brigham.

The men were ordered to camp on the field for that night, but Brothers Higbee and Klingensmith went with me to Hamblin's ranch, where we got something to eat, and stayed all night. I was nearly dead for rest and sleep, as I had rested but little since the Saturday night before. I took my saddle blanket and spread it on the ground after I had eaten my supper, and, using my saddle for a pillow, slept soundly until next morning. I was awakened by loud talking between Brother Haight and Bishop Dame.

They were much excited, and were quarreling with each other. I arose at once, but was unable to hear what they were quarreling about, for they cooled down as they saw that others were paying attention to them. I soon learned that Bishop Dame, Judge Lewis of Parowan, and Brother Haight, with several others, had arrived at the Hamblin ranch in the night, but I do not know what time they got there.

After breakfast we went back in a body to the Meadows, to hide the dead and take care of the property that was left there. When we reached the Meadows we rode up to that part of the field where the women were lying dead. The bodies of men, women, and children had been stripped naked. Knowing that Brothers Dame and Haight had quarreled at Hamblin's that morning, I wanted to know how they would act in sight of the dead. I was interested to know what Bishop Dame had to say, so I held close to them, without appearing to be watching them.

Bishop Dame was silent for some time. He looked over the field, and was quite pale, and looked uneasy and frightened. I thought then that he was just finding out the difference between giving and executing orders for wholesale killing. He spoke to Brother Haight, and said:

"I must report this matter to the authorities."

"How will you report it?" asked Brother Haight.

"I will report it as it is."

"Yes, I suppose so, and implicate yourself with the rest?" said Brother Haight.

"No," replied Bishop Dame. "I will not implicate myself, for I had nothing to do with it."

"That will not do," said Brother Haight, "for you know better. You ordered it done, and I will not be lied on."

Bishop Dame was much excited; he knew Brother Haight to be a man of determination, and one who would not stand any foolishness. As soon as Bishop Dame could collect himself, he said:

"I did not think there were so many of them!"

At this I felt that it was time for me to chip in, so I said:

"Brethren, what is the trouble between you? It will not do for our chief men to disagree."

Brother Haight stepped to my side, a little in front of me, and facing Bishop Dame. He was very angry, and said:

"The trouble is just this: Bishop Dame counseled the thing, and now he wants to back out. He cannot do it. He must not try to do it. He has got to stand to what he did, like a man."

Bishop Dame was cowed; he did not make any denial again, but said:

"Isaac, I did not know there were so many of them."

"That makes no difference," said Brother Haight.

It was now time to stop the fuss, for many of the young Danites were coming around. So I said:

"Brethren, this is no place to discuss such a matter. You will agree when you get where you can be quiet, and talk it over."

"There is no more to say; he has got to stand by it," said Brother Haight.

We went along the field, and passed by where the brethren were at work covering up the bodies. They piled the dead bodies in heaps, and threw dirt over them. The bodies were only lightly covered, for the ground was hard, and the brethren did not have proper tools to dig with. I suppose the first rain washed the bodies out again, but I never went back to examine whether it did or not.

We went along the field to where the corral and camp had been, and the wagons were standing. We found that the Indians had carried off the wagon covers, clothing, and provisions, and had emptied the feathers out of the feather-beds, and carried off all the ticks.

After the dead were covered up or buried (it was not much of a burial) the brethren were called together, and a Council was held at the emigrant camp. All the leading men made speeches; Bishop Dame, President Haight, Bishop Klingensmith, Brothers Higbee, Hopkins, and myself. The speeches were first: Thanks to God for delivering our enemies into our hands; next, thanking the brethren for their zeal in God's cause; and lastly, the necessity of saying that the Indians did it alone, and the Mormons had nothing to do with it.

153

Most of the speeches were in the shape of exhortations and commands to keep the whole matter secret from everyone but Brigham. It was voted unanimously that any Danite who should divulge the secret, or tell who were present, or do anything that might lead to discovery, should suffer death. The brethren all took a solemn oath, binding themselves under the most dreadful and awful penalties, to keep the whole a secret from every human being, as long as they should live. No man was to know the facts. The brethren were sworn not to talk of it among themselves, and each was to kill any who proved a traitor to the Church or to the people in this matter.

It was agreed that Brigham should be informed of the business by someone selected by the Church Council, after the brethren had returned home. It was also voted to turn all the property over to Klingensmith, as bishop of the Church at Cedar City, and he was to take care of the property for the benefit of the Church, until Brigham gave further orders what to do with it. Bishop Dame then blest the brethren and we prepared to go to our homes. I took my little Indian boy, Clem, up on the horse behind me, and started home. I crossed the mountains and returned the same way I had come.

When I got within two miles of Harmony I overtook a body of about forty Indians, on their way home from the massacre. They had a large amount of bloody clothing, and were driving several head of cattle that they had taken from the emigrants. The Indians were glad to see me, and said I was their captain, and that they were going to Harmony with me as my men.

It was the orders from the Church authorities to do everything we could to pacify the Indians and make them the fast friends of the Mormons, so I concluded to humor them. I started on and they marched after me until we reached the fort at Harmony. We went into the fort and marched round inside, after which they halted and gave their whoop of victory, which means much the same with them as cheers do with the whites. I then ordered the Indians fed; my family gave them bread and melons, which they ate, and then they left me and went to their tribe.

From that day to this it has been the understanding with all concerned in that massacre that the man who divulged the secret should die; he was to be killed, wherever found, for treason to the brethren who killed the emigrants, and for his treason to the Church. No man was at liberty to tell his wife, or anyone else; nor were the brethren permitted to talk of it even among themselves. Such were the orders and instructions from Brigham down to the lowest in authority. The orders to lay it to the Indians were just as positive. This was the counsel of all in authority, and for years it was faithfully observed.

The children that were saved were taken to Cedar City and other settlements and put out among different families. I did not have anything to do with the property captured from the emigrants, or the cattle, until three months after the massacre, and then I took charge of the cattle, being ordered to do so by Brigham. There were eighteen wagons in all at the emigrant camp. They were wooden axles but one, and that was a light iron axle; it had been hauled by four mules. There were over five hundred head of cattle, but I never got the half of them. The Indians killed a number at the time of the massacre, and drove

154

others to their tribes when they went home from Mountain Meadows. Bishop Klingensmith put the Church brand on fifty head or more of the best of the cattle.

The Indians got about twenty head of horses and mules. Brother Samuel Knight got a large sorrel mare; Brother Haight got a span of average American mules; Brother Joel White got a fine mare; Brother Higbee got a good large mule; Bishop Klingensmith got a span of mules. Brothers Haight, Higbee, and Allen each took a wagon. The people took what they wanted, and had divided and used up over half the property before I was put in charge.

The first time I heard that a messenger had been sent to Brigham for instructions as to what should be done with the emigrants was three or four days after I returned home from the Meadows. Then I heard of it from Brother Haight, when he came to my house and had a talk with me. He said:

"We are all in a muddle. Brother Haslem has returned from Salt Lake City, with orders from Brigham to let the emigrants pass in safety." In this conversation Brother Haight also said: "I sent an order to Brother Higbee to save the emigrants, after I had sent the orders for killing them all, but for some reason the message did not reach him. I understand that the messenger did not go to the Meadows at all." I at once saw that we were in a bad fix, and I asked Brother Haight what was to be done.

Brother Haight told me it was the orders of the Council that I should go to Salt Lake City and lay the matter before Brigham. I asked if he was not going to write a report of it, as he was the right man to do it; for he was in supreme command of the Danites in that section of the country, and next to Bishop Dame in command of the district. He refused to write a report, saying:

"You can report it better than I could write it. You are like a member of Brigham's family, and can talk to him privately and confidentially. Do this, Brother Lee, and you shall receive a celestial reward for it, and the time will come when all who acted with us will be glad for the part they have taken, for the time is near at hand when the Saints are to enjoy the riches of the earth. And all who deny the faith and doctrines of the Church of Jesus Christ of Latter-day Saints shall be slain - the sword of vengeance shall shed their blood; their wealth shall be given as a spoil to our people."

CHAPTER XXII
THE DANITE CHIEF REPORTS TO BRIGHAM

Accordingly, I went to Salt Lake City to report. I started about a week or ten days after the massacre, and was on the way about ten days. When I arrived in the city I went to Brigham's house and gave him a full, detailed statement of the whole affair. He asked me if I had brought a letter from Brother Haight, with his report of the affair. I said:

"No, Brother Haight wished me to make a verbal report of it, as I was an eye-witness. Brother McMurdy, Brother Knight, and myself killed the wounded men in the wagons, with the assistance of the Indians. We killed six wounded men."

Brigham asked me many questions, and I told him every particular - everything I knew. I described everything very fully. Brigham then said:

"Isaac [referring to Haight] has sent me word that if they had killed every man, woman, and child in the outfit there would not have been a drop of innocent blood shed by the brethren; for they were a set of murderers, robbers, and thieves."

While I was talking with him some men came into his house to see him, and he requested me to keep quiet until they left. I did as he directed. As soon as the men went out I continued my recital. I gave him the names of every man that had been present at the massacre. I told him who killed various ones. In fact, I gave him all the information there was to give. When I had finished talking, he said:

"This is the most unfortunate affair that ever befell the Church. I am afraid of treachery among the brethren that were there. If anyone tells this thing so that it becomes public, it will work us great injury. I want you to understand now, that you are never to tell this again, not even to Heber C. Kimball. It must be kept a secret among ourselves. When you get home I want you to sit down and write a long letter, and give me an account of the affair, charging it to the Indians. You sign the letter as Farmer to the Indians, and direct it to me as Indian Agent. I can make use of such a letter to keep off damaging and troublesome inquiries." He then said: "If only men had been killed, I would not have cared so much. I suppose the men were a bad set, but it is hard to kill women and children for the sins of the men. I must have time to reflect upon it."

Brigham then told me to withdraw and call next day, and he would give me an answer. I said to him:

"Brother Brigham, the people all felt, and I know that I believed, I was obeying orders, and acting for the good of the Church, and in strict conformity with the oaths that we have taken to avenge the blood of the Prophets. You must either sustain the Danites in what they have done, or release us from the oaths and obligations we have taken." The only reply he made was:

156

"Go now; come in the morning, and I will give you an answer." I went to see him again in the morning. When I went in he seemed quite cheerful. He said:

"I have made that matter a subject of prayer. I went right to God with it. I have evidence from God that He has ruled it all for good, and the action was a righteous one. The brethren acted from pure motives. The only trouble is they acted prematurely; they were a little ahead of time. I sustain you and the brethren in what was done. All I fear is treachery on the part of someone who took a hand with you, but we will look to that."

Then I was again cautioned and commanded to keep the whole thing a sacred secret, and again told to write the report as Indian Farmer, laying the blame on the Indians. That ended our interview, and I left him and started for my home at Harmony. When I reported my interview to Brother Haight, and give him Brig- ham's answer, he was well pleased; he said I had done well. I remember a circumstance that Brother Haight then related about Brother Dan McFarland. He said:

"Dan will make a great warrior."

"Why do you think so?"

"Well," returned he, "Dan came to me and said, 'You must get me another knife, because the one I have has no good stuff in it, for the edge turned when I cut a fellow's throat at the Meadows. I caught one of the devils that was trying to get away, and when I cut his throat it took all the edge off my knife.' I tell you that boy will make a warrior."

Next I wrote the letter to Brigham and laid the massacre to the Indians. It was as follows:

Harmony, Washington Co., U. T., November 20th, 1857. To His Excellency, Gov. B. Young:

Dear Sir: My report under date May 11th, 1857, relative to the Indians over whom I have charge as farmer, showed a friendly relation between them and the whites, which doubtless would have continued to increase had not the white men been the first agressors, as was the case with Capt. Fancher's company of emigrants, passing through to California about the middle of September last. When they were on Corn Creek, fifteen miles south of Fillimore City, Millard County, the company poisoned the meat of an ox, which they gave the Pah Vant Indians to eat, causing four of them to die immediately, besides poisoning a number more. The company also poisoned the water where they encamped, killing the cattle of the settlers. This unguided policy, planned in wickedness by this company, raised the wrath of the Indians, which soon spread through the southern tribes, firing them for revenge till blood ran in their path, and as the wrong, according to their tradition, was a national one, any portion of the white nation was liable to atone for that offense. About the 22d of September, Capt. Fancher and company fell victims to the Indians, near Mountain Meadows; their cattle and horses were shot down in every direction, their wagons and property mostly committed to the flames. Had they been the only ones that suffered we would have less cause of complaint. But the next company passing through had many of their men shot down near Beaver City, and had it not been for the interposition of the citizens at that place the whole company would

157

have been mas- sacred by the enraged Pah Vants. From this place they were protected by military force, by order of Bishop Dame, who also provided the company with interpreters, to help them through to the Los Vaagus. On the Muddy some three to five hundred Indians again attacked the company, and drove off several hundred head of cattle, telling the company that if they fired a single gun they would kill every soul. The interpreters tried to regain the stock, or a portion of it, by presents, but in vain. The Indians told them to mind their own business, or their lives would not be safe. Since that occurrence no company has been able to pass without carrying along some of our interpreters to explain matters to the Indians.

Friendly feelings yet remain between the natives and settlers and I have no hesitancy in saying that it will increase so long as we treat them kindly, and deal honestly with them. I have been blest in my labors the last year. Much grain has been raised for the Indians. I herewith furnish you the account of Bishop Dame, of Parowan, for cattle, wagons, etc.

Furnished for the benefit of the Chief Owanup (ss.),
for Two yoke of oxen, $100 each, one wagon and chain $75.
Total...$275.00
Two cows $30 each, for labor $80............................140.00
___
$415.00
P. K. Smith, Cedar City, Iron County:
For two yoke cattle $100 each, and Mo. 2 Weekses Band.....$200.00
One cow $35, do one wagon $80, total......................115.00
___
Total...$315.00
Jacob Hamblin's account for the benefit of Talse Gobbeth Band,
Santa Clara, Washington Co. (ss.): Two yoke of cattle,
$100 each, do one wagon, two chains, $100, total..........$300.00
Two cows $35 each, total...................................70.00
___
Total...$370.00
Henry Barney's account for the benefit of Tennquiches Band,
Harmony (ss.): For two yoke cattle $100....................$200.00
Do one wagon $100, do one plow $40, total..................140.00
Do four cows at $35 each, total............................140.00
For labor in helping to secure crops, etc..................40.00
___
Total...$520.00
For my services the last six months, and for provisions,
clothing, etc........... $600.00
___
Sum total..$2,220.00

From the above report you will see that the wants of the natives have increased with their experience and practice in the art of agriculture. With sentiments of high consideration.

I am your humble servant,

John Doyle Lee, Gov. B. Young. Farmer to Pah Utes Indians.

Having signed, I forwarded that letter, and thought I had managed the affair nicely. I put in this expense account of two thousand two hundred and twenty dollars just to show off, and help Brigham to something from the Government. It was the way his Indian farmers all did. I never gave the Indians one of the articles named in the letter. No one of the men mentioned had furnished anything to the Indians, but I did it this way for safety. Brigham never spent a dollar on the Indians while he was Indian Agent. The only money he ever spent on the Indians was when we were at war with them. Then they cost us some money, but not much.

Brigham, knowing that I wrote this letter solely for the protection of the brethren, used it in making up his report to the Government. I obeyed his orders in this, as I did at the Mountain Meadows. I acted conscientiously, and have nothing to blame myself for.

The following winter I was a delegate to the Constitutional Convention that met in Salt Lake City to form a constitution preparatory to the application of Utah for admission into the Union. I attended during the entire session, and was often in company with Brigham at his house and elsewhere, and he treated me with kindness and consideration.

At the close of the session of the Convention I was directed by Brigham to assume charge of the cattle and other property captured from the emigrants, and take care of it for the Indians. When I got home I gathered up about two hundred head of cattle and put my brand on them, and gave them to the Indians as they needed them, or rather when they demanded them. I did that until all of the emigrant cattle were gone.

The taking care of that property was unfortunate, for afterward when the Indians wanted beef they thought they owned everything with my brand on. So much so, that I quit branding my stock. I preferred leaving them unbranded, for everything with my brand on would be taken by the Indians. I know it has been reported that the emigrants were very rich. That is a mistake. Their only wealth was in cattle and teams. The people were comfortably dressed in Kentucky jeans and lindsey, but they had no fine clothing that I ever saw. They had but few watches.

While in Cedar City Brigham preached one night. In his sermon, when speaking of the Mountain Meadows Massacre, he said:

"Do you know who those people were that were killed on the Mountain Meadows? I will tell you who those people were. They were fathers, mothers, brothers, sisters, uncles, aunts, cousins, and children of those who killed the Saints and drove them from Missouri, and afterwards murdered our Prophets in Carthage jail. And yet after all this, I am told there are some of the brethren who are willing to swear against those who were engaged in that affair. I hope there is no truth in this report. I hope there is no such person here, under the sound of

159

my voice. But if there is, I will tell him my opinion of him, and the fact so far as his fate is concerned. Unless he repent at once of that unholy intention, and keep the secret, he will die a dog's death, and go to hell. I must not hear of any treachery among my people."

These words of Brigham gave great comfort. They insured our safety and took away our fears.

CHAPTER XXIII
LEE NEARS THE END

Many people think that Brigham cut me off from the Church and refused to recognize me following the massacre. I will relate a circumstance that took place ten years after the facts were known by him.

In 1867 or 1868 I met Brigham and suite at Parowan, seventy miles from Washington, the place where a part of my family resided. Brother James Pace was with me. The Prophet said that he wanted uncle Jim Pace to go with me and prepare dinner for him, and to go by my herd and take several fat kids along and have a good dinner for him by the time he got there.

Brigham's will was our pleasure. We rode night and day, and felt thankful that we were worthy the honor of serving the prophet of the Living God. The time designated for dinner was one o'clock. The company arrived at eleven o'clock, two hours ahead of time. The Prophet drove to Bishop Covington's house, in the block where I lived; he halted about five minutes there, instead of driving direct to my house according to previous arrangement. Then he turned his carriage around and got out with Amelia, his beloved, and went into the Bishop's house, leaving his suite standing in the street. Brigham felt his dignity trampled on because I was not present to the minute to receive him with an escort, and welcome and do homage to him upon entering the town.

As soon as I learned of his arrival I hastened to make apologies. The Prophet heard my excuses, and said that his family and brethren, all except himself and Amelia, could go to my house to dinner; that he would not eat until about two o'clock. He then whispered to me and said:

"Cut me a chunk off the breast of the turkey, and a piece off the loin of one of the fat kids, and put some rich gravy over it, and I will eat it at 2 p. m."

At two o'clock I again made his will my pleasure, and carried his dinner to him as requested, when he did me the honor of eating it. The rest of the company went to my house and took dinner. Among my guests that day were Bishop Hunter, Brothers John Taylor, W. Woodruff, several of the Prophet's sons and daughters, and many others.

At dinner Brother Smith and others of the twelve apostles laughed about the anger of Brigham, and said that if the Old Boss had not got miffed they would have lost the pleasure of eating the fat turkey. The party enjoyed themselves that day, and had many a laugh over the Prophet's anger robbing him of an excellent dinner.

At that time part of my family was at Washington, but I also had quite a family living at Harmony, where several of my wives were staying. The next morning the Prophet asked me if I was going to Harmony that night. I told him that I did intend going.

"I wish you would go," said he, "and prepare dinner for us."

Brigham then gave me full instructions as to what to prepare for dinner, and how he wanted his meat cooked, and said the company would be at my house in Harmony the next day at 1 o'clock, p. m. I at once proceeded to obey his instructions. I rode to Harmony through a rain storm, and I confess I was proud of my position. I esteemed it a great honor to have the privilege of entertaining the prophet of the Lord.

My entire family in Harmony were up all night, cooking and making ready to feed and serve the Lord's anointed and his followers. I killed beeves, sheep, goats, turkeys, geese, ducks, and chickens, all of which were prepared according to instructions, and eaten by Brigham and his party next day.

Prompt to time, the Prophet and his suite and an escort on horseback came into the Fort. There were seventy-three carriages, besides the Danite escort. I entertained the entire party, giving them dinner, supper, and breakfast.

In 1858 Brigham called upon me to locate a company of cotton growers, of which Brother Joseph Ham was captain. This company was sent out by Brigham and the leading men of Salt Lake City, to test the growing of cotton on the Santa Clara and Rio Virgin bottoms. In obedience to counsel, I located the company at the mouth of the Santa Clara River, about four miles south of where St. George now stands.

In 1859 or 1860, the first trip that Brigham took from Salt Lake City to southern Utah, he went by way of Pinto, Mountain Meadows, Santa Clara, and Washington. I was at Washington, building a gristmill, some two miles west of the town, when he came along. I was sitting on a rock about thirty steps from the road. His carriage was in the lead, as was usual with him when traveling. When he came opposite where I was sitting he halted and called me to his carriage, and bid me get in. I did so. He seemed glad to see me, and asked where I lived. I told him I lived in the same block with Bishop Covington, and that he would pass my door in going to the Bishop's. I then thought he would put up with the Bishop, and not with a private person.

In crossing the creek, on the way into town, the sand was heavy. I was about to jump out and walk. He objected, saying:

"Sit still. You are of more value than horseflesh yet."

When we neared my residence, he said:

"Is this where you live, John?"

"It is. That is where the Bishop lives." The old man made no reply, but continued on. Then he said:

"You have a nice place here. I have a notion to stop with you."

"You are always welcome to my house," I replied.

161

Then he said to the company, which consisted, I think, of seventy-three carriages:

"Some of you had better scatter round among the brethren."

About half the company did so. The rest, with the Prophet, stayed at my house. The next day the whole company went on to Tokerville, twenty miles from my residence. I went with them to that place. In the evening all went to St. George, and held a two days' meeting. At the close of the meeting the Prophet called me to the stand, and said:

"John, I will be in New Harmony on Wednesday next. I want you to notify the Saints, and have a bowery built, and prepare for my reception."

Brother Imday was President of that place, and was at the meeting. I traveled all night, and reported the orders of the Prophet to the people. Great preparations were made for his reception. A committee of arrangements was appointed, with a committee to wait on his Honor. Also an escort of fifteen Danites was selected to accompany this committee. They went out fifteen miles, where they met the Prophet and his followers and made a report of our proceedings. He thanked them, and said:

"I am going to stop with Brother John D.," as he often called me. "John, I am going to stop with you."

"You know you are always welcome," I said. Brigham drove to the center of the town and halted; then he said:

"John, where do you live?" I pointed across the field about half a mile.

It being his will, we went to my house, sixteen carriages going with us. Quite a number of Brigham's company had gone by Kanab, to Cedar City, to hold meetings in what settlements they would pass through. The arrangements of the committee were treated with indifference by Brigham and his party. All the company but one carriage went to my house; that one stopped at Brother James Pace's. During their stay at my house all were friendly. Brigham asked me to go with them to Cedar City, which I did.

In 1870, some time in the fall, I went from Parowan by way of Panguich, up the Severe River with Brigham, on a trip to the Pareah country. On this trip I was appointed a road commissioner, with ten men to go ahead, view out and prepare the road for Brigham and his company to travel over. While at Upper Kanab I had a private interview with him, concerning my future. Brigham said he thought I had met with opposition and hardships enough to entitle me to have rest the balance of my life; that I had best leave Harmony, and settle in some good place farther south; build up a home and gather strength around me. After a while we would cross over into Arizona Territory, near the San Francisco Mountains, and there establish the order of Enoch, or United Order. We were to take a portable steam sawmill and cut lumber with which to build up the southern settlements, and I was to run the mill in connection with Bishop Stewart. This I consider an additional honor shown me by the Prophet.

From Upper Kanab I was sent across the mountains to Lower Kanab, to Bishop Stewart's, to have him carry supplies for the Prophet and company. I had to travel sixty miles without a trail, but I was glad of a chance to perform any duty that would please the Prophet. I again met the company, and went with the party to Tokerville, where I closed arrangements with Brigham about the sawmill. All was understood and agreed upon, and we parted in a very friendly manner. About two weeks after leaving Brigham and party at Tokerville, I was notified that I had been suspended from the Church because of the Mountain Meadows affair.

The following spring I visited the Prophet at St. George, and asked him why they had thus dealt with me, without allowing me a chance to speak for myself; why they had waited seventeen years and then cut me off; why I was not cut off at once, if what I had done was evil?

"I never knew the facts until lately," he said.

"Brother Brigham, you know I told the whole story to you a short time after it happened."

The reply he made was this:

"Be a man, and not a baby. I am your friend, and not your enemy. You shall have a rehearing. Go up to the office and see Brother Erastus Snow, and arrange the time for the hearing."

We arranged the time of meeting. It was agreed that all parties interested were to be notified of the meeting, and required to be in St. George on the following Wednesday, at 2 p. m. All parties agreed to this, and after talking over the whole thing I again parted with Brigham in a very friendly manner. I went to Washington and stayed with my family there. The next morning I started for Harmony, to visit my family at that place, and make arrangements for the rehearing that was to me of the greatest consequence. I then considered that if I was cut off from the Church I might better be dead; that out of the Church I could find no joys worth living for.

Soon after I left Washington Erastus Snow, one of the twelve apostles, arrived at my house and asked for me. My family told him I had gone to Harmony to arrange for the new hearing and trial before the Church authorities. He appeared to be much disappointed at not meeting me, and told my family that Brigham had reconsidered the matter, and there would be no rehearing or investigation; that the order cutting me off from the Church would stand; that he would send a letter to me which would explain the matter, and the letter would reach Harmony about as soon as I did. On the next Tuesday night an anonymous letter was left at my house by one of the sons of Erastus Snow, with orders to hand it to me. The letter read as follows:

John Doyle Lee, of Washington:

Dear Sir: If you consult your own interest, and that of those that would be your friends, you will not press an investigation at this time, as it will only serve to implicate ones who would otherwise be your friends, and cause them to suffer with, or inform upon you. Our advice is to make yourself scarce, and keep out of the way.

There was no signature, but I knew it came from Apostle Snow, written by orders of Brigham. When I read the letter I saw that I had nothing to hope from the Church, and my grief was as great as I could bear. To add to my troubles, Brigham sent word to my wives that they were divorced from me and could leave me, if they wished to do so. This was the hardest blow I ever

163

received in my life, for I loved my wives. As the result of Brigham's advice eleven of my wives deserted me, and have never lived with me since that time.

Afterwards I was arrested (on or about the 9th of November, 1874) and taken to Fort Cameron, in Beaver County, Utah Territory, and placed in prison there. A few days after my arrest I was visited in prison by Brothers George A. Smith, Orson Hyde, Erastus Snow, A. F. McDonald, and many other leaders of the Church. They each and all told me to stand to my integrity, and all would come right in the end.

At this time the Prophet was stopping with Bishop Murdock, in Beaver City. My wife Rachel went under cloud of night to see him and have a talk about my case. He received her with kindness, saying:

"Sister Rachel, are you standing by Brother John?"

"Yes, sir, I am," was her reply.

"That is right," said he. "God bless you for it. Tell Brother John to stand to his integrity to the end, and not a hair of his head shall be harmed."

What is there more? I wait within the reach of death. There is no help for the widow's son. Still, all is for the best.

Camp Cameron, March 23rd, 1877.

Morning clear, still and pleasant. The guard, George Tracy, informs me that Col. Nelson and Judge Howard have gone. Since my confinement here I have reflected much over my sentence, and as the time of my execution has come, I feel composed. I hope to meet the bullets with manly courage. I declare my innocence. I have done nothing wrong. I have a reward in Heaven, and my conscience does not accuse me. This to me is a consolation. I place more value upon it than I would upon an eulogy without merit. If my work be finished on earth, I ask God in Heaven, in the name of His Son Jesus Christ, to receive my spirit, and allow me to meet my loved ones who have gone behind the veil. The bride of my youth and her faithful mother; my devoted friend and companion, N. A.; my dearly beloved children, with whom I parted in sorrow, but shall meet in joy - I bid you farewell. Be true to each other. Live faithful before God, that we may meet in the mansions that God has prepared for His servants. Remember the last words of your most true friend on earth, and let them sink into your aching hearts. I leave my blessing with you. Farewell. John Doyle Lee

APPENDIX I
BLOOD ATONEMENT

As exhibiting the Mormon position on the doctrine of "Blood Atonement," the following extracts are taken from the sermons and preachings of the Prophet Brigham Young:

"I could refer you to plenty of instances where men have been righteously slain in order to atone for their sins."

"Now, when you hear my brethren telling about cutting people off from the earth, that you consider is strong doctrine; but it is to save them, not to destroy them."

"All mankind love themselves; and let these principles be known by an individual, and he would be glad to have his blood shed. That would be loving themselves even unto eternal exaltation."

"This is loving our neighbor as ourselves; if he needs help, help him; if he wishes salvation, and it is necessary to spill his blood upon the ground in order that he be saved, spill it."

"Any of you who understand the principles of eternity - if you have sinned a sin requiring the shedding of blood, except the sin unto death - would not be satisfied or rest until your blood should be spilled, that you might gain the salvation you desire. This is the way to love mankind."

"It is true the blood of the Son of God was shed for sins through the fall and those committed by men, yet ye men can commit sins which it can never remit. As it was in the ancient days, so it is in our day; and though the principles are taught publicly from this stand, still the people do not understand them; yet the law is precisely the same."

"I have known a great many men who have left this Church, for whom there is no chance whatever of exaltation; but if their blood had been spilled, it would have been better for them. The wickedness and ignorance of the nations forbid this principle being in full force, but the time will come when the law of God will be in full force."

"Will you love your brothers and sisters likewise, when they have committed a sin that cannot be atoned for without the shedding of their blood? Will you love that man or woman well enough to shed their blood? That is what Jesus Christ meant. He never told a man to love his enemies in their wickedness. He never intended any such thing."

"I have known scores and hundreds of people for whom there would have been a chance in the last resurrection if their lives had been taken and their blood spilled upon the ground as a smoking incense to the Almighty, but who are now angels to the devil, until our elder brother, Jesus Christ, raises them up, and conquers death, hell, and the grave."

"There are sins that can be atoned for by an offering upon an altar, as in ancient days; and there are sins that the blood of a lamb, of a calf, or of turtle doves cannot remit, but they must be atoned for by the blood of the man. That is the reason why men talk to you as they do from this stand; they understand the doctrine, and throw out a few words about it. You have been taught that doctrine, but you do not understand it."

"Now, take a person in this congregation, who has a knowledge of being saved in the kingdom of our God and our Father, and being an exalted one, - who knows and understands the principles of eternal life, and sees the beauty and excellency of the eternities before him, compared with the vain and foolish things of the world; and suppose he is overtaken with a gross fault - that he has committed a fault which he knows will deprive him of that exaltation which he desires; and that he cannot attain to it without the shedding of his blood; and

165

also knows that by having his blood shed, he will atone for that sin and be saved, and be exalted with the gods, is there a man or woman in this house but what would say, 'Shed my blood, that I may be saved and exalted with the gods'?"

APPENDIX II
THE STORY OF LEE'S ARREST

United States Marshal's Office, Beaver City, Utah, April 1st, 1877.

My Dear Sir: As requested, I send you the facts of the arrest of John Doyle Lee, from the time the warrants were placed in my hands until I arrested him and brought him to Beaver City. I tell it in my own way, and you can use it as you see proper.

About the 1st of October, 1874, warrants were placed in my hands for the arrest of Lee, Haight, Higbee, Stewart, Wilden, Adair, Klingensmith, and Jukes (the warrant for the arrest of Dame not being placed in my hands at that time). I received instructions from General George R. Maxwell, United States Marshal for the District of Utah, that Lee was the most important one of all those indicted, and that he wanted him arrested first, if possible, but that it was a dangerous undertaking, for he was satisfied by what he could learn that Lee would never be taken alive. He wanted me to take him alive, if possible, but not at too great a risk; that he did not want to give me any plan of operations or particular instructions how to act, as he believed I knew more about that kind of business than he did, and that he did not wish to give any officer under him any plans when he was sure, as he was in this case, that it would be laying a plan to have one of his own officers killed. I took the case in hand, thinking at that time that I would have to go to Lee's place on the Colorado River. I was arranging for that trip.

On the 28th day of October, 1874, I started south from Beaver City, to summon jurors for the November term of the District Court for the Second Judicial District of Utah Territory, to be held at Beaver City. I also intended to procure a guide, if I could do so, and go to the Colorado River to make the arrest. When I reached Parowan I learned that it was currently reported that Lee had come from the Colorado River, and was then in the southern counties of Utah. He was supposed to be at Harmony, because it was known that he had some accounts due him there, which he was then probably collecting, in the shape of provisions, to take back with him to the river. I at once started again, on my way south, determined to arrest him at Harmony, and to do so alone, for I did not know where reliable aid could be had. I considered there was no time to lose, and that I was taking no more chances in attempting the arrest alone than I would be taking if I found him at the Colorado River, at his stronghold, even if backed by a strong force.

166

On my way I met Thomas Winn. I told him what I was intending to do. I told him I was going to arrest Lee. Winn said he considered it madness, as it was reported that several of Lee's sons were with him, and all armed. He volunteered to go with me and take even chances.

We finally decided that he should go to Iron City and get help, as there were then several men there that we could depend on. He was to get these men and be at Harmony by daylight on the morning of the 30th of October. I was to go to Harmony and get there soon after dark the night of the 29th of October, and make the arrest, if I thought I could do so and get away in safety under the cover of night. If not, I was to find out where he was, and wait for assistance.

When I got to Hamilton's Fort, eight miles south of Cedar City, I learned that Lee had left Harmony and gone back to the Colorado River, by the way of Toquerville, and was then several days ahead of me. I then sent a boy out on the Iron City road to stop Winn and send him back. I proceeded on my way and summoned my jurors. I could hear nothing of Lee in the southern country. On my way back I stopped at Thomas Winn's house, and got him to go over on the Severe River, to see if Lee had not gone by the way of Panguitch, and stopped there to lay in more supplies.

Winn started on the 5th day of November, and took Franklin R. Fish with him. They pretended to be looking for stock. They were to report to me at Parowan, on the night of the 7th of November. I returned to Beaver City, and made my returns.

On the morning of November 7th I started for Parowan to meet my men, Winn and Fish. That same day Brigham Young went from Beaver to Parowan. He passed me near the Buck Horn Springs. I have no doubt but that he thought I was there to assassinate him, for he had four of his best fighting Danites with him as a guard. They were armed with Henry rifles, and as they came up to me the Danites rode between me and their beloved Prophet's carriage; but they had no reason for alarm. Brigham Young was not the man that I was after at that time. I met Winn and Fish at Red Creek. As they were coming out of Little Creek Canyon Winn remarked:

"Your man is there!"

As the men had found that Lee had made everything ready for a start, we rode on to Parowan, where I arranged my plan of action. Fish was to go back over the mountains to Panguitch that night, with instructions to come out and meet us, in case Lee should start away from Panguitch. I was to start back toward Beaver City until I had passed Red Creek settlement, and then go up Little Creek Canyon. The others, Thomas Winn, Thomas LaFever, Samuel G. Rodgers and David Evans, were to go into the mountains in different places, and all to meet near Thompson's Mill on Little Creek. We followed this plan, and met at the mill. We then went over the mountains towards Panguitch.

The snow on the way would average fully two feet in depth, and the night was very cold. We stopped at a place about three miles from Panguitch for the night. I sent David Evans into Panguitch to see Fish, and find out if all was right. Long before daylight we saddled our horses and started on, for the night was bitter cold. We had no blankets with us, and dared not build a fire, for fear it would alarm Lee and notify him that we were there. We reached the place where Evans was to meet us sometime before daylight; he was not there. We waited until after the sun was up, but still Evans did not come. Then thinking that my plans had been found out in some way, and that my two men, Fish and Evans, were captured, and more than likely Blood Atoned, I concluded to act quickly and effectually.

We mounted our horses and dashed into the town at full speed. We found Evans, and learned that Fish had not been able to locate Lee, but knew that he was in town. I then ordered my men to go to different parts of the town, and keep a good lookout, and not to let any wagon go out of town until they had searched the wagon. I inquired of the citizens about Lee, but could learn nothing from them about him. Some said they never knew him, others that they never heard of such a man, had not even heard the name.

The citizens soon came crowding around in disagreeable numbers. I saw I must resort to strategy, or I and my friends were in danger; so in order to disperse the crowd, I took out my book and pencil and took down the names of those around me. I then summoned them to assist me in finding and arresting Lee. They each and all had some excuse, but I refused to excuse any of them and ordered them to go and get their arms and come back and aid me. This worked well, for in less than five minutes there was not a Mormon to be seen on the streets of Panguitch. About this time I rode near Thomas Winn, when he said:

"I believe I have Lee spotted. I asked a little boy where Lee's wife lived, and he showed me the house."

This was something to work on. I rode around to the house that Winn pointed out to me. As I turned the street corner I saw a woman looking into a log pen, and when she saw me she turned back towards the house, then turned and walked back to the pen, and appeared to be talking to someone in the pen. She seemed to be very much excited. I rode by the house and around the lot, and while doing so I saw a little girl go out and look into the pen for a little while; she then took up a handful of straw and went back into the house. I, like Winn, was then satisfied that Lee was in that pen. I then told Winn to keep the place in sight, but not appear to be watching it, while I was getting ready to search for Lee. I soon afterwards met Samuel Lee. I took down his name and ordered him to assist me in searching for and arresting John D. Lee.

"John D. Lee is my father, sir," said he.

At that I told him it made no difference to me if he was his grandmother, that I was going to search the house and wanted him with me. He said he was going down to the threshing machine to see his brother Al, and started off. I drew my revolver and told him to stop. He walked right along, looking back over his shoulder at me all the time. I then spurred my horse and went in front of him. He said:

"You can shoot and be hanged. I am not heeled, but I am going down to see my brother Al."

While we were talking, Alma Lee came up and asked what was up. Sam said:

"This is the officer come to arrest father."

168

"Is that all! I thought there was a dog fight."

He then took Sam one side and talked to him for a time. Sam soon came back and said he was ready to go with me. I then dismounted and had Winn do the same. I first went into the house, where I found several women. I searched the house thoroughly, but found no one in it that I wanted. I then said to Sam:

"We will go over to the other house."

"All right, come on," said Sam, and started out ahead of me.

When I got into the yard I stopped, saying:

"Hold on; here is a corral out here, let us examine that."

At this Sam came to a standstill, and was very much excited. I was then certain that my man was there. I had to urge Sam considerably to get him to go up to the corral with me. Henry Darrow, one of Lee's sons-in-law, followed us. I took a circle around the corral, and then walked up to the log pen. This pen was about seven feet wide, nine feet long, and four feet high in the clear. There was a hole close to the ground, just about large enough for a man to crawl through. I first went to this hole and looked through into the pen, but I could see nothing but some loose straw in the back end of the pen. I then discovered a little hole between the top logs, near the back end, where the straw covering was off. I went to this hole and put my eye down to it, and then I saw one side of Lee's face, as he lay on his right side; his face was partly covered with loose straw. I waited a few seconds, until Winn came near enough for him to hear me without my speaking over a whisper. I then said:

"There is someone in that pen."

"I guess not," said Darrow.

"I am certain there is a person in there."

"Well, if there is, it is likely one of the children," said Darrow.

By this time Winn was in position and holding his Henry rifle ready for instant use. Winn and myself were alone. All my other men were in other parts of the town. Just then I saw Fish coming. I then said:

"Lee, come out and surrender yourself. I have come to arrest you."

He did not move. I looked around to see if any of my men were coming. I saw Fish sitting on his horse in front of the door, his gun in his hand. I motioned my hand for him to come to me, but he remained still and kept watch of the house, as if he was going to shoot, or expected danger from that quarter. His action surprised me, for he was a brave man, and quick to obey orders. I then looked at the house to see what was attracting his attention, and I soon saw there was enough there to claim his full time. I saw two guns pointed through the logs of the side of the house and aimed directly at me, and Fish was watching the people who held those guns. That looked like business. I instantly drew two pistols from my overcoat pocket, taking one in each hand. I put one pistol through the crack in the roof of the pen, with the muzzle within eighteen inches of Lee's head. I then said to Winn:

"You go in there and disarm Lee, and I promise you that if a single straw moves, I will blow his head off, for my pistol is not a foot from his head."

Winn was going into the pen. Darrow then commenced to beg me not to shoot. Lee also spoke and said:

"Hold on, boys, don't shoot, I will come out."

He then commenced to turn over to get out of the pen, at the same time putting his pistol (which he had all the time held in his hand and lying across his breast) into the scabbard. I said to Winn:

"Stand back and look out, for there is danger from the house."

Darrow continued to beg us not to shoot. I told Darrow that I would not hurt a hair of Lee's head if he surrendered peaceably, but that I was not going to die like a dog, nor would I permit Lee to get away alive. Lee came out of the pen, and after straightening up, he asked very coolly:

"Well, boys, what do you want of me?"

"I have a warrant for your arrest, and must take you to Beaver with me," I said,

Lee then asked me to show him the pistol that I put through the pen and pointed at his head. He said:

"It was the queerest-looking pistol that I ever saw. It looked like a man's hand with the fingers cut off short."

It was a dragoon pistol, with the barrel cut off short. He laughed when he saw it, and was not at all excited. We then went to the house. The women seemed wild, some of them crying and all unreasonable in their language. Lee told his family to be quiet, and did all that he could to pacify them. I sent and bought some wine, and took a pitcher of the liquid into the house to the women. They all took a drink. When I got to one of his daughters, who was crying bitterly, she took the glass and said:

"Here is hoping that father will get away from you."

"Drink hearty, miss," I said.

By the time all the family had taken a drink a large number of people had gathered around the house. I think fully one hundred and fifty Mormons were there. I turned to one of my men and told him to find some place where we could get something to eat. Lee heard me, and apologized for not thinking to ask us to have something to eat before that time.

"But," said he, "the women folks have been making so much fuss that I have thought of nothing."

Lee then ordered breakfast for us all. His sons gathered around him and told him that if he did not want to go to Beaver, to say so, and they would see that he didn't go. Lee then took me one side and told me what his friends proposed, and wanted to know what answer he should give them. I thought he did this to see if there was any chance to frighten me. I told him to tell the boys to turn themselves loose; that I knew I had no friends in that place, except those who came with me, but we were well armed, and when trouble commenced we would shoot those nearest to us, and make sure of them, and then keep it lively while we lasted. Lee said he did not want anything of that kind to happen, and would see that the boys behaved themselves.

We started from Panguitch soon after breakfast. We put two of our animals in the team, making a four-horse team. Darrow drove. Lee and Rachel, one of his wives, and two of my men rode in the wagon. It was about 11 a. m., on Monday, the 7th day of November, 1874, when we left Panguitch with Lee as a prisoner. We reached Fremont Springs that night at 11 o'clock, and camped there until daylight. The roads were so bad that we had been twelve hours in making thirty miles. The night was dark and cold, and having no blankets with us we could not sleep.

We left Fremont Springs at daylight, and reached Beaver about 10 o'clock, a. m., November 10th, 1874. We had been twenty-four hours without food. Lee and Rachel had fared better, for they had a lunch with them. When we reached Beaver the people were thunderstruck to know that Lee had been arrested. After the arrest Lee was in my custody the greater portion of the time that he was in prison. He never gave any trouble to me or his guards. He never tried to escape, but at all times assisted the guards to carry out the instructions received from the officers.

I remain your most obedient servant,
William Stokes.

APPENDIX III
DEATH OF JOHN DOYLE LEE

John Doyle Lee was executed on Mountain Meadows, Washington County, Utah Territory, at the scene of the massacre, on the 23d day of March, 1877. On Wednesday preceding the day fixed upon for the execution the guard having Lee in charge started from Beaver City, where Lee had been imprisoned, for Mountain Meadows, where it had been decided to carry the sentence into execution. The authorities had received information that an attempt to rescue Lee would be made by his sons, and precautions were taken to prevent the success of any such attempt. The place of execution was kept a secret, and a strong guard procured. Lee was cheerful and seemed to have but little dread of death.

The party reached Mountain Meadows about 10 o'clock Friday morning, and after the camp had been arranged Lee pointed out the various places of interest connected with the massacre, and recapitulated the horrors of that event. A more dreary scene than the present appearance of Mountain Meadows cannot be imagined. The curse of God has fallen upon it and scorched and withered the luxuriant grass and herbage that covered the ground twenty years ago. The Meadows have been transformed from a fertile valley into an arid and barren plain, and the Mormons assert that the ghosts of the murdered emigrants meet nightly at the scene of their slaughter and re-enact in pantomime the horrors of their taking off.

As the party came to a halt at the scene of the massacre sentinels were posted on the surrounding hills, to prevent a surprise, and preparations for the execution were at once begun. The wagons were placed in a line near the monument, and over the wheels of one of them army blankets were drawn to serve as a screen or ambush for the firing party. The purpose of this

171

concealment was to prevent the men composing the firing party from being seen by anyone, there being a reasonable fear that some of Lee's relatives or friends might hereafter wreak vengeance upon his executioners. The rough pine boards for the coffin were next unloaded from a wagon, and the carpenters began to nail them together. Meanwhile Lee sat some distance away.

At 10.35, the arrangements having been completed, Marshal Nelson read the sentence of the Court, and at its conclusion turned to Lee and said:

"Mr. Lee, if you have anything to say before the sentence of the Court is carried into effect, you may now do so."

"I wish to speak to that man," said Lee, pointing to the photographer, who was adjusting his camera near by. "Come over here," said Lee, beckoning with his hand.

"In a moment, Mr. Lee," replied Mr. Fennemore.

"I want to ask a favor of you," said Lee. "I want you to furnish my three faithful wives each a copy," meaning the photograph about to be taken. "Send them to Rachel A., Sarah C., and Emma B." Lee then repeated the names of his three wives carefully, saying to the artist, who had approached him: "Please forward them - you will do this?"

Mr. Fennemore responded affirmatively.

Lee then seemed to pose himself involuntarily, and the picture was taken. He then arose from his coffin, where he had been seated, and, looking calmly at the soldiers and spectators, said in an even tone of voice:

"I am on the brink of eternity; the solemnities of eternity rest upon my mind. I have made out - or have endeavored to do so - a manuscript, abridging the history of my life. This is to be published. In it I have given my views and feelings with regard to these things. I feel resigned to my fate. I feel as a summer morn. I have done nothing wrong; my conscience is clear before God and man. I am ready to meet my Redeemer and those that have gone before me, behind the veil. I am not an infidel. I have not denied God and His mercies. I am a believer in these things. Most I regret is parting with my family; many of them are unprotected and will be left fatherless." Here he hesitated. "When I speak of these things they touch a chord within me. I declare my innocence of anything wrong. I am only a victim - a victim must be had. I do not fear to die; I trust in God; Death has no terror. No mercy have I asked. I do not fear eternity. I am a believer in the gospel of Jesus Christ. It is my last word - it is so. I believe in the gospel that was taught in its purity in former days. I regret leaving my family; they are near and dear to me. These are things which touch me - those poor orphaned children! I ask the Lord, my God, if my labors be done, to receive my spirit."

Lee was informed that his hour had come. He looked at the small group of spectators, exchanged a few words with Marshal Nelson, saying:

"I ask one favor of the guards - center my heart."

The Marshal then bound a handkerchief over Lee's eyes, but his hands were allowed to remain free. Lee straightened himself up, faced the firing party as he sat on his coffin, clasped his hands over his head, and exclaimed:

"Remember! The balls through my heart!"

172

The Marshal gave the order to the guards, Fire! As the word "fire!" rang out on the morning air a report was heard and Lee fell back, dead. There was not a cry, not a moan.

THE END.

Made in the USA
Las Vegas, NV
27 January 2023

66364902R00098